HOLDING THE BULLY'S COAT

HOLDING THE

ALSO BY LINDA MCQUAIG

It's the Crude, Dude:
    War, Big Oil, and the Fight for the Planet
All You Can Eat: Greed, Lust and the New Capitalism
The Cult of Impotence: Selling the Myth of Powerlessness in the
    Global Economy
Shooting the Hippo: Death by Deficit and Other Canadian Myths
The Wealthy Banker's Wife: The Assault on Equality in Canada
The Quick and the Dead: Brian Mulroney, Big Business and
    the Seduction of Canada
Behind Closed Doors: How the Rich Won Control of Canada's Tax
    System—and Ended Up Richer

DOUBLEDAY CANADA

LINDA McQUAIG

BULLY'S COAT

CANADA AND THE U.S. EMPIRE

Doubleday Canada and colophon are trademarks.

Library and Archives Canada Cataloguing in Publication

McQuaig, Linda,
Holding the bully's coat : Canada and the U.S. empire / Linda
McQuaig.

Includes bibliographical references and index.
ISBN 978-0-385-66012-9

1. Canada—Social conditions—21st century. 2. Canada—Politics and
government—2006-. 3. Canada—Foreign relations—United States. 4. United
States—Foreign relations—Canada. I. Title.

FC640.M36 2007   971.07   C2007-900294-3

Jacket images:
(maple leaf) Geostock/Photodisc/Getty Images
(stars and stripes) Digital Vision/Getty Images
Printed and bound in the USA

Published in Canada by
Doubleday Canada, a division of
Random House of Canada Limited

Visit Random House of Canada Limited's website: www.randomhouse.ca

BVG   10   9   8   7   6   5   4   3   2   1

For my wonderful brother
Don McQuaig
who will forever be missed

and, as always, for my precious
Amy

CONTENTS

INTRODUCTION

Although it received almost no attention in the Canadian media, the appointment of Gen. Bantz Craddock as NATO's top military commander in December 2006 had a significance for Canadians. Craddock had been in charge of the U.S.'s notorious Guantánamo Bay prison in Cuba, where hundreds of suspected terrorists have been stripped of their most basic human rights in defiance of international law. His appointment as NATO's military chief meant that Canadian troops serving in the NATO mission in Afghanistan were being brought under the ultimate command of a U.S. general deeply connected to the worst aspects of American foreign policy carried out in the name of defeating "terror."

This development should help dispel the comforting notion that Canada has stayed clear of the reckless and illegal course embarked on by the administration of George W. Bush in the post–9/11 era. In fact, there has been a significant shift in how Canada operates in the world, as we've moved from being a nation that has championed internationalism, the United Nations and UN peacekeeping to being a key prop to an aggressive U.S. administration operating outside the constraints of international law.

In his book *Lawless World*, Philippe Sands, a law professor at University College London, describes the actions of the Bush administration as amounting to "a full-scale assault, a war on law."[1] This rejection of the rule of law and the global rules created following the Second World War has freed up a boisterous crowd of neoconservatives operating within the U.S. administration to unabashedly pursue policies aimed at enhancing America's global dominance. The administration's plans, the *Wall Street Journal* noted in March 2005, envision "a military that is far more proactive, *focused on changing the world* instead of just responding to conflicts" (italics added).[2] The distinguished U.S. journalist Mary McGrory captured this aggressive U.S. behaviour colourfully in a column in the *Washington Post* when she described America as the "SUV of nations. It hogs the road and guzzles the gas and periodically has to run over something—such as another country—to get to its Middle Eastern filling station."[3]

As Canada has backed this SUV of nations as it goes about changing the world to suit its own needs, Ottawa has repositioned Canada in the world, with implications for us as Canadians. Our close alignment with Washington also has implications beyond our borders. It is fashionable in Canadian media circles to denigrate the importance of Canada as a world player and scoff at the idea that anything we do would matter one way or another. But in fact we are a player of some significance on the global stage, owing to our reputation—partly deserved and partly undeserved—as a fair arbiter and promoter of just causes, as a decent sort of country. By lining itself up so uncritically with Washington, even as the Bush administration has become a renegade in the world and highly unpopular on its own home turf, the Canadian government has played a role in enabling a regime that is considered by many around the world to be the major obstacle to peace and security.

The government of Stephen Harper has come to the aid of the beleaguered White House, which has become more and more isolated as it pursues its "war on terror." On the eve of a NATO summit in Latvia in late November 2006, the growing reticence among NATO allies about the mission in Afghanistan came out into the open, with Belgian defence minister André Flahaut calling for "an exit strategy." Flahaut gave voice to a view that had been gaining strength in Europe and elsewhere: "The situation is deteriorating," he noted, "and, over time, NATO forces risk appearing like an army of occupation." But with European support flagging, Canada stepped forward to defend the war, pressuring other NATO countries to make Afghanistan the top priority, and berating them for their reluctance to beef up their troop commitments. Harper's strident advocacy has been very useful to the Bush administration, since it allows the voice of another country—and one that has considerable international legitimacy—to make the case for America's war. This leaves the White House looking less isolated, to both the world community and the domestic American audience.

In tilting so strongly towards Washington, Ottawa has moved us further and further away from our European allies, with whom we actually have a great deal in common. While we are always reminded of how similar we are to Americans, there's been a tendency to overlook the compelling similarities between Canadian and European society. As Canadian political scientist Philip Resnick has argued, Canada "would fit remarkably well into the European Union, were it located on the European continent."[4] Indeed, there are similarities between Canada and Europe in our desire for strong social programs, our aspirations for greater social equality and our desire to move towards a world of peaceful co-existence among nations. Meanwhile, America has become an intensely unequal society, and one that is focused on decisively crushing its enemies in the world. Resnick also notes that Canadians share with Europeans a self-doubt, and a sense of limitations and the need for compromise in politics, while the Americans plow ahead with a fierce certainty about themselves and their rightful place at the centre of the world.

All this suggests that Canada could be making common cause with the Europeans on many fronts—on strengthening our social welfare systems, on championing collective international efforts to combat climate change and on standing united in opposition to U.S. actions that violate international law. Canada could have, for instance, joined the European Union in June 2006 in calling for the closure of Guantánamo Bay. Instead, however, we have lined up ever more closely with Washington, even embracing the notion of fencing ourselves off from the world behind the tight security boundaries of a "Fortress North America." Our ties with Europe, once actively cultivated in Ottawa, have been largely left untended. Inside the Canadian government, there's been a significant diversion of focus and resources away from Europe and towards the United States.

This growing closeness to the United States has crept up on many Canadians a little unexpectedly. Indeed, in the past few years, most Canadians have taken satisfaction in the decision, made by the Liberal government of Jean Chrétien in February 2003, not to send Canadian troops to participate in Bush's "coalition of the willing" in the invasion of Iraq. As the U.S. invasion and subsequent occupation of Iraq has turned into a debacle of momentous proportions, resulting in the deaths of hundreds of thousands of Iraqis and more than three thousand U.S. troops, the Chrétien government's decision has proved extremely popular among Canadians. There's been a tendency to forget that, at the time, some of our leading political figures—including our current prime minister, Stephen Harper—actively favoured the U.S. invasion and encouraged our participation.

It's worth recalling how keenly Harper supported the invasion, and how he publicly rebuked the Canadian government—even in front of U.S. audiences—for failing to participate in it. In a letter published in the *Wall Street Journal* in March 2003, Harper and Stockwell Day, now minister of public safety, sharply criticized

Chrétien's decision not to join the "coalition of the willing," presenting it as a treacherous failure of loyalty to Britain and the U.S. "This is a serious mistake. For the first time in history, the Canadian government has not stood beside its key British and American allies in their time of need." The next month, Harper told U.S. TV network Fox News that he endorsed the war, as did most Canadians outside Quebec. "Outside of Quebec, I believe very strongly the silent majority of Canadians is strongly supportive." It was only later, when the war became extremely unpopular and began to look unwinnable, that Harper started to back off. Appearing on CTV's *Question Period* in April 2004, Harper said that Canada lacked the military capacity to become involved, and that if he were elected prime minister he would not send troops to Iraq.

Since becoming prime minister in February 2006, Harper has put Canada on a course that has been most helpful to the Bush administration. Although Canada has not sent troops to Iraq, it has become a leading contributor to another prong of Washington's "war on terror"—the war in Afghanistan. Launched by Washington in October 2001, that war is now carried out largely under the auspices of NATO, with the approval of the UN Security Council. But it remains very much Washington's war. Washington has long dominated NATO, and U.S. troops make up the bulk of the NATO force in Afghanistan, with an additional eight thousand U.S. soldiers serving there under a separate U.S. command. The war embodies the worst aspects of Bush's "war on terror," and is increasingly coming to resemble the disastrous and failed war in Iraq, with its emphasis on hunting down and killing radical Islamic insurgents.

While the war is often defended as beneficial to Afghanistan, it has become harder and harder to make this case. Violence and civilian deaths rose dramatically in 2006. As the insurgency grew in strength, the NATO force responded with devastating air strikes. According to U.S.-based Human Rights Watch, an estimated 1,000 civilians were killed in 2006 in the southern Panjwai district. In one instance, when nine people were killed in a NATO attack on the village of Ashogha, west of Kandahar city, a NATO investigation concluded that the attack was "within the rules of engagement and the village was a legitimate target."[5] Legitimate to whom? It's easy to see how this sort of behaviour has alienated Afghans and made the NATO force seem to them like an army of occupation, not all that different from the Soviet army they fought in the 1980s. Even Afghan president Hamid Karzai, a close ally of Washington's, openly wept on national television in December 2006 as he described his inability to protect the Afghan people from violence by the U.S. and NATO, as well as by the Taliban insurgents. "We can't prevent the [NATO] coalition from bombing the terrorists," he said, "and our children are dying because of that."

Canada's tilting towards the foreign policies of the Bush administration was already under way under Paul Martin, who replaced Chrétien as Liberal prime minister in December 2003 and who emphasized from the outset his desire for more harmonious relations with Washington. To highlight this more pro-Washington approach, the Martin government prepared a defence policy review in April 2005 that emphasized the integration of the Canadian and U.S. militaries. "Today our ships integrate seamlessly with U.S. Navy formations," the review noted enthusiastically. The review also showed that Canada had adopted Bush's view of the world, claiming that "failed states" and "weapons of mass destruction" had made the world dangerous to Canadians: "Most of the new dangers to the United States are no less risks to Canada." In fact, there was little reason to make such a claim, other than to encourage the notion that a common vulnerability tied Canada and the United States together. It was also the Martin government that in 2005 approved the redeployment of

Canadian troops in Afghanistan from the Kabul district, where they were largely involved in peacekeeping, to the southeastern region, where they have been fighting insurgents and contributing to the broader U.S. "war on terror."

It should be mentioned that this "war on terror," in addition to being an aggressive war fought outside the rules of international law, is also based on an over-hyped threat. U.S. political scientist John Mueller has noted that, even including the September 11 victims, the number of Americans killed by international terrorism since the late 1960s (when the State Department began keeping count) is about the same as the number of Americans killed during the same period by lightning, accidents caused by deer or by severe allergic reactions to peanuts.[6] It has also been observed that far more Americans die each year from obesity than from terrorism. Of course, unlike these other causes of death, terrorism is an external threat, and we should take the appropriate measures to protect ourselves against it. But we shouldn't allow fear of terrorism to remake our lives and our society. As Toronto criminal lawyer Clayton Ruby astutely observed: "There is a marked parallel between the 'war on communism' that warped the economic, military, political and emotional life of the last half of the last century, and the 'war on terror' presently on offer at much the same price by much the same people."[7]

There is no evidence that Canada's embrace of this war is what Canadians want. Polls have shown that Canadians are increasingly wary of our involvement in Afghanistan and more broadly of aligning Canada too closely with the United States. The Harper government has managed to deflect some of the public dissatisfaction over its increasingly militarized pro-Washington stance by portraying any criticism of our Afghan role as a failure to "support the troops."

But support for the troops isn't the issue. The legitimacy of the war—and Canada's involvement in it—is the issue. And it is ludicrous to suggest that criticism of a government decision to commit our troops to war amounts to criticism of the troops, whose job it is to carry out government orders. The government is clearly hoping to shield itself from such criticism by hiding behind the troops, trying to make Canadians feel that any condemnation of the government smacks of ingratitude for the enormous sacrifices Canadian soldiers are being called upon to make.

This approach, so reminiscent of the Bush administration's own flag-pumping jingoism, has been helped along by the Canadian media. To a surprising extent, the media have taken on the role of championing the war effort to Canadians, as if they were cheering on the home team in a sports match. Nikolai Lanine, a veteran of the Soviet campaign in Afghanistan, has compared the Canadian media's upbeat, ever-supportive coverage of the war to the Soviet coverage two decades ago. "The Canadian media coverage seemed like an echo of the Soviet press," commented Lanine, now a resident of Victoria, B.C. Citing comforting phrases from the Canadian media suggesting the military situation is improving and that development is under way, Lanine wrote, "I have heard this all before . . . Like the Soviet–Afghan war, this one is fought in the name of state security, a peaceful Afghanistan, and women's rights. Canadians fight the same people the Soviets fought between 1979 and 1989: 'terrorists, extremists, insurgents and bandits.' This should make sense, except that, in the 1980s today's Taliban were supported by the West as 'freedom fighters.'"[8]

The disturbing notion of the media as war promoter is reflected in a statement made by the Canadian Journalism Foundation, a private organization that describes itself as dedicated to promoting "excellence in Canadian journalism." It's an odd sort of excellence the foundation seems to have in mind. In the late fall of 2006, it organized a public forum to address what it saw as baffling—the lack of public support for the war effort. In a release promoting the event, the foundation praised the media for "doing a credible job of reporting on the importance of Canada's role in the military operation." (Shouldn't the media be expected to do a credible job of reporting the facts of the war, and let Canadians decide for themselves the importance—and legitimacy—of Canada's role?) Yet, the foundation noted, Canadian public support for the war remained low, prompting the foundation to ask: "What's the disconnect?"

But is there any disconnect? Canadians are skeptical and even disapproving of the war—despite the enthusiastic and inappropriate cheerleading of many in our media. I suspect that's because Canadians have a sense of what they want Canada to stand for in the world, and attacking villages in faraway places as part of a broader U.S. campaign focused on changing the world isn't part of it.

Linda McQuaig
Toronto
January 10, 2007

CHAPTER 1

ANTI-CANADIANS AT HOME AND ABROAD

Even with the most sophisticated media techniques, carefully scripted attempts by politicians to portray themselves as heroes have a way of backfiring.

So it was with President George W. Bush when he appeared in full battle gear, strutting and swaggering aboard a U.S. aircraft carrier beneath the banner Mission Accomplished, after the mighty U.S. military had defeated the feeble Iraqi army in the spring of 2003. In a similar grand gesture of self-drama, our own Prime Minister Stephen Harper, on his way home from the G8 summit in Russia, redirected his private jet to Cyprus in a supposed attempt to rescue some of the thousands of Canadians trapped in Lebanon during the Israeli air bombardment of July 2006.

Unfortunately, Canadian officials running the evacuation effort had switched the destination for most of the fleeing Canadians to Turkey. But here was Harper in Cyprus. In the midst of the chaotic evacuation endeavour, Canadian officials working frantically to get desperate Canadians out of war-torn Lebanon were put to work instead shifting schedules in order to spare Harper the embarrassment of leading a rescue mission to Cyrpus, only to find no one there to rescue.

As the *Globe and Mail* reported from Cyprus, Harper's "rescue mission ended up adding confusion and delay to an evacuation effort that was already running into serious snags . . . *A special diplomatic effort was needed, involving dozens of officials, to shift schedules so that at least some [evacuees] would arrive in Cyprus during the PM's visit*" (italics added).[1]

Finally, after hours of delay, a shipload of Canadians—exhausted, nauseated and dehydrated after many hours waiting in the hot sun in Beirut and then tossed all through the night in a gruelling sea voyage—showed up in Cyprus, where some of them were welcomed by the prime minister onto his jet for the journey home.

Fortunately, amongst the skeletal staff the prime minister had brought with him, he'd had the foresight to include a photographer—an essential member of any rescue team.

Harper's failure to provide meaningful help for desperate Canadians trapped in Lebanon actually went beyond his awkward mission to Cyprus.

Ever since he had become prime minister, in February 2006, Harper had followed the United States in tilting strongly towards Israel, abandoning Canada's traditional attempt at even-handedness in the Arab–Israeli conflict. One of the first foreign acts of the newly elected Harper government was to cut off aid to the Palestinian government led by the group Hamas, after Hamas had been democratically chosen by Palestinians in parliamentary elections that winter—ironically by a larger margin than Harper's own government had received in the Canadian election.

But Harper's strong pro-Israel bias took on a dramatic new dimension in the summer of 2006 when Israel launched its devastating attack on Lebanon, after the capture of two Israeli soldiers by Hezbollah, the Lebanese guerilla army.

Suddenly, some fifty thousand Canadians were in harm's way, trapped in a country that Israel was relentlessly bombing. Now, one would have thought that the first priority of a Canadian prime minister is the safety of Canadians. One would have thought that Harper, faced with a choice of expressing his support for Israel or doing everything he possibly could to protect tens of thousands of vulnerable Canadians, would opt for protecting the Canadians. After all, he is prime minister of *Canada*, not Israel.

But, astonishingly, Harper refused to do the very minimum necessary—to add his voice to those of other world leaders and the UN secretary-general in calling for a ceasefire in the conflict.

Let's stop for a minute to consider what that ceasefire would have entailed. It simply would have meant an end to the killing. Israel would have stopped bombing Lebanon, and Hezbollah would have stopped firing rockets into Israel. These assaults were killing civilians on both sides of the border—although the carnage was about ten times higher in Lebanon, which was defenceless against Israel's overwhelming air power. Lebanon was desperately pleading for a ceasefire. But Israel didn't want a ceasefire, at least not yet. It wanted to continue its assault, in order to destroy or at least cripple its bitter enemy Hezbollah, and it was getting solid support from the Bush administration on this. Despite international pressure, Bush adamantly refused to call for a ceasefire, giving Israel the green light to continue its assault on Lebanon, where hundreds of civilians were dying, about one third of them children.

Stephen Harper followed Bush's lead—as he has in so many areas—in refusing to call for a ceasefire. The message was clear: let the killing continue! In fact, Harper actively defended Israel's bombing, calling it a "measured" response, a description he refused to withdraw even after eight members of a Canadian family and a Canadian UN peacekeeper were killed by Israeli strikes in Lebanon.

Harper's stance amounted to giving encouragement to a foreign army whose actions were directly endangering the lives of Canadians.

Earlier that summer, Harper had announced massive new military spending, which was ostensibly all about making Canadians safer in the world. But if the prime minister really wanted to make Canadians safer in the world, one would have thought that a good place to start would have been calling for a ceasefire when thousands of Canadians were directly in the line of fire.

––––––

However commercialized and corrupt the Olympics has become, it's hard not to feel a twinge of pride when one of your nation's athletes, having endured years of brutally rigorous training, mounts the podium and is celebrated as the best in the world. So when hurdler Perdita Felicien, Canada's brightest hope for a gold medal at the 2004 Olympics in Athens, tripped moments into her race and ended up lying startled and devastated on the ground, it's probably safe to say that most Canadians felt some disappointment, sadness or even compassion.

A very different sort of emotion evidently went through David Bercuson, a well-known historian at the University of Calgary. Oddly, this moment seemed to be something Bercuson had been waiting for—a moment when Canada was prostrate in defeat, humiliated in front of the world.

"Mr. Bercuson dashed straight to his computer," according to a recounting of the incident in a *New York Times* feature article about Canada. "He knocked out a screed declaring that her sad performance, and that of the entire Canadian Olympic team, was just another symptom of 'the national malaise' that is making Canada a second-rate, uncompetitive nation."[2]

So, with Perdita—and symbolically Canada—lying defeated on the track, Bercuson's response was to seize the moment. Gotcha now, Canada, you nation of losers!

––––––

Peddling the notion of Canada as a nation in decline—uncompetitive and second-rate—has become the stock-in-trade of Bercuson and a number of other high-profile, neoconservative Canadian media and academic commentators. They tend to be full of disdain for the Canadian public's fondness for medicare and for universal social programs in general. But perhaps their central theme in recent years has been that this country has slipped badly from the glory days of the First and Second World Wars, when Canada was a significant military power fighting alongside the great powers Britain and the United States. Since then, they complain, we've allowed our military to decline, we've gone too far in our embrace of peacekeeping and the United Nations and we've shown too little loyalty to our old Anglo allies and too little willingness to support them in their wars. All this, these critics allege, has weakened Canada's position in the world. Their mantra can be summed up by the title of a book by Andrew Cohen: *While Canada Slept: How We Lost Our Place in the World.*

It's a powerful lament, but is there any substance to it?

I'd argue that far from being a nation in decline, we are a nation that, overall, works, and works well. It is one of our charms as a nation that we are not particularly focused on achieving an elevated stature for ourselves on the world stage. We've managed to earn some respect in the world not by eagerly seeking it out but rather by going about our business for the most part without intruding on others, by often promoting worthwhile causes in the international arena—and on occasion by rising to a leadership role on issues that matter. Canada's Lester Pearson played a key role in solving the Suez Crisis in 1956, averting a war in the Middle East and effectively inventing "UN peacekeeping" (and winning a Nobel Peace Prize) in the process. In more recent years, Canada has been pivotal in establishing an international treaty against land mines and the International Criminal Court, and at times played a significant role in negotiations for nuclear disarmament. In fact, when it comes to developing and support-ing international treaties—in areas from disarmament to human rights—Canada is always a contributor of time and resources, is often in the forefront of shaping treaties and is a "serial complier," according to Trevor Findlay, a political scientist at Carleton University and executive director of the Canadian Centre for Treaty Compliance.[3] And, perhaps this is stretching the definition of a Canadian role, but it strikes me that there is something quintessentially Canadian about Stephen Lewis and his leader-ship of the UN-sponsored crusade against AIDS. What makes these various Canadian actions important is not that they impressed the neighbours but that they were worthwhile con-tributions to the world community.

It should be noted that Canada has also performed badly in some ways, mostly by not living up to the image of ourselves that we've projected in the world—a subject we'll return to later. Overall, however, the Canadian approach to the world that has evolved in the past fifty years—promoting internation-alism, the United Nations and the rule of law—has been a good one. But it is also almost completely at odds, and potentially in conflict with, the American approach to the world crafted by the Bush administration in the wake of 9/11—an approach largely embraced by the Harper government.

Indeed, what is lamentable is not the rather likeable Canada that emerged in the postwar years, but rather the recent switch in direction that has brought Canada more into line with the U.S. empire, even as Washington has become a belligerent and lawless force in the world. As the U.S. has rejected the rule of international law and become a law unto itself, Ottawa has followed in close step, ever eager to please our powerful neighbour. To this end, we have abandoned our traditional role as a leading peacekeeping nation and adopted a more militaristic, warlike stance as a junior partner in the U.S. "war on terror." We've also abandoned our traditional attempt to be a fair-minded mediator and conciliator, most notably in the Middle East conflict, where, like the U.S., we've adopted a hardline anti-Palestinian position that will make a peaceful, just solution all the more evasive. We've also joined the U.S. in becoming a leading obstructionist in worldwide efforts to deal with climate change—perhaps the most pressing issue on the international agenda. The switch in direction evident in these and other positions has redefined the way Canada operates in the world, transforming us into a helpful assistant to an aggressive U.S. power, increasingly out of sync with our European allies and the rest of the world.

This new, more aggressive role for Canada is also at odds with our own sense of ourselves and the Canadian identity that has emerged in the last five or six decades—an identity that is partly reflected in our laws and institutions, and partly reflected in our aspirations (difficult as these are to measure). This Canadian identity takes its inspiration from Lester Pearson and the useful role he carved out for Canada in the world, and from Tommy Douglas, the father of Canadian medicare. For what it's worth, let's not forget that 1.2 million Canadians cast votes in a nationwide poll organized by the CBC in the fall of 2004 to select "the Greatest Canadian of all time," and they passed over prime ministers, inventors and star athletes and instead chose Tommy Douglas, the former Saskatchewan premier who gave us our public health care system.

The importance that Canadians attach to medicare has long gotten under the skin of our neoconservative commentators. "A country is not just a health system," scoffed military historian Jack Granatstein, one of the critics quoted in the *New York Times* article mentioned above, who apparently feels that the size of a country's military is a more appropriate measure of greatness. True, a country is not just a health system. But how a country organizes its health care system—that is, how it deals with something as basic and important to its people as their physical well-being—reveals a lot about what kind of country it is. Canada's system is founded on the principle that everyone should have access to health care and everyone should be treated equally. Our system sometimes fails to live up to this ideal, but that is the ideal, and it's an ideal Canadians value. It's also an ideal that is strikingly absent from the U.S. system. As much as we may resemble Americans in many ways, there is an undeniable difference in the way we have organized something as important as our health care systems. Canadians would have no stomach for a system so riddled with inequality that more than 42 million Americans lack health insurance, leaving them unsure of access to medical care in the case of serious illness or injury.

The Canadian health care system typifies values that, I would argue, are central to Canadians—equality, fairness and inclusiveness. These are the values Canadians want in their own society and also want to promote in the world. I'd also add to the list: a commitment to the rule of law (both domestically and internationally) and a distaste for imperialism. These "Canadian" values are not the same as the values espoused by many of our high-profile commentators. Indeed, this gulf between "ordinary" Canadians and members of the elite has been evident for some time. Ekos Research Associates, an Ottawa-based polling firm, has demonstrated this difference by interviewing Canadians in general and then asking the same questions of those who could be loosely described as members of the elite—business executives, senior civil servants, editorial writers, and so on. The gap between the views of the two groups is striking. While the elite favours a neoconservative agenda of tax cuts, privatization and deeper integration with the United States, the general Canadian public favours a more egalitarian agenda of public investment, universal social programs and keeping Canada distinct from the U.S. Another pollster, Michael Adams, president of Toronto-based

Environics, also points to the strong egalitarian inclination of the majority of Canadians, who, he notes, are deeply attached to the Canadian Charter of Rights, with its emphasis on equality.

But it is the views of the elite—as expressed by Andrew Coyne, Margaret Wente, Rex Murphy, Robert Fulford, Jack Granatstein, David Bercuson, to mention a few of its more prominent media voices—that tend to dominate the national debate. Their views are given an extraordinary amount of media time and space, which gives them considerable influence in shaping the debate and making palatable a neoconservative political agenda that has little natural resonance with the broad Canadian public. It is important to pay attention to these voices so we can understand the message they're promoting—and how antithetical it is to the aspirations of most Canadians. It is also important that we be able to filter out these over-amplified voices so that we can hear our own voices, and bring into focus a vision of a country that appeals to most of the rest of us: a vision based on equality and inclusiveness, and on finding our own way in the world.

––––––

With the retirement of British prime minister and key Bush ally Tony Blair, Stephen Harper emerges as arguably George W. Bush's staunchest and most important international supporter, indeed one of his few international supporters. Bush's gratitude towards Harper was evident in a video tribute the U.S. president sent to a dinner honouring Harper in Calgary in October 2006. In the video, Bush thanks Harper for his leadership in the "war on terror," and ends with the words "God bless Steve."[4]

Being chief ally to the Bush administration is not a role most Canadians want, and indeed it's one that Ottawa has taken on incrementally and without consulting the Canadian public. Many Canadians, relieved that the Chrétien government decided in 2003 not to send troops to join the U.S. invasion of

Iraq, have simply assumed that we are not participating in America's dangerous and lawless crusade in the name of fighting terror. Our involvement in Afghanistan somehow seemed more benign. In chapter 2, we will challenge this assumption.

At this point, however, I want to highlight one particularly serious aspect of our involvement in Afghanistan, namely our complicity in the torture of Afghans—a complicity that raises profound questions about our new, more aggressive role in the world. As a signatory to international treaties and as a morally responsible nation, Canada has a duty to ensure that the Afghans we take into custody are not tortured or mistreated. It was ostensibly to meet this duty that Ottawa signed an arrangement with the Afghan government in December 2005, outlining conditions under which Canada would transfer detainees to the custody of the Afghan government. The arrangement, signed for Canada by General Rick Hillier, specified that the Afghan government would treat our detainees according to the Geneva Conventions and allow the Red Cross access to them.

But Michael Byers, a political science professor at the University of British Columbia, notes that the arrangement actually envisages that some detainees will be transferred to the custody of other countries, and puts no restrictions on what these other countries do to them. This means that detainees can end up in U.S. custody. Notes Byers: "Given what we now know about practices at Abu Ghraib [in Iraq] and elsewhere, the possibility that our detainees will be tortured in U.S. custody is real."[5]

For that matter, the likelihood of torture is actually higher for detainees who are not transferred but who remain in the custody of Afghanistan, which has a notorious human rights record. Even the Afghanistan Independent Human Rights Commission—an agency of the Afghan government—reports that Afghanistan routinely tortures its prisoners. There have been bone-chilling reports of Afghanistan housing prisoners in steel shipping containers, with only a hole cut in the bottom for them to defecate. Yet, despite widespread reports of horrendous abuses in Afghan prisons, Ottawa's arrangement with the Afghan government contains only the most minimal protections—far fewer than a similar agreement between Afghanistan and the Netherlands, another contributor of troops to the NATO mission in Afghanistan. The Dutch agreement requires that Dutch officials be permitted to visit its detainees, and to be notified in advance of any plans to transfer them. There are no such provisions in the Canadian agreement, even though Canadian authorities reviewed drafts of the Dutch agreement prior to signing theirs. Amir Attaran, a law professor at the University of Ottawa, describes the Canadian arrangement as a "detainee laundering agreement" that "has no adequate safeguards to prevent torture from occurring."[6]

In an interview, Lieutenant Carole Brown, a spokesperson for Canada's Department of National Defence, acknowledged that Canada doesn't follow up on what happens to its detainees. "It would not be our mandate to track them in any way." She also refused to reveal any information about Canada's detainees, including even how many there have been.[7]

In fact, Canada has left its detainees in a particularly dangerous situation. Attaran notes that, by refusing to reveal any information about these people, Canada is actually making their situation even more perilous than those held by the U.S. at Guantánamo Bay. The Pentagon at least lists the names of Guantánamo prisoners on its website. By not revealing the names of those it hands over to Afghanistan, Ottawa makes it impossible for lawyers or human rights organizations to contact them or their relatives or to in any way take up their cause, thereby denying them any hope of access to the courts. They simply disappear into a black hole, beyond any possible legal protection. Says Attaran: "We are doing something [denying them access to the courts] that has not been done in the common law in centuries."

This alone should make our involvement in Afghanistan intolerable.

Exxon, the world's richest and mightiest corporation, was the leading force behind a massive ten-year campaign to block the Kyoto accord and ensure the world remained hooked on the product that Exxon has made its fortune selling. This was no easy battle, even for Exxon. Lined up against it was virtually the entire scientific world—and, for that matter, most of the world community. In the end, not even Exxon was able to block the signing of the historic Kyoto Protocol, as the world came together in 1997 in a far-reaching bid to shake our planet-endangering oil addiction.

But Exxon did score one huge victory in March 2001, when the newly elected administration of George W. Bush and Dick Cheney, close Exxon allies, withdrew U.S. support for Kyoto. The withdrawal of the United States, which emits roughly one quarter of the world's greenhouse gases, was a devastating blow. Still, the world community has pressed on with Kyoto.

Into this titanic, ongoing struggle between the world community and the Bush-Cheney-Exxon axis of oil, Canada has now definitively entered—on the side of the oil interests.

With the release of the Harper government's so-called Clean Air Act in October 2006, Ottawa signalled its abandonment of Kyoto. This amounted to a repudiation of the only serious effort under way to tackle global warming. What makes this repudiation all the more stunning is the fact that Ottawa had played a role of some significance in getting global warming onto the world agenda in the first place.

Although the scientific understanding of the global warming phenomenon began to take shape back in the 1820s, for well over a century the world did not recognize the scope and urgency of the problem. It wasn't really until the mid-1980s that the scientific community began to pay serious attention, and to focus on the extent to which the earth's warming was being driven by our industrialized lifestyles. A number of Canadian scientists, in government and in the academic world, as well as some Canadian environmentalists were among those who early on took a strong interest in the subject. This interest led to the organization of an international scientific conference on global warming in Toronto in June 1988. The significance of the event was underlined by the presence of then Prime Minister Brian Mulroney, who gave the opening address. At the end of the conference, the scientists attending released a consensus statement declaring that "humanity is conducting an unintended, uncontrolled, globally pervasive experiment whose ultimate consequences are second only to global nuclear war."

The Toronto conference had helped sound a worldwide alarm about the urgency of the global warming problem. In some ways it had seemed like a natural follow-up to another major environmental initiative—an international treaty to protect the earth's ozone layer—in which Canada had also been a major player the year before. Canada had chaired a key UN committee into the ozone problem in the early 1980s and been the first country to ratify a framework treaty. In September 1987, twenty-four countries came together in Montreal to sign what became known as the Montreal Protocol, restricting the use of substances that cause ozone depletion; the number of signatories has now grown to 175.

This spurt of Canadian leadership on environmental issues in the late 1980s is, sadly, not typical of the Canadian environmental record, a subject we will return to later. But it is particularly regrettable that Canada has failed to follow through with its initial impetus to try to spark worldwide efforts on global warming. Canada did go on to participate in the Earth Summit in Rio de Janeiro in 1992, in which leaders of 154 countries—including Mulroney and U.S. president George Bush (Sr.)—signed a legally binding convention committing themselves to address global warming. Five years later, the world reconvened in Kyoto, Japan, to continue the process begun in Rio. After marathon negotiating sessions, a treaty to reduce greenhouse gas emissions was finally reached, with U.S. vice-president Al Gore playing a crucial mediating role.

Canada was on board at Kyoto, and stayed committed to the process even after the new Bush administration withdrew from it. In December 2002, despite strong opposition from the Alberta government and the oil industry, the government of Jean Chrétien ratified the Kyoto Protocol, helping to keep it alive.

But despite these formal commitments to Kyoto, the Liberal governments of Chrétien and Paul Martin did a lacklustre job, to put it charitably, in actually moving Canada towards meeting our Kyoto targets. Both governments utterly failed to take serious steps to reduce Canada's greenhouse gas emissions. They backed off from adopting tough new laws—modelled on laws already introduced by the state of California—that would have forced automakers to design more fuel-efficient cars, settling instead for toothless voluntary agreements. The Martin government even opposed efforts by European countries to develop international standards for fuel efficiency in cars and energy efficiency in buildings. David R. Boyd, a Canadian environmental lawyer who worked as a special adviser in the Privy Council Office in Ottawa, recalls that the Europeans tried to get these proposed standards—and a tax on international air travel—onto the agenda of the G8 Summit in Scotland in 2005. "I argued vehemently that Canada should be siding with the Europeans at the G8 on global warming," says Boyd.[8] But the Martin government sided with the Bush administration, helping to kill the European initiative.

Similarly, the Chrétien and Martin governments failed to rein in the single biggest contributor to the growth of Canada's greenhouse gas emissions—Alberta's oil sands, the vast pool of oil that the coffin for Canada's Kyoto commitment. The Harper plan esn't even mention Kyoto; instead it calls for yet more consulta-ns with industry and sets actual reduction targets an incredible ty-four years into the future. By then, presumably even industry ll be sick of consulting. It won't matter much, though, since the rth will almost certainly have warmed to the point where the mage will be irreversible. Even the much more demanding dead-es set out in the Kyoto Protocol are a long shot at reversing the rrendously destructive course we're on before it's too late.

So Canada has gone from being an international leader this file, helping to alert the world to the need for action on obal warming, to being a major part of the problem, refusing en to co-operate with the world's efforts to address the prob-m. It now seems that Canada will be one of only a few nations ling to meet targets it agreed to in signing Kyoto. Our irre-onsibility on this issue is made worse by the fact that we have e of the highest levels of greenhouse gas emissions, per person, the world. Prominent British journalist and author George onbiot has described Canada as in danger of being considered n international pariah" for its refusal to take meaningful action global warming.[9]

Harper showed unequivocally which side he's on. He's aware at the Canadian public is on the other side, but he's hoping e'll be so dazzled by his talk of a "green" plan for "clean air" at we won't notice the Bush-Cheney-Exxon axis lurking in the ackground.

———

the heat of the federal election campaign in December 2005, tephen Harper declared that protecting Canada's sovereignty was)ttawa's most important duty. In surprisingly defiant language, Iarper pledged that a Conservative government would not allow oreign vessels—including U.S. submarines—to enter Canadian

lies embedded in a tarry muck beneath large
province. On the contrary, the Chrétien and Mart
supported ambitious plans by the oil industry a
government to triple oil sands production by 2015
barrels a day, even though such an increase would r
impossible for Canada to meet its Kyoto targets. '
ment plans were enthusiastically supported by Wasl
since almost all the oil from the oil sands will be
energy-hungry United States. So although the Libe
their political support for Kyoto—the Martin
endorsed plans to extend Kyoto at an international
Montreal in December 2005—they were unwilling
that would interfere with oil sands development. A
environment minister Stéphane Dion told the
Chronicle in May 2005, "There is no minister of the
on earth who can stop this [oil sands developmen
forward because there is too much money in it."

With the election Stephen Harper's Conservat
refusal to take action on Kyoto became even mor
Harper's political base is in Alberta, with strong t
industry, and he solidly backs an aggressive strateg
development. Furthermore, unlike his Liberal p
Harper has long been resistant to Kyoto, and has s
conclusion that human actions are causing global
conclusion that virtually every climate scientist i
considers about as open-and-shut as the case tl
causes cancer. Harper showed his contempt fo
appointing Rona Ambrose to be his first environm
thereby putting in charge of this key file a political
got her environmental training working on the anti-
paign of the fiercely anti-Kyoto Alberta governmen

With the announcement of its "clean air" plan, or "
in October 2006, the Harper government delivered t

Arctic waters without Canada's permission. Harper pledged to build three military icebreakers and a system of underwater sensors to detect unauthorized activities in our waters. "You don't defend national sovereignty with flags, cheap election rhetoric and advertising campaigns," Harper said. "You need forces on the ground, ships in the sea and proper surveillance."

This tough talk provoked a sharp rebuke from U.S. ambassador David Wilkins, who noted that Washington has never recognized Canada's claim to these Arctic waters. This American rebuke helped Harper shed his image as a pro-American water boy who'd be quick to cave in to the Bush administration.

What a difference a few months—and some private time with the president—make. Visiting the White House in July 2006, Harper was no longer the defiant nationalist vowing to block Yankee submarines from straying into our waters. Bush was so taken with the meeker, more co-operative Harper that he dubbed him "Steve"—a term of familiarity that even Harper's wife avoids. So, with the election over, Harper deftly shifted his military focus from defending our Arctic sovereignty against U.S. encroachment, to providing support for American troops on the battlefield.

Of course, the Canadian military would be getting a lot of new money, but it would be spent on things that please, rather than irritate, the Bush administration: aircraft and helicopters that would allow Canada to contribute more effectively to the U.S. "war on terror." Particularly pleasing to the Bush administration was a $3.4-billion contract for heavy-lift cargo planes, awarded—without competition—to U.S. aerospace giant (and major Republican contributor) Boeing. It's all part of Harper's plan to massively increase Canada's military spending, well beyond the substantial increases made by Paul Martin's government. By 2010, Harper's plan will raise our military spending to $21.5 billion a year from $13 billion in 2005.

This means significant additional taxpayer dollars will go to the military rather than to other Canadian priorities. Perhaps this sounds like a good idea. After all, we've heard a relentless chorus from commentators, academics and retired generals about our woefully underfunded military. But is this really the case?

Before the dramatic increases announced by Harper, Canada was already the seventh biggest military spender among the twenty-six nations of NATO, putting us clearly in the top one third of the organization, which is the world's strongest military alliance. NATO secretary-general Jaap de Hoop Scheffer noted on a visit to Ottawa in June 2006 that Canada was increasing its military spending even as most other NATO members were actually decreasing theirs.

The notion of Canada as a significant military spender may sound bizarre; it certainly doesn't fit with the popular perception. That's because the Harper government and a host of pro-military commentators have dominated the public debate with their portrayal of Canada as a laggard whose military spending ranks only above little Luxembourg among NATO nations.

This characterization is extremely misleading. As Steven Staples, a defence analyst with the Ottawa-based Polaris Institute has noted, the pro-military set has managed to make Canada's military spending look shrivelled by using an inappropriate method of measurement—measuring military spending *as a share of Gross Domestic Product (GDP), rather than measuring it in actual dollars.* That may sound reasonable, but here's the first clue that it isn't. As we all know, the biggest military spender in the world is the United States, which currently spends some $450 billion a year on its military—more than almost all the other nations in the world combined. But, using the measuring stick favoured by Canada's pro-military commentators (percentage of GDP), the biggest military spender in NATO isn't the United States. It's Turkey! And next biggest is another military powerhouse—Greece![10]

Turkey and Greece are not, of course, military powerhouses, but if we use the GDP measuring method, they appear to be big military spenders because they are relatively poor countries. Although they don't spend nearly as much as the U.S.—or even Canada—their military spending amounts to a large percentage of their GDPs, simply because they have such small GDPs.

GDP is often used as a measure of public spending in areas other than the military, and in many areas it is the appropriate measure, since it provides an indication of a country's overall wealth and therefore its ability to pay. So, for instance, if we are doing a cross-country comparison of health care spending, it is relevant to know how rich the country is. A rich country can presumably afford a more advanced health care system—something every nation wants but not all can afford. So, in a health care comparison, it is useful to measure a nation's health care spending as a percentage of its GDP (or ability to pay) to determine if it is spending as much as it can afford. But with military spending, a different measure should apply. The military is not something we necessarily want more of simply because we have more money. Presumably our military spending should be determined *on the basis of need*. Surely the relevant question then for measuring the adequacy of our military budget isn't the size of our GDP but rather the size of the military threat we face.

For a country that is by nature peaceful, has no aggressive intentions and is separated by huge oceans from any potentially threatening army, being the seventh biggest spender in the world's strongest military alliance should be adequate.

––––––––––

In the 1920s, an officer in the Canadian military by the name of Col. J. Sutherland-Brown was convinced that the United States was planning to invade Canada. Sutherland-Brown, a veteran of the First World War, was Canada's director of military operations and intelligence after the war, making him solely responsible for the nation's war planning. In fact, there wasn't much war planning going on at that point in Canada. But Sutherland-Brown, or Buster as he was known, insisted on developing a 200-page plan for defending Canada against a possible U.S. invasion.[11] For this, he was ridiculed by many of his contemporaries, who dismissed him as obsessive, archaic and almost pathological in his worry about an American threat to Canadian sovereignty. But it turns out that Buster had hit on something, because U.S. strategic planners had indeed considered how they might go about invading Canada, should they decide it was necessary.

In fact, in the 1920s, U.S. military planners developed an elaborate secret plan for invading and conquering Canada—a plan that was given Cabinet-level approval by the U.S. government in May 1930. This plan for war against Canada was part of a larger plan for war against Britain, which was code-named "Plan Red." In the event of such a conflict, "Plan Red" assumed that the British navy would seize the Philippines, Guam, Hawaii and the Panama Canal and that the United States would invade and take control of Canada, or "Crimson" as it was dubbed in the colour scheme.

It's interesting to note the aggressive nature of this plan. Certainly, it's hard to construe it as in any way defensive. U.S. strategists envisioned that Washington would start the war by in some way interfering with British commercial trade, "although other proximate causes to war may be alleged."[12] The planners speculated about the possibility that Canada might declare itself neutral. But this was considered irrelevant to Canada's fate. Regardless of whatever action Canada did or didn't take, the U.S. Army's mission, as spelled out in capital letters in a draft of the plan, was "ULTIMATELY, TO GAIN COMPLETE CONTROL OF CRIMSON."

"Plan Red" was one of several colour-coded war plans developed by the U.S. military between the First and Second World

Wars, in which strategies were set out for waging wars against Japan, Mexico and Britain, as well as a number of largely unarmed Latin American and Caribbean nations. Oddly, no plan was ever developed for war against Germany. Even as Germany became increasingly militarized and belligerent throughout the 1930s, building up a massive military and expanding beyond its borders, U.S. military planners kept their focus on plans for war against other nations. The largest, most developed and most detailed of all the U.S. war plans in these years was "Plan Red," which included plans for taking control of Canada, or "Crimson."

As late as 1935, Washington was actively refining "Plan Red," and had budgeted to build three bases for attacking Canada including a camouflaged military air base that could be used for a surprise attack against Canada. The plans for the base were inadvertently made public when the U.S. government printing office mistakenly published the minutes of secret hearings before the Congressional Committee on Military Affairs. The *New York Times* ran a front-page story about the plans for the camouflaged base. In Canada, the *Globe and Mail* quickly picked up the story.

Since then, the story—and the larger story of "Plan Red"— has resurfaced from time to time in the Canadian and American media, in 1975, in 1991 and most recently in 2005. Each time, the story has been reported with a slightly whimsical, even humorous tone, as if the building of a secret air base for attacking Canada was so far-fetched that we can all have a good laugh over it. Even the first *Globe* story, back in 1935, when the plan was still active, ran under the headline "U.S. Disavows Airport Yarn." The *Globe* was apparently satisfied with Washington's official denial of what its own Congressional committee records had disclosed.

Of course we know that the U.S. did not attack Canada, and in 1937 "Plan Red" was declared obsolete. But the plan did exist. (All the colour-coded war plans were declassified in 1974, and are now available through the U.S. National Archives.)[13] The response of dismissing the whole matter as a bit of entertainment is an odd one. There was nothing frivolous or harmless about the U.S. Army's plan for the invasion of Canada. On the contrary, the plan was extremely detailed and clearly aimed at doing extensive damage to Canada and causing Canadians great suffering. As a 1928 draft pointed out: "It should be made quite clear to Canada that in a war she would suffer grievously." In a 1930 draft, the plight of Canada was spelled out further: "Large parts of CRIMSON territory will become theatres of military operations with consequent suffering to the population and widespread destruction and devastation of the country." In an amendment in October 1934, both the U.S. secretary of war and the secretary of the navy approved plans for the bombing of Halifax, Montreal and Quebec City; later plans were approved for the bombing of Vancouver. Another 1934 amendment, which also received U.S. Cabinet-level approval, authorized the use of poison gas to ensure the quick surrender of Canada, and therefore the saving of American lives. Accordingly, the amendment directed the U.S. Army, in capital letters, "TO MAKE ALL NECESSARY PREPARATIONS FOR THE USE OF CHEMICAL WARFARE FROM THE OUTBREAK OF THE WAR. THE USE OF CHEMICAL WARFARE, INCLUDING THE USE OF TOXIC AGENTS, FROM THE INCEPTION OF HOSTILITIES, IS AUTHORIZED."

Quite a yarn.

———

One can only imagine how much of a chuckle the Americans would have had if they'd discovered Canada had done some serious thinking about how we might use chemical weapons against them. One suspects that the Canadian laughter is, in some ways, nervous laughter. After all, we know we would be unable to defend ourselves against a U.S. invasion. By laughing it off, dismissing it as far-fetched nonsense given our long-standing friendship, we take the sting out of it. We convince ourselves that it was all just a joke (even though clearly it wasn't). If we treat it as an amusing little yarn, then we don't have to confront what it may reveal about our neighbour on the other side of that long, undefended border.

My point in raising all this isn't to suggest that the U.S. is currently contemplating invading Canada. I doubt very much that it is. Of course, if we were to elect a provocative, Hugo Chavez–style nationalist as prime minister and align ourselves with nations challenging U.S. economic (or, hard to believe, military) hegemony, that could change. But as long as Canada remains a friendly, pro-U.S. nation that welcomes and protects the rights of international capital, it is inconceivable that Washington would attack. Indeed, the U.S. has no reason to invade Canada. Not only is it getting our co-operation and support in its military adventures abroad but we have granted the Americans extensive rights over our energy through NAFTA, and we are currently offering them even more extensive rights to these crucial resources in negotiations connected with the Security and Prosperity Partnership (SPP). (More on this later.)

My point in raising "Plan Red" is, first, to note how utterly disrespectful, to say the least, the U.S. has been of our sovereignty as recently as the 1930s. Even though everything was ostensibly peaceful between our two countries, and we were dismissing our own Colonel Sutherland-Brown as a paranoid fruitcake for worrying about aggressive U.S. intentions, in fact U.S. military authorities were making detailed plans for conquering Canada—and using chemical weapons, no less!

Secondly, and more importantly, "Plan Red" illustrates something about the U.S. that Canadians often prefer to ignore: that there is, somewhere deep in the American psyche, a profoundly militaristic and aggressive bent. "What is the mentality and line of illogic that leads ranking military professionals, executive cabinet officers, and congressmen to plan and prepare war on an ally and good neighbour?" asks Floyd Rudmin, a U.S.-born psychologist who teaches at the University of Tromsø in Norway. Rudmin argues that the U.S. militarism on display today in Iraq runs deep in American culture, and goes well beyond the specifics of current geopolitics or the Bush administration. "There is something wrong at a much deeper level in American political culture. The American malady of militarism extends across decades, across generations, and is so deeply rooted in the American mind that attacking another nation seems to be the natural, spontaneous reaction of choice."[14]

Let's immediately acknowledge that this militarism by no means represents the views of all Americans. For instance, as the success of the Democrats in the 2006 mid-term elections shows, a majority of Americans are now opposed to U.S. actions in Iraq. Similarly, a strong anti-war movement developed across the United States during the era of the Vietnam War. Still, it can be said that, despite the opposition of large numbers of Americans, there is an aggressive militaristic bent that has been integral to American foreign policy over many decades, and under both Republican and Democratic administrations. While this aggressiveness has usually been more pronounced under Republican reigns, it has also been central to Democratic administrations. It was, for instance, Democratic president Lyndon Johnson who grossly escalated the U.S. military involvement in Vietnam, and Democratic president Harry Truman who dropped not one but two nuclear bombs on tens of thousands of Japanese civilians. The truth is that a bipartisan consensus has long existed between Republicans and Democrats in favour of an aggressive U.S. military stance in the world, and this stance presumably has the support of large numbers of Americans. Even in the debate over Iraq leading up to the 2006 mid-terms, it is important to note that the critique advanced by Democrats and other mainstream critics of the war focused on the fact that the Bush administration's policies had failed to produce victory. None of these critics ever raised the more important issue: that the U.S. invasion had been illegal and immoral, that Washington has no right to invade and occupy other countries. One suspects that, had the U.S. succeeded in quelling the insurgency and bringing Iraq under control, little criticism would have come from the Democrats.

Rudmin uses the analytical techniques of psychology to explain the "malady of American militarism." He notes that American military ventures are typically motivated by material or political goals, such as expanding trading opportunities or taking control of the resources of another country. But U.S. strategists soon begin to concoct theories that the victims of this planned aggression are actually thinking of attacking the U.S.—in other words, that the victims are planning to do to America what America is in fact planning to do to them. Rudmin calls this "classic psychopathic projection."

So, for instance, in the secret 1935 testimony before the Congressional Committee on Military Affairs, U.S. captain H. L. George set out a hair-raising scenario in which Canadian seaplanes, positioned on lakes deep in the Canadian interior, take off and swoop down to bomb Boston and Baltimore. As George's testimony continues, his vision of Canadian treachery grows more vivid, until finally he concludes that the U.S. must find these Canadian planes and attack them before they attack American targets. He describes "the vast number of sheltered water areas that are available deep in Canada . . . from which pontoon-equipped aircraft could operate at will . . . There is no necessity for starting with an observation in order to know what they [the Canadians] are going to bomb. They know what they are going to bomb. They know where every railroad crosses every river [in the U.S.]. They know where every power plant is located. They know all about our water supply systems . . . Now they are dispersed widely out over this area. Their location is most difficult for us to learn, for our own air force to learn. We have to hunt them up. We have to find out where they are *before we can attack them*" (italics added).

In fact, there were no such Canadian plans. But the U.S. Army's "Plan Red" called for just this sort of destruction of Canadian targets. The congressmen listening to Captain George didn't question his assertion about aggressive Canadian intentions. On the contrary, they complimented him on his testimony and, on June 6, 1935, approved appropriations for the new camouflaged air base so that the duplicitous Canadians could be stopped in their tracks.

Rudmin sees this as evidence of the "militarized imagination" of those in the American government, and of their tendency to project their own violent intentions onto others. He notes that the United States, which is obsessed with its own security, is in fact the least threatened nation on earth. Its sheer power and its favourable geographic location give it a far greater level of security than just about any other nation. Most others have been attacked from many sides or even invaded—the Russians, for instance, lost 23 million citizens in World War II—and remain vulnerable to future attack. And yet other nations are considerably less fearful than super-armed, well-protected America. "The U.S.A. is now the only nation with two defense departments; one to defend the homeland and one to . . . to do what?" asks Rudmin. "To project 'defense' of America outside of our borders into other nations? That is normally called 'aggression.'"

Rudmin argues that this mentality leads to an accelerating cycle of belligerence and fear, where aggression is presented as defence. "We imagined that Nicaragua's Sandinistas would invade Texas. We imagined that a socialist government in Grenada would destabilize the Western Hemisphere. We imagined that Iraq would put nuclear bombs into New York subways. These are all comic claims, but many in America did not laugh. Instead, we attacked these nations."

In fact, the U.S. has been "defending" itself for decades, intervening aggressively both economically and militarily around the world. If we just take the example of the Persian Gulf, where so many of the current geopolitical problems are located, we can observe that the U.S. has long intervened in the region, where two thirds of the world's oil is located. In the early 1950s, Washington overthrew the democratically elected government of Iran because it had nationalized the country's oil industry. For decades, Washington has propped up the military dictatorship in Saudi Arabia in exchange for U.S. oil companies being granted exclusive access to Saudi oil. In 1980, President Jimmy Carter declared what became known as the Carter Doctrine, establishing that the U.S. would intervene militarily if necessary to preserve its access to the Persian Gulf, which it had declared vital to its national security. In 2003, Washington invaded and took control of Iraq, in a plan that Rudmin notes is strikingly similar to its earlier "Plan Green" for the invasion of Mexico. (U.S. plans for both Iraq and Mexico featured the seizure of oil resources, propaganda claims that the invasion was for benevolent purposes, the establishment of a new government in the conquered country that would serve U.S. interests, and the creation of a local army that would provide the security for the new regime and that would be paid for by the new regime. A draft of "Plan Green," approved by the U.S. secretary of war in August 1919, states: "It is therefore important to seize these oil fields at once.")

Yet despite an obvious pattern of aggressive U.S. interventions in the Persian Gulf—and with fourteen U.S. permanent military bases under construction and some 150,000 U.S. soldiers in Iraq—Washington still presents its behaviour there as basically defensive. Iraq had to be attacked, we were told, because it harboured weapons of mass destruction that would be used to attack

America. Although this turned out to be false, Washington now makes the same allegations against Iran. Washington claims that Iraq and Iran are planning to attack America when in fact America has been planning to attack them.

Of course, America actually was attacked on 9/11, not by a nation but by al Qaeda, whose avowed purpose was to drive the U.S. out of the Islamic world and overthrow pro-U.S. governments there. One can deplore the terrorism of 9/11 and still recognize that this vicious attack was a response to U.S. military involvement in the region, or, to use the CIA term, that it was "blowback."

But this larger picture of U.S. aggression is obscured in the popular narrative, which instead tells a tale of U.S. vulnerability. America is under attack, we're told, because it represents Western freedoms, which are resented by Muslim fundamentalists or "Islamofacsists." The whole history of U.S. intervention, and the interventionist nature of current U.S. actions in the Middle East, is dropped out of the story, allowing the deeply aggressive intentions of the U.S.—the malady of American militarism—to go unnoticed. Instead, the U.S. is portrayed as big, powerful and benevolent, just minding its own business, when resentful, evil-doing foreigners insist on attacking it. No wonder America must devote so many of its resources to "defence."

The war plans developed by Washington strategists in the 1930s help shine a light on aggressive U.S. tendencies—tendencies that, as Rudmin notes, are "rooted in [the American] psyche and political culture." One can note that these aggressive tendencies have been deliberately cultivated by the powerful military-industrial lobby, which clearly benefits from keeping Americans perpetually (and needlessly) worried about their own security. But the point is, however it has come about, a "militarization of the American mind" has taken place. While it certainly does not apply to all Americans, many of whom deplore it, this way of thinking clearly runs deep in American political culture.

Americans often argue that Canadians are free riders who take advantage of America's massive defence spending so that we don't have to invest heavily in our own defence. But is America's massive defence spending necessary, or is it even about defence? As Rudmin points out, much of what the United States calls defence is thinly disguised aggression. In what sense is that helpful to Canada? On the contrary, by generating so many enemies, Washington's projection of military power around the world is putting Canadians—as well as Americans—at greater risk.

By any logic, Canada should answer U.S. requests for us to increase our military spending with Canadian requests that they diminish theirs.

—————

As Canadians have become more skeptical of the exercise of U.S. power, our elite commentators have attempted to shut down discussion. The slightest criticism of the U.S. is quickly branded "anti-Americanism." Indeed, even the suggestion that Canada has different values than the United States or a different way of doing things is likely to provoke a mini-tantrum in some commentators. *Globe and Mail* columnist Margaret Wente mocks the Canadian penchant for internationalism, suggesting it reeks of smugness since it "allows us to congratulate ourselves that we disapprove of the lone gunslinger approach . . . It allows us to believe that the world needs us, because even though we are neither powerful nor rich, we are good."[15] The logic here is intriguing. Internationalism—that is, the promotion of peace and understanding among nations—is derided, while there is no criticism of the "lone gunslinger approach." Wente has twisted things around so that what is being ridiculed is not the "lone gunslinger approach"—with its overtones of gangsterism and hooliganism—but rather Canadians for "congratulat[ing] ourselves that we disapprove" of it.

Thus Canadians are given a good smack for showing any sign of disapproval of U.S. behaviour, even when that behaviour resembles that of a swaggering gunslinger. Such disapproval is automatically attributed to some annoying Canadian sense of "moral superiority." In a column in the *National Post*, commentator Robert Fulford referred, for instance, to "that collection of self-adoring notions we sometimes [call] 'Canadian values.'"[16] *Self-adoring?* Fulford's contempt is palpable. He appears to be offended by the very attempt to identify something distinctive about this country, to try to establish what we stand for and strive for as a nation. (Equality? Inclusiveness? The rule of law? Don't get him going!)

Oddly, frequent chest-thumping claims by prominent Americans—such as *New York Times* columnist Thomas Friedman's insistence that the U.S. is a "beacon of freedom" in the world—don't prompt Canadian commentators to dismiss Americans as "self-adoring."

Our alleged anti-Americanism is mocked as the glue that holds Canada together, that, as Fulford puts it in another *National Post* commentary, "spreads happiness from sea to sea."[17] Fulford goes on to paint this glue as a poisonous adhesive, as a "polite and acceptable form of bigotry. People who would die of shame before tolerating homophobia, racism or anti-Semitism will cheerfully join in denunciations of the unlovable characteristics of 'the Americans.'" Anti-Americanism, according to Fulford, is "bred in the bone," like some deeply ingrained primal hatred, passed from generation to generation.

Whoa, Nelly. This is absurd.

Let me offer myself as a case in point. I am not anti-American. I like many aspects of American culture; I admire many of its political traditions, its literature, its energy and its creativity. But I am opposed—fiercely opposed, in fact—to American *exceptionalism*. By that I mean that I am opposed to the notion that the United

States is above the rule of law, that it enjoys some exemption from the rules that apply to other nations in the international community. On the contrary, I believe that the U.S. enjoys exactly the same rights as other nations—and not one single right more.

The term "American exceptionalism," first coined by Alexis de Tocqueville in 1831, has been used to suggest that America is somehow unique in the world—that, as Friedman maintains, it represents a "beacon of freedom" that gives it a moral authority to set its own rules—rather than it being, as I would suggest, just another nation promoting its own self-interest in the world, often very aggressively. Thus, behaviour that would not be tolerated in other nations is considered acceptable and even held up as commendable when the U.S. engages in it.

Take, for instance, the U.S. invasion of Iraq. International law, as set out in the United Nations charter, prohibits a country from attacking another country unless it has been directly attacked by that country, or unless the UN Security Council has authorized that particular military action as necessary to preserve world peace or security. The U.S. was not attacked by Iraq. And, despite intense U.S. efforts to pressure Security Council members to support a resolution authorizing it to attack Iraq, it became clear in the winter of 2002–2003 that there was not sufficient support for the resolution. So the U.S. simply withdrew it and proceeded with its war plans on its own. It rounded up a group of countries to join its "coalition of the willing." But the invasion by the U.S.-led coalition had no legitimacy in international law and was, by any reasonable reading of the UN charter, an illegal act of war, as Secretary-General Kofi Annan pointed out.

Still, many people—including Stephen Harper and Michael Ignatieff—considered the U.S invasion acceptable and even commendable. Such people believe in U.S. exceptionalism. They would have heartily condemned an invasion of Iraq by the Soviets, but they apply a different set of rules to Washington. I don't.

That doesn't make me anti-American. It makes me anti-American-exceptionalism.

Similarly, those who believe in American exceptionalism tend to condone—or ignore—Washington's failure to abide by international laws, as set out in the Geneva Conventions, against torture and long-term detention of prisoners without trial. Washington has defied these conventions in operating its Guantánamo Bay and Abu Ghraib prisons, as well as a number of others, including secret prisons in undisclosed locations.[18] The U.S. has also handed detainees over for interrogation in other countries known for human rights abuses, under a program it has called "extraordinary rendition." Those who believe in U.S. exceptionalism, including Harper and Ignatieff, have essentially condoned these violations as a necessary part of Washington's "war on terror" and continue to treat the U.S. with a respect that they would not extend, for instance, to other human rights violators like China or Syria.

Another example would be tolerance for U.S. defiance of the international treaties aimed at preventing the spread of nuclear weapons. Even as Washington demands that others, particularly enemies like Iran, be held to their obligations under the Nuclear Non-Proliferation Treaty, Washington flouts its own obligations under the treaty, which requires nuclear-armed nations to make real efforts to move towards disarmament. Washington, which has by far the world's largest nuclear arsenal, has moved in the opposite direction, setting out its plans, in its 2001 Nuclear Posture Review, to maintain and modernize its large nuclear force indefinitely into the future. Washington has also withdrawn from the Anti-Ballistic Missile Treaty. Furthermore, it has refused to co-operate with international efforts through the UN to establish a treaty banning weapons in space, and has instead announced its intention to build such weapons. Those who support American exceptionalism keep their focus on Iran's obligation to follow the international community's rules on nuclear weaponry, while condoning Washington's active defiance and rejection of treaties the international community has established, or seeks to establish, to control the spread of nuclear weapons.

These are just three of the many areas where the United States has shown an indifference, if not an active resistance, to the laws and standards of the international community. There's an irony in this, since the very existence of the United States as a country was founded on the rejection of arbitrary power, such as that of an unelected monarch, and the establishment instead of a system of the rule of law governed by a constitution. Furthermore, the U.S. was one of the architects of our modern system of international laws.

At the same time, however, there have long been strong elements in U.S. political culture resisting international laws and conventions when these rules have been seen as interfering with U.S. interests and sovereignty. This resistance was evident back in the early part of the twentieth century, when President Woodrow Wilson championed a system of international governance enforced by a League of Nations, only to have the U.S. Senate refuse to ratify the treaty establishing the league, amid complaints that it encroached on U.S. sovereignty. The U.S. attitude towards the United Nations has also been a mixture of support and opposition. Although Washington played a key role in establishing the world body after the Second World War, there has long been resistance and even hostility to the UN within U.S. political circles. In the 1980s and 1990s, Washington refused to pay its UN dues. More recently, John Bolton, Washington's ambassador to the UN in 2006, has been almost openly contemptuous of the world body, as are many commentators in the mainstream U.S. media.

The U.S. also opposes the International Criminal Court, mostly because it doesn't want its own officials and soldiers to be subject to possible prosecution, and it has even tried to intimidate other nations into not supporting the court. (The American Servicemembers' Protection Act allows for a ban on U.S. military assistance to nations that ratify the court, and authorizes any necessary action to free U.S. soldiers handed over to the court.) The U.S. has also been reluctant to accept the authority of the International Court of Justice, the judicial branch of the UN. Although Washington accepted the court, with some reservations, when it was established in 1946, that acceptance was withdrawn in the 1980s after the court ruled that it had jurisdiction to decide a case brought by Nicaragua charging that the U.S. had illegally supported groups trying to overthrow the Nicaraguan government.

The U.S. has also refused to ratify the Kyoto Protocol. Similarly, despite its professed concern about biological weapons, it has walked away from international negotiations aimed at strengthening the 1972 Biological Weapons Convention through a protocol with strict new rules for site inspections. An analysis by the U.S.-based Institute for Energy and Environmental Research and the Lawyers' Committee on Nuclear Policy concluded that Washington abandoned the negotiations because it wanted to be free to develop biological weapons itself and not be subject to tough international inspections: "The United States would like to be completely exempt from oversight by any other party, while creating its own ways to enforce others to comply with its wishes on an ad hoc basis."

In other key areas the U.S. has been resistant to or defiant of international efforts that are clearly aimed at improving human welfare. The U.S. Senate imposed a number of significant reservations and conditions when it ratified the Covenant on Civil and Political Rights and the Convention on Torture. The U.S. still refuses to ratify the Convention on Discrimination Against Women, as well as the Covenant on Economic, Social and Cultural Rights. And it joins Somalia as the only other nation in the world that has declined to ratify the Convention on the Rights of the Child and a protocol to that convention aimed at banning the use of children as soldiers in armed conflicts.

Of course, in general, the U.S. is not the only nation failing to abide by or help develop important international laws. But it has been unusually resistant. The analysts from the Institute for Energy and Environmental Research and the Lawyers' Committee on Nuclear Policy point out that there's been a "trend of powerful states to erode existing international legal regimes and to resist the development of new ones, to the detriment of security, disarmament, international justice, human rights and the protection of the environment. The United States is foremost among these states."[19] What makes this particularly of concern is the enormous power that the U.S. wields in the world. As the analysts conclude: "The importance and weight of the United States makes a U.S. withdrawal from the global legal process, except when it gets its own way, a dangerous course for security as well as the environment."

There is a longstanding pattern—more pronounced under the Bush administration—of Washington refusing to abide by or to remain within international law and conventions. This attitude that the United States is above the law was perhaps best expressed by former U.S. ambassador John Bolton when he declared: "It is a big mistake for us to grant any validity to international law even when it may seem in our short-term interest to do so—because, over the long term, the goal of those who think that international law really means anything are those who want to constrict the United States."[20] This stunning statement reveals a deep contempt for the very notion of international law. It openly states the idea that the U.S. answers only to itself.

Is it so surprising that Canadians have sought to distance themselves from—and even criticize—this sort of cavalier indifference to the rule of law? Is this really evidence of a personality disorder on our part, of an anti-Americanism "bred in the bone," of a "form of bigotry" that runs deep in our genes? Or is it, on the contrary, evidence that we believe laws are fair only when they apply equally to all, and that certain people or nations don't have more rights because they're richer or more powerful?

Refusing to remain silent when the powerful throw their weight around, when our muscular neighbour behaves lawlessly, is surely evidence of moral sanity, of our ability to think clearly and independently. Branding such critical commentary "anti-American" is a transparent attempt to shut it down, to intimidate Canadians from criticizing the United States or even suggesting that there are things we like about Canada.

Perhaps the real problem afoot in the land isn't anti-Americanism but rather *anti-Canadianism*.

———

Rex Murphy is no TV pretty boy. Lacking the square jaw, symmetrical good looks and well-modulated voice common to men who typically make careers in television, Murphy comes across as a break-the-mould kind of character. With Murphy, it feels like you're getting something real. His bulging, intense eyes, combined with his irreverent manner and willingness to go for the jugular, give him the look and feel of a fearless, determined animal, a terrier who simply won't let go. This is no highfalutin' commentator. This isn't someone you'd call Mr. Murphy. This is just plain Rex. Rex tells it like it is.

And Rex is everywhere. Certainly, anyone following the mainstream Canadian media will soon come across him. He enjoys two of the most prestigious positions in the Canadian media, as the only regular commentator on CBC-TV's flagship nightly news program *The National*, where he delivers a highly personalized opinion piece, as well as a choice weekly spot as an op-ed columnist in the *Globe and Mail*'s Saturday edition. He's also the host of CBC Radio's weekly phone-in show *Cross Country Checkup*. It is hard to imagine a Canadian media commentator with more of a perch from which to shape the Canadian debate.

So a match-up between this tough-talking icon of Canadian journalism and Paul Cellucci, who served for five years as the public face in Canada of George W. Bush, presented some intriguing possibilities. As U.S. ambassador to Canada, Cellucci had been an outspoken advocate of the very militarism and unilateralism that has made the Bush administration so wildly unpopular here. And he had repeatedly pressured Canada to ramp up its military spending and become a fuller partner in the U.S. "war on terror"—a message that Cellucci made clear came directly from the president.

But if Cellucci is a fierce advocate for the Bush administration, we've got that bulldog Rex to take him on. How appropriate, then, that the *Globe and Mail* selected Rex to review Cellucci's book, *Unquiet Diplomacy*, in September 2005. The book was Cellucci's parting shot at Canada as he left the ambassadorship, and in it he continues his rather condescending lecture on how Canada should behave. So let Rex at him!

Yet, reading Rex's review, one is struck by the strongly sympathetic tone. Indeed, Rex has barely begun when he starts tipping his hat to Washington, even helping Cellucci put Canadians in their place.

A central strategy of the Bush administration has been to invoke the tragic events of September 11, 2001, to justify a whole set of hawkish foreign policies long favoured by the Republican right. Rex jumps right in and helps Cellucci make the "world has changed" argument that underlies the Bush administration's case for doing pretty much whatever it wants in the world. "From September 11 on, the world's only superpower elevated the matter of its own security, the safety of its citizens at home and abroad, to be the absolute fundamental of its foreign policy."

The fact that the Bush administration paid only minimal atten-tion to the most basic safety of tens of thousands of its citizens—abandoned in flooded New Orleans for days after Hurricane Katrina, in the same month that Rex wrote his review—apparently didn't prompt him to question the sincerity of the administration's commitment to ensuring "the safety of its citizens at home and abroad." By this point, even the mainstream U.S. media had begun to grow skeptical about the administration's alleged focus on protecting Americans. But not our Rex. His con-fidence in the sincerity of the White House apparently hadn't wavered with the administration's dawdling pace in rescuing tens of thousands of people stranded on rooftops, trapped in attics or jammed into filthy stadiums without food, water, medicine or san-itation. Instead, he blamed Canadians for not appreciating the horrors of September 11, thereby allowing a "gulf" to develop between the two countries—a gulf that was based, according to Rex, on the fact that "they were attacked and we were not."

But is the gulf really due to the failure of Canadians to empathize with the horrors of September 11? In reality, Canadians were overwhelmingly sympathetic, with thousands sending supplies and even opening their homes to take in Americans stranded here in the days after the attack. The falling-out between Canada and the U.S. came later, when the Bush administration began thumbing its nose at international law, invading Iraq on the flimsiest of pretexts and showing a callous indifference to detainees held in its "war on terror."

But Rex was taking Cellucci's side, dismissing Canadian resist-ance to this above-the-law behaviour as nothing more than (here we go again) knee-jerk anti-Americanism: "Neither Cellucci nor the Americans are stupid," he writes. "They know that occasional spasms of anti-Americanism, or 'standing up to the White House,' offer an easy harvest of electoral popularity. Why did we stay out of Iraq? Was it because we thought it was wrong? Or was it because the Chrétien government could not, politically, contemplate going along with the Americans? I'd say the second was the more puissant recommendation than the first. Decorate the choice with a few anti-Bush comments, and you've hit the sweet spot of Canadian politics."

Rex may be right that the Chrétien government's decision to stay out of Iraq was largely based on its perception that that was what Canadians wanted. But he fails to go on and ask the obvious question: *why did Canadians want that?* Why was refusing to go along with the U.S. invasion of Iraq close to the "sweet spot" of Canadian politics? He seems to be suggesting that the resistance amounts to some sort of "spasm," some kind of irrational anti-Americanism. Nowhere does he consider the possibility that Canadians might have a reason for wanting to avoid participating in an illegal war that most of the world considered provocative, unnecessary and morally repugnant.

Without examining this possibility—that is, giving Canadians credit for rational thought and authentic moral revulsion—Rex goes on to insinuate that our resistance was mere posturing, that we were "gaming" the Americans on Iraq. He writes: "It is almost impossible to believe that if the Americans thought we were gaming them on Iraq, deprecating the 'legitimacy' of the invasion, avoiding missile defence—not on the merits of these cases, but on their 'optics' for Canadians—they would not respond on other fronts." Before we deal with the "other fronts" that the Americans responded on, let's just stop here and note that, in his convoluted way of expressing himself, using a lot of big words, Rex is clearly implying that Canadians were not criticizing the U.S. over the merits of the case (against Iraq and missile defence) but rather were criticizing it for some other reason. Presumably we were falling prey to that old irrational demon that allegedly haunts the Canadian psyche: rampant, uncontrollable anti-Americanism.

Rex never considers that there could be any substance to Canadian resistance to the war. Having blithely discarded this possibility, he goes on to suggest that Washington then responded on "other fronts." He points to the softwood lumber dispute, and notes: "We pay for our posturing."

So, Canadian resistance to supporting a U.S. military invasion and the restarting of the nuclear arms race has been reduced, in Rex's view, to "posturing." What's more, it's clear that Rex feels we deserve a little punishment for this "posturing," that it is something we must "pay for." His willingness to take the American side here is striking, given the strength of the Canadian case on softwood lumber. As Rex knows, NAFTA rulings on softwood lumber have consistently favoured Canada, and his book review appeared only weeks after a top NAFTA panel—the one reserved for "extraordinary challenges"—ruled unanimously in Canada's favour, concluding that the U.S. had violated its own trade laws in collecting more than $5 billion in penalties on our softwood lumber. Given this background, one might have expected Rex—who is after all a Canadian—to at least acknowledge the strength of the Canadian case on softwood lumber. Instead, he suggests that, because of our failure to co-operate with U.S. military plans (in Iraq and on missile defence), we are getting the punishment we deserve from the Americans on softwood lumber.

Rex just can't see any reason why Canadians don't simply co-operate with Washington. He recognizes that, with the more aggressive U.S. stance since 9/11, "a majority of Canadians probably feel that the Americans are overreacting." It's okay for us to feel this way, as long as we confine our response to simply noting how the Americans feel differently about these things (presumably because we have no ability to imagine what it feels like to be attacked). So, he writes, "some Canadians will scold and even mock the Americans for their post-9/11 intensity." Note how Rex trivializes our resistance, presenting it sneeringly as scolding or mocking. He goes on to say that our resistance will be seen by Americans as "posing, as haughty and preachy." He clearly takes pleasure in laying out the American case against Canadian resistance, once again suggesting it has a schoolmarmish, puffed-up quality about it. Utterly absent is any acknowledgement of the possibility that Canadians expressing disagreement with U.S. militaristic actions are simply asserting a genuine, deeply felt disagreement about some of the most serious issues in the world, about matters of war and peace, of life and death.

Rex clearly sides with the Americans, who, he notes, "would take our fears at face value."

Really? So, presumably, we can count on Washington taking seriously our fears about its decision to abrogate the anti-ballistic missile treaty (thereby sparking a renewed nuclear arms race), or undermining international law or contributing to the proliferation of firearms in North America? Could we really expect the U.S. to take any of these fears seriously—or at least to not dismiss them out of hand, and with annoyance at us for even mentioning them? Or is it just that Washington would take seriously any fears we might have of terrorism, or fears that North Korea might attack us with missiles? In other words, is Washington only willing to take seriously any fears we have that fit perfectly into its agenda?

Our bulldog Rex isn't without criticism of Cellucci. He faults the bombastic U.S. ambassador for not having a sufficiently pleasing writing style! He also maintains that Cellucci was not very effective over the years in delivering his message that the world had changed fundamentally with 9/11. There is no questioning or challenging by Rex of the basically anti-Canadian message.

Rex even goes on to blame Cellucci's communication shortcomings on Canadians—for failing to pay attention! It's that old Canadian insensitivity to American suffering. Rex ends up concluding that Cellucci's book is "stuffed with home truths for both countries." This sounds almost balanced, until you think about it. The central message of Cellucci's book, like his public remarks throughout his tenure as ambassador, is that Canada should be more accepting of U.S. leadership, that we should be more accommodating to U.S. power. Rex apparently sees this as containing important "home truths" for Canadians.

Rex is a journalist, so he no doubt values his independence, which might explain his reluctance to take the side of his home country. But does he feel no qualms about so unabashedly taking the other side—the side of a foreign country that has long dominated his own?

————

Rex Murphy's defence of the U.S.—and his put-down of Canadians who differ with the U.S.—provoked no controversy here. Why would it? If there's one thing we're used to in Canada it's watching members of our elite—from the media, academic and corporate worlds—pander to Washington. It's an unusual phenomenon when you think about it. One would expect members of our elite to identify with, even to take pride in, their own country. But instead they seem to identify with a foreign government and foreign elite, and comfortably take on the role of drumming Canadians into line, giving us a dressing-down when we show any resistance to this foreign dominance.

If this sounds overstated, let's drop in on a little gathering in Toronto, the day after George W. Bush was re-elected president. To most Canadians, this was a grim day; the prospect of four more years of the Bush administration was anticipated with about as much enthusiasm as a colonoscopy. But to the small group gathered at the C. D. Howe Institute, a business-funded think tank in downtown Toronto, Bush's re-election was clearly an energizing tonic.

Along with the *National Post*, the C. D. Howe Institute serves as a kind of spiritual home for neoconservatives and others who want deeper social spending cuts and more U.S.–Canada integration. Among this crowd, Bush's re-election was regarded as a useful tool to whip into line all those who had clung to the prospect that a John Kerry victory would spare us from pressure to participate in far-fetched missile defence schemes and "wars of liberation." As a *National Post* headline put it that morning: "Life with Bush: Get used to it." More pointed still was the headline on an article in the *Globe and Mail*, written by two commentators associated with the C. D. Howe Institute: "Why Ottawa must curry U.S. favour now."

So it seemed fitting that the very day after the U.S. election, the campaign to push Canada deeper into the U.S. orbit was revved up with a C. D. Howe–sponsored lecture by former Canadian ambassador to the U.S. Allan Gotlieb. John Kerry had barely delivered his eloquent concession speech in Boston when Gotlieb held forth before the supportive Toronto business audience with a lengthy lecture about how Canada is a faded power in the world and that we must learn to accept the reality of "transcendant U.S. power."[21]

This boils down to a choice for Canadians, Gotlieb said, between "realism" and "romanticism." The "realistic" approach involves accepting U.S. power, even when it violates international law. Indeed, Gotlieb seems to feel we're far too fixated on the UN and international law. Loosening our attachment to the UN is part of Gotlieb's formula for improving our relations with the U.S. He urges Canadians to "liberate themselves from the belief that the UN is the sacred foundation of our foreign policy."

But hold it. *Shouldn't* international law, as embodied in the charter of the United Nations, be the sacred foundation for our foreign policy? Not according to Gotlieb. He continues: "The UN is not the only begetter of multilateral action nor the only authority that can confer legitimacy on armed intervention." Is some sort of armed action *outside the law* acceptable? Gotlieb clearly appears willing to accept the legitimacy of "coalitions of the willing." Would it be legitimate then for any group of countries to form a coalition and invade another country, or is it only legitimate for the United States to do so?

The "romantic" approach involves championing international law and treaties, like those protecting children in conflict zones and banning land mines, despite the lack of U.S. support for these initiatives. Gotlieb dismisses this approach—which most Canadians would probably consider "principled"—as "narcissistic" and "sanctimonious." And he insists that, by following this course, we have marginalized ourselves in the world, leaving Canada a washed-up power with little influence.

In order to restore our influence in the world, he argues, we must draw closer to Washington, to play on the special historical, cultural, linguistic and geographic ties that we have with the U.S., to work our way deeper into the inner sanctum of U.S. power. "Our potential for influencing the world's greatest power is our comparative advantage in the world. It gives us credibility in other capitals. As U.S. power grows, so does Canada's opportunity."

Gotlieb's notion that Canada would gain stature in the world by its ability to influence Washington is odd. First, it assumes that it's possible to influence the Bush administration, which is notoriously impervious to outside opinion and apparently indifferent to, if not contemptuous of, any contrary points of view. As Bush announced in his first press conference after his re-election—even as Gotlieb was delivering his address in Toronto—"I'll reach out to everyone who shares our goals." That's apparently as far as his reach goes—to those on his side. As he's suggested before, you're either with him or against him.

But even those who are clearly "with him" have had little luck influencing him. Tony Blair, Bush's chief foreign ally, apparently felt he could win the president's ear, thereby allowing Britain to shape events in Iraq and also to push Washington to focus on the

Israeli–Palestinian problem. Both goals have proved elusive. In the end, Blair's co-operative stance won him nothing—not even an exemption for British steel from U.S. tariffs imposed by the Bush administration.

So it's hard to imagine how Canada could somehow exert influence where Britain has failed to, even if Canada is as pleasing and supportive of the Bush administration as Britain has been. It's even harder to imagine how this would "give us credibility in other capitals." The Bush administration has managed to alienate governments around the world with its bullying tone and actions. For Canada to be seen as more closely co-operating with Washington, as a kind of trusted assistant, would hardly help us command respect elsewhere in the world. Since the bully has little credibility in world capitals, it's hard to imagine how its pandering helpmate would have much either. Indeed, it's hard to imagine that we'd be viewed with anything but contempt, as the bully's unctuous little sidekick.

An alternative path would be for us to simply remain committed to the values we hold—and to try to advance them in the world—regardless of the contrary direction the United States might take. Gotlieb rejects this approach, suggesting instead that we avoid taking positions aimed at creating "counterweights to U.S. power." Rather, Canada should simply accept U.S. power as "the dominant feature of the contemporary international order" and avoid asserting positions—even on morally important issues—that put us at odds with Washington. Even when the U.S. does things that offend our sensibilities and our sense of justice, Gotlieb would apparently have us keep our eyes cast demurely downward.

So if the United States chooses to invade Iraq, to launch a lawless "war on terror," to start an arms race in space or to obstruct worldwide efforts on climate change, Canada should quietly stand by her man. Similarly, we should avoid supporting causes—like banning land mines or protecting children in combat zones—for fear that this sort of "sanctimonious" behaviour might annoy Washington. If we want to disagree with our powerful boyfriend, we should whisper softly in his ear, not embarrass him in public. We should confine ourselves to being the manipulative little woman behind the scenes, using our wiles to get what we want from him and using our position of influence over him as our ticket to status in the outside world.

Leaving aside for a minute any skepticism about the effectiveness of such a role—whether the manipulative little woman really does manage to influence her man—there is the aching question of what it means for us as a nation to take on this role.

It is hard to imagine a more demeaning vision for a woman—or a country.

"In its relations with the U.S. these days, Canada feels a bit like a woman having an affair with the big rich man next door. She depends on him and he's a good provider, but he has a roving eye and a lot of other offers."

Here, then, is an even more demeaning depiction of Canada, the little woman. In this view, Canada is the anxious mistress, always fearful that her wealthy playboy-lover will wander off, attracted by some more curvaceous, accommodating starlet. The above lines were written by an American—*New York Times* columnist James Reston, in a 1973 column—but they fit with an image of Canada promoted by members of Canada's own corporate elite as part of a campaign to get Canadians to overcome their resistance and accept deeper economic integration with the U.S. The basic strategy was to make Canadians feel vulnerable, like the anxious mistress.

Spearheaded by the C. D. Howe Institute with back-up support from the Canadian Council of Chief Executives, the campaign launched in 2003 played on the notion that Canada is particularly vulnerable to being tossed aside by the U.S. in the new tight-border atmosphere of the post-9/11 era. Access to the U.S. market is "less assured than it was," warned the lead-off paper in a C. D. Howe series on closer Canada–U.S. ties, highlighting the theme of vulnerability that runs throughout the series, hinting ominously at the heightened levels of economic insecurity Canadians should feel in the post-9/11 world. One can sense those exotic beauties (Britain, Australia, Spain, Uzbekistan) prettying themselves up, plumping up their cleavages, as they jockey for the chief mistress suite at the presidential ranch. If Canada wants to keep her man from wandering, she better remember the tricks for pleasing a guy: laugh at his jokes, stroke his ego, admire his plans to invade Iraq . . .

All this raises some intriguing questions: *why* is our elite so keen to promote the idea of Canada as weak and vulnerable? What is it about members of our elite that motivates them to put their own country in such a deferential position?

The notion of a "comprador class" might be useful here. The *Concise Oxford Dictionary* defines a comprador as the "chief native servant in a European house of business." The term "comprador class" was a nineteenth-century colonial term used to describe a local elite that served the interests of a foreign business class. Members of this comprador class acted as intermediaries, presenting the goals of the foreign interests to the local population in a positive light. By putting a local face on foreign interests, the compradors helped sell the foreigners' agenda to the local population, often compromising the national or public interest of their own country in the process.

Important segments of the Canadian elite have, it seems, at least some of the characteristics of a comprador class. This would include some high-ranking members of our corporate world, who work for or even head up Canadian divisions of U.S.-owned corporations. Overall, 28 per cent of the non-financial sectors of the Canadian economy were foreign-controlled in 2004, with 20 per cent U.S.-controlled. In the key oil and gas sector, the degree of foreign control is higher—45 per cent, with 33 per cent in U.S. hands. So while Imperial Oil Company of Canada sounds Canadian, it is owned by ExxonMobil of Texas. Similarly, the Canadian Council of Chief Executives (CCCE), which is made up of the CEOs of the 150 most powerful corporations in the country, sounds like a thoroughly Canadian entity, but roughly 25 per cent of the Canadian CEOs who sit on this council head up companies that are subsidiaries of foreign companies, about 18 per cent of them American.[22] (Interestingly, the council changed its name in 2003, dropping its old name, the Business Council on National Issues. This strange move, in which a well-recognized name was scrapped for an unknown one, was perhaps done to get the word "Canadian" into the title, just in case there were any doubts.)

This degree of U.S. ownership of the Canadian economy is significant, but not overwhelming. And it has declined from the early 1970s. At its peak in 1971, total foreign control of non-financial industries in Canada was 35 per cent, with 26 per cent U.S.-controlled. At the same time as the level of U.S. ownership has declined, however, a new form of economic dependence on the U.S. has developed in Canada through our ever-growing reliance on selling to the U.S. market. Whereas our exports to the U.S. amounted to 59 per cent of our total exports in 1954, our exports to the U.S. today account for an astonishing 87 per cent. This growing reliance on the U.S. market has been encouraged by our business elite, through its championing of the Free Trade Agreement (FTA), the North America Free Trade Agreement (NAFTA), and now through a new plan to further integrate the economies called the Security and Prosperity Partnership (SPP). This increasingly deep integration of the two economies has left our business elite feeling highly dependent and anxious to cater to the whims of the U.S. business and political elite, since our access to their market is so crucial to our economic fortunes. This could be said to have created a new type of comprador class mentality in our business elite, which has used its influence with Ottawa to press for policies—both domestic and foreign—that please the U.S. elite.

Certainly parts of our business elite have operated hand-in-glove with U.S. business interests, particularly in key areas like the energy sector. Thus, the Trudeau government's 1980 National Energy Program (NEP) was fiercely resisted by both Canadian-owned and U.S.-owned energy corporations in Alberta. The NEP sought to increase Canadian ownership, both private and public, in the Canadian oil patch. Whether Canadians, including Albertans, might have derived any benefit from the NEP became a moot point, as the corporate world quickly turned the issue into one of the federal government's meddling in provincial affairs. Resentment against the NEP in Alberta became so great that Ottawa beat a full retreat, and has been resistant ever since to developing any sort of national policy on energy. This has only emboldened Washington to push for ever greater control over Canadian energy. With help from the corporate world on both sides of the border, Washington has succeeded in blocking Ottawa from giving Canadians any sort of preferential access to our own energy resources. In the 1993 NAFTA treaty, for instance, Ottawa agreed to section 605, which effectively prevents Canada from cutting back our energy exports to the U.S., no matter how great the Canadian need may be. (Mexico, also a partner to NAFTA and also well endowed with oil, refused to agree to this provision and was granted an exception.)

And now, with negotiations under way to further integrate our economies under the SPP, Canada seems poised to surrender even greater control over our energy. Remarkably, the task of working out the details for the deeper integration has been handed to business leaders from Canada, the U.S. and Mexico. One of the chief goals identified by these business leaders has been deeper energy integration. Documents released by the business teams working on the SPP refer to the "North American energy market" and "North American energy security"—making no distinction between Canadian and U.S. energy supplies and security.

It's important to note that "North American energy security" is about meeting U.S. energy needs. With its voracious energy appetite, the U.S. has been rapidly devouring Canada's once-ample energy reserves, leaving our energy future somewhat precarious. At current consumption, Canada is now estimated to have less than a ten-year supply of conventional oil, and less than nine years proven natural gas reserves. (Yes, we have huge unconventional oil and gas reserves, in the oil sands and the Arctic, but developing them poses major environmental and feasibility problems.) Meanwhile, there are plans to build the Mackenzie Valley pipeline to bring our Arctic gas south, but almost all this gas is slated to be used (along with copious amounts of our fresh water) to produce oil from the oil sands, which will then be shipped to the U.S. This raises the question of whether there will be enough gas left to heat Canadian homes—or whether we'll have to rely on precarious plans to import liquefied natural gas from abroad.

Our corporate elite, led by the CCCE's Thomas d'Aquino, rejects the idea of giving priority to Canadian energy needs—as does Stephen Harper. Speaking to the Canada-UK Chamber of Commerce in London in July 2006, Harper endorsed "continental energy security" and rejected "self-serving monopolistic political strategies" that put Canadian requirements first. So the idea of government planning to meet our own needs is dismissed as "self-serving" and "monopolistic." Even though both the U.S. and Mexico have national energy strategies aimed at ensuring their domestic needs, Canada's elite fiercely resists such planning in the Canadian national interest.

So whether the members of our Canadian corporate elite are behaving like a comprador class or are simply choosing to make common cause with a set of powerful foreigners, one thing is clear: they're not on *our* side. By that, I mean that the Canadian corporate elite is defending its own interests as a business class, and this can and has put it at cross-purposes with the interests of the country and the broader public—or what used to be called "the public interest." Hence, our corporate elite is pushing for "North American energy security," even though this will limit our ability to ensure Canada's own energy security, something that will surely become more important in the coming worldwide energy crunch. Furthermore, Canadian energy companies are eagerly reaping the rich rewards of developing the oil sands and resisting any attempts to slow down that development, despite the disastrous impact on our environment, on our water resources and on our ability to meet our Kyoto commitments. So, in the key case of energy, the Canadian corporate elite could be said to be operating *at odds* with the Canadian public interest.

The corporate elite is also pushing for policies that make Canada more like the U.S., even though this is again at odds with what the broader Canadian public wants. Remaking Canada more in the U.S. image is partly about facilitating a deeper integration between the two countries and partly about replicating in Canada the kind of economic and tax policies that have rewarded the American elite so handsomely. Members of the Canadian elite—in the corporate as well as the media, academic and political worlds— enjoy a privileged position in Canadian society, and have a stake in preserving and enhancing that privileged position, creating for themselves the kind of richly advantaged position that the U.S. elite enjoys.

This desire to redesign Canada as a more unequal society is captured neatly in the writings of Canadian financier Conrad Black, who unabashedly expressed his contempt for the Canadian penchant for equality. Although Black's influence has waned with his mounting legal problems, he was for many years an influential Canadian commentator and spokesman for the business world, even creating the *National Post* as a vehicle (which it remains today) for business and right-wing advocacy in Canada. Black used the *Post* to ridicule the importance Canadians attach to programs like medicare, deriding the Canadian taste for equality and inclusiveness, and insisting instead that "we must create a society more able to contain and reward its greatest talents," presumably people like himself. Black routinely insisted that to reward our talented people, we had to lower their taxes or else they'd join the "brain drain" to the U.S., and we'd be left here all alone, barely able to figure out how to turn on the lights. Black, who gave up his Canadian citizenship to become a British baron, portrayed the Canadian taste for equality as some sort of resentment against the talented, even arguing that Canadians seem to be jealous of greatness.

Sadly, the Canadian elite has been successful in pushing Canada towards the U.S. model of inequality, moving us farther and farther from the more egalitarian European social model. While polling data consistently show that Canadians value social programs, the elite managed to convince Canadians that we had to cut social spending if we wanted to remain competitive in the global economy. It should be mentioned that, in reality, there is little connection between a country's level of social spending and its ability to compete in the global economy—as the European countries have proven. The high-spending social welfare nations of northern Europe, particularly the very high-spending Scandinavian countries, consistently rank among the top globally competitive nations, as ranked by the World Economic Forum in Geneva. Indeed, Finland has often scored No. 1, even ahead of the United States. In the 2006–2007 ranking, three Scandinavian countries scored in the top five.

Nonetheless, our elite has succeeded in pushing us to follow the U.S. example in cutting taxes and social spending, leaving us with ever-growing disparities between the rich and the poor. The extent of these disparities was captured vividly in a research report put out in the fall of 2005 by Citigroup Global Markets, a New York–based investment house. The report, prepared for Citigroup's investors, describes how the developed world is increasingly being divided into two blocs. On one side is the "egalitarian bloc," made up of Europe and Japan. On the other side are the "plutonomies"—economies where economic growth is largely consumed by the wealthy few. The key plutonomies, the report notes, are the U.S., the U.K.—and *Canada*.[23]

The report goes on to explain how striking the inequality has become in the plutonomies: "There are rich consumers, few in number, but disproportionate in the gigantic slice of income and consumption they take. There are the rest, the 'non-rich,' the multitudinous many, but only accounting for surprisingly small bites of the national pie." This level of inequality isn't entirely new, the report notes: "Plutonomies have occurred before in sixteenth century Spain, in seventeenth century Holland, the Gilded Age and the Roaring Twenties in the U.S." In other words, the extreme level of inequality in today's plutonomies is found only rarely in history. What's more, it's likely to continue into the future, according to the report: "We project that the plutonomies (the U.S., the U.K. and Canada) will likely see even more income inequality."

Members of our elite can clearly see the advantages of living in a plutonomy, and are no doubt frustrated by the deeply rooted taste for equality in so many of their compatriots.

If only all those infuriating Canadians weren't so jealous of greatness.

———

Time magazine selected George W. Bush as "Person of the Year" for 2004. At the same time, its Canadian edition, in selecting a "Canadian Newsmaker of the Year," chose Maher Arar. It's hard to imagine two men more different than Bush and Arar. While Bush is the swaggering frontman for the American empire, Arar is a modest immigrant, who became known in Canada only because he was tortured in Syria under the U.S.'s "extraordinary rendition" program. Arar went on to achieve a stature in Canada for boldly confronting the injustice he had endured and demanding accountability for what had happened to him—ultimately for raising his voice against the lawlessness of Bush's "war on terror."

Time was not endorsing either of these two individuals, merely drawing attention to the impact of their contributions. Bush's impact was obvious; Arar's less so. But in selecting Arar, the editors of *Time Canada* captured an essential aspect of Canadian political culture. They perceptively understood the significance of Arar to Canada: he was admired for having the guts to publicly challenge the injustice of the U.S. "war on terror" as well as our own government's complicity in that injustice.

The striking difference between Bush and Arar may also point to an important difference between Canadians and Americans that has not properly been appreciated. In the traditional stereotype, Canadians are polite, orderly and deferential to authority. (Question: What's the one word that will get a crowd of Canadians out of a swimming pool? Answer: "Please.") On the other hand, Americans, according to the stereotype, are bold, brash and defiant. But extensive data on the attitudes of Canadians and Americans, collected by pollster Michael Adams, reveal a different story. In his book *Fire and Ice*, Adams argues that Canadians and Americans are increasingly diverging in their values and attitudes. While Canadians have become skeptical and questioning of authority, Americans have become more deferential. Adams notes, for instance, that Canadians are less accepting of religious authority, and more egalitarian in their notions of the family, while Americans have become more accepting of religious authority and have come to see the family in more traditionally patriarchal terms. "The once-shy and deferential Canadians, who used to wait to be told by their betters what to do and how to think, have become more skeptical of traditional authority and more confident about their own personal decisions." Meanwhile, says Adams, Americans are "becoming more and more willing to Wait Till Their Father Comes Home to find out if it's okay to watch *The Simpsons*."[24]

We see this difference in the political domain as well. Americans fell in line behind their government to a surprising extent after 9/11, even as it embarked on a lawless course in the world. Canadians showed considerably more resistance to this lawlessness, in their reaction, for instance, to the treatment of Arar by U.S. authorities and by Canadian authorities co-operating with them. The mistreatment of Arar quickly became a *cause célèbre* in Canada in a way that the massive mistreatment of detainees at Guantánamo Bay and other U.S. prisons abroad failed to in the United States. In the Arar case, the demands for justice and accountability across Canada became so intense that the government of Paul Martin eventually felt obliged to call an inquiry—even over fierce objections from Washington. By contrast, in the United States, there's been no serious pressure for a probe of what amounts to a system of U.S. political prisons.

The Canadians who demanded a thorough probe into Arar's mistreatment could be said to represent a new Canadian character—a character who refuses to simply defer to those with power, even the vast power of the U.S. government.

Perhaps it is the spunkiness and independent-mindedness of this new Canadian character that so irritates members of our elite, who prefer us to be deferential to U.S. authority. Despite the efforts of our elite to drum Canadians into line and convince us that resistance to the U.S. empire is futile—so we might as well engage in what Canadian journalist Murray Dobbin has dubbed "pre-emptive surrender"—there seems to be a new, defiant Canadian afoot in the land.

This new Canadian is neither anti-American nor self-adoring—just resistant to bullies, on both sides of the border.

CHAPTER 2

NO MORE GIRLIE-MAN PEACEKEEPING

It is early on a Saturday morning in the north Toronto neighbourhood of Armour Heights, and most of the residents are no doubt still sleeping. But at the Canadian Forces College, a pleasant campus that fits unobtrusively and almost unnoticed into the quiet residential neighbourhood, the coffee has already been served and a wide-awake crowd of senior Canadian military officers, soldiers, defence analysts and lobbyists listen with rapt attention as a U.S. general lays out a stark vision of global conflict.

Lt.-Gen. Thomas Metz, an Iraq-hardened commanding general from Fort Hood, Texas, presents the audience with "a quick trip around the world." Using slides, he flashes a series of maps that highlight, one at a time, India, China, the Pacific Rim, the Western Hemisphere, Europe and sub-Saharan Africa. Then he comes to his final map, the one that really matters. Unlike all the others, this isn't just a map of a geographic area. It's a map of a religion: the Islamic World.

"The Islamic faith is not evil," says the general, then quickly adds, "but it's been hijacked by thugs . . . Most of the Islamic world believes the suicide bombers of the World Trade Center are now in the land of milk and honey." The general notes that there are almost a billion people in the Islamic world, and that if only one per cent of them are radical, "that's ten million radicals."

He then shows a chart depicting the military challenges America faces, measured in terms of level of danger and level of likelihood. At the very apex—the most dangerous and the most likely—sits just one: radical Islamic terrorism. "Radical Islam wants to re-establish the Caliphate," says Metz. "Just as Hitler wrote *Mein Kampf*, you can read what they want to do."

If the residents of the sleepy enclave of Armour Heights are like most other Canadians, they are attached to the notion of Canada as a peaceful nation, indeed a world leader in peace-keeping. And as they wake up and begin to go about their day on this cold, sunny Saturday morning in January 2006, they are not likely thinking much about going to battle against ten million Muslims. But Lt.-Gen. Metz—and the Canadian military types gathered to hear him—have been up early, working hard to change that.

———

In the midst of his talk about the dangers of Islamic terrorism, Lt.-Gen. Metz abruptly shifts gears and starts talking about America's dependence on oil.

In his southern drawl, the general notes how much oil the U.S. consumes—roughly 25 per cent of the world's consumption, even though Americans make up only 5 per cent of the world's population—and how central this is to the country's high standard of living. To dramatize the importance of energy, the general points out that one can put a pint of gasoline into a chainsaw and then go out and cut a huge amount of wood before the gasoline runs out. The next day, he says, one could feed a big, strong man an enormous breakfast and send him out to cut wood—and he'd be able to cut only a fraction of what the gasoline-fired chainsaw had been able to cut in far less time. The lesson from this little fable is clear: America needs oil to go on being the rich, advanced society that it enjoys being. Without oil, Americans would be like that big strong man with the big breakfast—with only a tiny pile of wood to show for it.

The general's little discourse on the importance of energy to America is certainly interesting. But what is it doing in a speech about military threats to the United States? The connection between America's voracious oil consumption and the dangers of radical Islamic terrorism are never explicitly stated by Lt.-Gen. Metz; he simply notes that the Islamic world has a lot of oil and what happens there has an impact on energy markets. But an important element has clearly been added to the picture: the U.S. needs what lies under the ground in the Islamic world if Americans are to go on living the bounteous life that lies at the heart of the American dream—a life that has them devouring the lion's share of the world's energy.

Given that Lt.-Gen. Metz is a military man and he is addressing a military gathering at a military college, one might be tempted to conclude that gaining control over the Islamic world and its oil is regarded as something of a military matter, that the United States is inclined to use its vast military power to ensure itself access to this vital resource. That sounds very aggressive. It smacks of old-style imperialism—plundering the resources of another country. Indeed, Metz's thinking sounds similar to the "militarized imagination" that psychologist Floyd Rudmin described in the last chapter. Metz is suggesting that the Islamic world is planning to do to America what America is in fact planning to do to the Islamic world.

Of course, we're told that the U.S. isn't acting aggressively; it's simply defending itself against the aggression of the Islamic world—a world full of people who wish to harm America. Don't forget there are some ten million of these people, "thugs" who want to destroy America. What choice does America have but to fight back, to defend itself? Suddenly, what might have seemed like a war of aggression has become a war of self-defence, a war to wipe out the scourge of terrorism.

America's vigilance against terrorism, it seems, just happens to coincide with its need for oil.

————

There was a buzz of excitement in the packed hall of the Ottawa Congress Centre as newly anointed Chief of Defence Staff General Rick Hillier delivered his inaugural address to more than two thousand Canadian soldiers from National Defence headquarters. It had been a long time since members of the Canadian Forces, disheartened after years of budget cuts and feeling ignored by politicians and the public, had felt this kind of energy. And it had a lot to do with Hillier himself, a Newfoundlander whose presence that day seemed to fill the room. Hillier was a whole new kind of general—tough, brash, straight-talking, ready to take on any enemy, exuding a kind of warrior bravado rarely seen in a Canadian general. And the audience lapped it up. "When Canadian troops go overseas," declared the general, "they expect sex." Within a split second, Hillier had corrected himself: "success." It was a slip of the tongue, nothing more. But it also somehow fit the mood in the room. After years of feeling like an emasculated army of peacekeepers, the Canadian Forces now had a real fighting man at their helm. No more girlie-man peacekeeping, boys! We're gonna make war!

For years, many in our military have chafed under the notion that their main function in the postwar era is peacekeeping. They've been gripped by a fear of losing their "warrior ethic," by what retired Canadian general John Arch MacInnis, writing in *Canadian Defence Quarterly*, described as the "morbid fear of being transformed into a peacekeeping force." Military historian Jack Granatstein perhaps comes closest to getting at the primal emotions involved when he describes the "devastating effect" that peacekeeping has had on the Canadian military, creating what he calls "a flaccid military."[1] There is no mistaking Granatstein's deliberate invoking of notions of masculinity and sexual potency, and his implication that only by engaging in real combat will our "flaccid" military once again teem with testosterone.

The instalment of Hillier as Canada's top soldier in February 2005 signalled the transformation of the Canadian military into a combat force, and one that would mesh neatly with the U.S. military. The threadbare Canadian military has long looked to the amply funded, amply armed U.S. military as the big time, as the ultimate in military sophistication and fighting power. It's long been Canadian military policy to send high-level officers for training at the U.S. Army War College in Pennsylvania, to the U.S. Army Staff School in Kansas or to U.S. military bases. Increasingly, this U.S. training seems to have become a key qualification for high command in the Canadian Forces. It's interesting to note that both Hillier and the vice chief of defence staff, Lt.-Gen. W. J. Natynczyk, have done high-level postings in the United States. (Natynczyk even served in Iraq as deputy commanding general of the Multinational Corps.)

Hillier had the distinction of being the first Canadian to be appointed deputy commander general at Fort Hood, the Texas military base that Lt.-Gen. Metz hails from. Fort Hood is also the home base of the elite III Corps, the self-styled "counter-attack corps," known for its heavy artillery and fighting skills and referred to fondly in military circles as "America's Hammer." (Former U.S. defense secretary Donald Rumsfeld once referred to members of the corps as "some of the most highly respected warriors in the world.") Hillier, a lifelong soldier and member of the prestigious armoured corps within the Canadian Forces, was clearly thrilled to be deputy commander of one of the most respected units in the U.S. military, and he fully absorbed its fighting credo—and appears to have also absorbed its contempt for "radical Islam."

Hillier's public remarks have shown an enthusiasm for war and for fighting Islamic insurgents that have had a distinctly un-Canadian ring, or at least have been strikingly different from what Canadians have heard in the past from our top military officials. Brazenly thumbing his nose at the Pearsonian peacekeeping tradition, Hillier, as chief of defence staff, publicly stated that the role of the Canadian military is "to be able to kill people." And he publicly referred to insurgents in Afghanistan as "scumbags," a term even more hostile and demeaning than Metz's term "thugs." While there have been mixed reactions to Hillier's "straight-talking" approach in the Canadian media and among the public, this sort of macho tough talk is definitely popular within the military, even in the officer ranks. Amongst themselves, officers in the Canadian military sometimes refer to Muslims as "ragheads," and express great enthusiasm that Canadian soldiers are finally getting more "trigger time." The U.S. notion, as articulated by Lt.-Gen. Metz, that the West must engage in a long-term war against radical Islam is a common one in our military ranks.

Certainly the military seems to be gearing itself up for a drawn-out battle against Third World insurgents. One indication of this is a somewhat bizarre book called *Crisis in Zefra*, produced by the Department of National Defence and available on the department's website. Designed to showcase high-tech weapons and tactics of the future, the book tells the story of Canadian troops, fighting as part of a coalition, battling insurgents in the imaginary war-torn city of Zefra in the year 2025. While the account is clearly fictional, there is no mistaking the non-Western nature of the enemy. The accompanying drawings depict mean-looking characters in turbans and sandals; the distinctive outlines of a mosque are clearly visible. In one scenario in the book, a Canadian commander encounters a toothless Zefran man who offers him "a reeking paper bag" filled with a curry dish, which the man is hoping to sell for $20. The transaction is completed; the man gets the money while the Canadian army gets a curry dinner and a shot at winning "the hearts and minds of the people."

Crisis in Zefra is simply a fictional version of the "Three Block War" concept, which was the theme of Lt.-Gen. Metz's speech to the Canadian Forces College. This is the model for battling "terrorists" in "failed states." It involves the U.S. and its allies engaging in various efforts—all in the space of three city blocks—that include high-intensity combat, tracking down insurgents and winning the hearts and minds of the local population. Metz's keynote presentation to the day-long event—hosted by the Canadian Institute for Strategic Studies, an influential lobby group for the military—outlined for Canadians how to fight the Three Block War.

The Canadian military has eagerly taken on the role of partner in the U.S. "war on terror." Projecting this new image seems to have been the purpose of an advertising campaign, developed by the Canadian Defence Department and aimed at Washington and the American public. The campaign, which included ads on Washington bus shelters and a website, steers clear of the word "peacekeeping" and instead emphasizes Canada's war fighting, specifically as America's ally in the "war on terror." The website, CanadianAlly.com, points to the 21,250 personnel and 22 warships deployed in the Afghan war since 2001—as well as the 43 Canadian deaths (a number that is constantly being revised upward). Reading the website, it's hard not to get the feeling that our war dead are being offered up as tokens of our devotion to our American friends.

Under a section called "Facts Which May Surprise You," the website provides a history of Canada's military engagements, going back to the First World War. Reading this, one would have little sense that Canada has, until recently, been a world leader in peacekeeping. Instead, the emphasis is on Canadian battlefield heroics in both world wars, in Korea (where a Canadian battalion was awarded a U.S. Presidential citation, the website notes), in the first Gulf War, in the Balkans and in Kosovo (where Canadians carried out 10 per cent of the NATO bombing campaign, the website says). Another feature of the website, under a section called "Did You Know?" (right below a picture of a group of Canadian soldiers in full combat gear, carrying machine guns), highlights the fact that Canada is America's largest supplier of oil, gas, electricity and uranium. The message seems to be that Canada is a full-service ally; whether America is looking for troops for its "war on terror" or oil to feed its energy habit, Canada is standing by, ready to help.

This attempt to reposition the Canadian Forces as a robust war-fighting U.S. ally has been under way for some time within the Canadian military, but it has come to fruition under the governments of Paul Martin and Stephen Harper. It was the Martin government that appointed Hillier chief of defence staff and began pumping large amounts of new money into military spending. Soon after his appointment, Hillier began pressuring Martin to agree to U.S. requests to increase and intensify Canadian involvement in the Afghan war. Martin was initially hesitant, but agreed to the deeper commitment in Afghanistan, only after extracting from Hillier a promise that the Canadian military would also have sufficient troops available to participate in vital UN peacekeeping missions. At a meeting with Hillier and the defence and foreign affairs ministers on March 21, 2005, Martin stressed the importance of the Canadian Forces being prepared to help the UN intervene, particularly in the brutal fighting in Darfur, where hundreds of thousands of people had been killed. Despite Hillier's assurances that troops would be available for peacekeeping, the general argued the following spring—with the support of the newly elected Harper government—that the military was so overworked by the Afghan deployment that it lacked the soldiers to contribute to a UN mission to Darfur.[2]

Under Harper, the military's desire to transform itself into an adjunct of the U.S. "war on terror" was now perfectly in sync with the government in Ottawa. Just as Harper's appointment of Rona Ambrose to be environment minister signalled his government's resistance to Kyoto, Harper signalled his active support for the army's transformation with the appointment of Gordon O'Connor as defence minister, as well as with further increases in the military budget. O'Connor, a retired brigadier general with a thirty-year military career, also has an extensive background lobbying for defence contractors. O'Connor lobbied for such major contractors as Airbus Military, United Defense and General Dynamics Canada. He also was a senior associate for the Canadian subsidiary of Hill & Knowlton, the giant U.S. marketing firm notorious for concocting a report about Iraqi soldiers tossing Kuwait babies out of incubators, as part of a massive disinformation campaign during the first Gulf War. In addition to what influence his past lobbying connections might have on the army's actual procurements, O'Connor's background shows how deeply tied he is to the Canadian military and to the defence lobby. Past federal governments have typically chosen civilians as defence ministers, thereby putting a little distance between the military and the politician overseeing it. O'Connor is the first Canadian defence minister in twenty years to have actually served in the military. He also belonged to the same armoured corps unit within the military that Hillier comes from.

Harper himself has directly encouraged the new image of Canada as a war-making U.S. ally, and has even deliberately aped Bush's warrior style. Showing up to speak to Canadian troops in Afghanistan in March 2006, Harper donned full combat body armour and carried a helmet under his arm—just as George W. Bush did in his Mission Accomplished photo-op after the fall of Saddam. "We don't make a commitment and then run away at the first sign of trouble," Harper told the troops, echoing Bush's constant theme that the U.S. military won't "cut and run." Harper also used the fifth anniversary of 9/11 to position Canada more firmly as an ally in the U.S. "war on terror." He surrounded him-self that day with Canadian relatives of 9/11 victims and of soldiers serving in Afghanistan, just as Bush frequently surrounds himself with 9/11 victims and U.S. soldiers serving in Iraq. "As the events of September 11 so clearly illustrate, the horrors of the world will not go away if we turn a blind eye to them, no matter how far off they may be," said Harper. "And these horrors cannot be stopped unless some among us are willing to accept enormous sacrifice and risk to themselves."

With the prime minister, the defence minister and the Canadian military all wanting to align Canada fully with the U.S. "war on terror," all the ducks in the pond seem to be lined up in the same direction. The only duck that might destroy the neat formation is the Canadian public.

———

In the advertising world, bait and switch is a classic strategy. The advertiser has a product that is difficult to sell, so he lures in prospective customers by showing off another product that he knows they'll find appealing. Only when he's got them inside the showroom does he deftly try to switch their attention to what he's really hoping to sell. The Canadian military has been using bait and switch for years, baiting the Canadian public with peacekeeping in the hopes of selling its real agenda: war making.

Canada's military has long understood the Canadian fondness for peacekeeping. Polls have shown over the years that close to 90 per cent of Canadians enthusiastically endorse Canada's involvement in UN peacekeeping—a role that Canada played prominently for decades after Lester Pearson organized the first real UN peacekeeping mission in 1956. Hanging on a wall upstairs at the Canadian Forces College, not far from where General Metz made his speech, is an outdated Canadian military poster featuring a Canadian soldier on a peacekeeping mission.

Tall and strong and wearing the distinctive blue beret of a UN peacekeeper, the soldier protectively holds a crying boy who is clutching a teddy bear. The poster neatly captures the Canadian public's image of its soldiers intervening to protect the vulnerable in troubled parts of the world. Over time, the notion of Canada as a peacekeeping nation has become, for many Canadians, an essential part of their self-image.

The Canadian public's fondness for peacekeeping has long grated on many in our military establishment, but they largely kept quiet about their resentment of being saddled with Pearson's legacy. They even deliberately highlighted the peacekeeping image with the public, realizing that it was crucial to maintaining support for military budgets among Canadians who might otherwise have seen little relevance for significant military spending in a peacetime era. And the federal government was also traditionally eager to keep the peacekeeping model front and centre with the public, knowing its appeal.

But with the arrival of the Harper government and its overt support for war making, members of the Canadian military establishment have grown bolder. They no longer seem to feel obliged to dangle peace in front of Canadians, in the hopes of winning support for war. Now they make the case directly for war, and insist that peacekeeping is passé in today's world, that it no longer really exists. "It died in Rwanda" says Michael Ignatieff, the runner-up in the federal Liberal leadership race of 2006. Ignatieff supported the U.S. invasion of Iraq and insists that Canada now needs a "more muscular policy."[3] This theme has been echoed by others, including Jack Granatstein and retired Lt.-Gen. George Macdonald, who have both argued that traditional UN peacekeeping no longer exists.

This is patently untrue, as is clear at UN headquarters in New York. From his large office, Jean-Marie Guéhenno, under-secretary-general for peacekeeping operations, oversees 18 missions involving

71,823 peacekeepers from 108 nations. In fact, UN peacekeeping activities are near an all-time high. What has changed in recent years is not the number of conflict zones requiring UN peace-keeping but the willingness of Western nations, including Canada, to participate. "I regret that Canada has so little involvement with peacekeeping," says Guéhenno.[4]

For decades, Canada was a star international performer on the peacekeeping front, participating in virtually every UN mission and providing substantial numbers of troops. Since 1947, a total of 125,000 Canadian military personnel have served in UN missions. That amounts to more than 10 per cent of the UN total. (And 120 of those Canadian peacekeepers were killed performing their duties.) But in recent years, Canada has virtually disappeared from the UN peacekeeping scene. By March 2006, for instance, Canada ranked 49th, out of 108 nations, providing only 169 soldiers, considerably less than one per cent of the total UN force. So it's not just that Canada is no longer a star performer on the peacekeeping stage; it's actually a laggard, ranking well below the troop contributions of tiny nations like Benin (412 troops), Togo (326) and Fiji (197).

Canada's failure to step up to the plate for UN operations is part of a larger retreat by Western nations that has left UN peacekeeping missions increasingly reliant on the Third World. The leading contributor to peacekeeping is now Bangladesh, with 10,255 troops, followed by Pakistan, India, Jordan and Nepal. The first Western nation to show up on the UN peace-keeping list is Poland, at No. 19 (with 712 troops). The only other Western nations in the top thirty are Ukraine (658 troops), France (584) and Ireland (467). Guéhenno argues that this lack of Western support is debilitating for UN efforts, partly because it leaves UN missions often lacking in specific technical capacities, since Third World nations tend to have less-sophisticated mili-tary equipment. "In the Congo, we needed attack helicopters," said Guéhenno. "We looked for more than a year to find them. Eventually we got some from India."

Equally if not more important, according to Guéhenno, is the political significance of the West's declining involvement. "It sends a powerful signal," he notes, pointing out that in any conflict where the UN intervenes, its peacekeeping forces represent "the stakes the international community puts on the table." So a minimal representation from the West sends the message that the rich, powerful Western nations have only limited interest in the crisis. "Yes, the Security Council cares, yes the international community cares, but only up to a point—not to the point where the whole world is going to come together to really address the situation." This lack of interest is understood by those involved in the conflict, who, according to Guéhenno, often think they can get away with more since they're only dealing with countries that aren't "at the head table."

So, contrary to the declarations of Ignatieff and others that UN peacekeeping is dead, it's very much alive—with Canada missing in action. And Guéhenno makes no secret of his belief that greater Canadian involvement would make a significant positive difference: "It would send a very strong and powerful signal if Canada showed it was going back into peacekeeping. In the credibility of peacekeeping, it would not go unnoticed, because of the historical role of Canada in the creation of peacekeeping, and because of what Canada represents today."

It's not that the powerful, influential Western nations have been staying away from global hot spots. Not at all. It's just that they've increasingly been making their interventions through NATO (the North Atlantic Treaty Organization), rather than through the UN. Commentators often talk about the UN and NATO as if they're similar organizations, both intervening in conflict zones around the world. In fact, they're very different. The UN is the closest thing we have to a body representing the world, whereas NATO is a military alliance essentially representing the West, and it is effectively controlled by the United States. Established after the Second World War with a mandate to protect Europe from potential Soviet aggression, NATO has continued to exist despite the demise of the Soviet Union, and its troops are now being deployed in faraway Afghanistan. But its new role as a kind of world police force fighting in the "war on terror," rather than as a defensive alliance, changes the nature of NATO substantially, and raises the question of what role it can and should play. Its mission in Afghanistan has been given the approval of the UN Security Council, so officially it has the sanction of the world body. But how does NATO come across in the non-Western world—in the Muslim world, for instance?

By participating in NATO missions rather than UN missions, Canada—along with other nations—is choosing to be part of a Western force, essentially operating under the direction of the United States, rather than being part of a more broadly based and inclusive UN force. We are choosing to be part of what amounts to an army of the West. It's not hard to see how this could fuel the notion of a "clash of civilizations."

In the hierarchy of most-wanted terrorists, Abu Musab al-Zarqawi was up there in the stratosphere. He was believed to be the leader of al Qaeda in Iraq and was therefore held responsible for much of what had gone so terribly wrong with the U.S. occupation. He was also reportedly an extremely brutal man who pioneered beheadings as a terrorist method in Iraq and who personally beheaded American businessman Nicholas Berg, an execution which was captured on video and shown around the world. So when the U.S. Air Force dropped two massive bombs on a house in Iraq in June 2006, killing al-Zarqawi (as well as six others, including a woman and child), it was perhaps not surprising that there was much celebrating in the U.S. media. What was surprising, however, was the widely expressed belief that al-Zarqawi's death would take the steam out of the insurgency.

This reflected a view of the insurgency as a cult-like group of religious fanatics who hate us in the West because of our freedoms and our lifestyles, the way we dress, the music we play and the movies we watch. Theirs is an irrational hatred, based on a fanatical loyalty to the leader, we're told. If the leader is killed, the theory seems to go, the religious spell will be broken, and the group will become dispirited and lose its sense of direction and purpose.

Within days of al-Zarqawi's death, media pundits were expressing disappointment and puzzlement that the insurgency just kept right on going, that his demise hadn't stopped or even reduced the violence in Iraq. (In fact, it increased.) Typically, however, none of the puzzled pundits seemed to consider that the answer to their confusion—just like their ongoing confusion over the U.S. failure to "win" in Iraq—lay in their misunderstanding of the nature of the enemy in the "war on terror."

One of the few systematic studies of terrorism provides evidence that refutes the theory of terrorists as a fanatical group of irrational zealots. Robert Pape, a political scientist at the University of Chicago and director of the Chicago Project on Suicide Terrorism, has put together a comprehensive data bank of every suicide terrorist attack—there have been 315 such attacks, at last count—in the world since 1980.

"What nearly all suicide terrorist attacks have in common," notes Pape in his book *Dying to Win*, "is a specific secular and strategic goal: to compel modern democracies to withdraw military forces from territory that the terrorists consider to be their homeland." In other words, their motivation isn't irrational or religious. It's rational and political. Pape also notes that once a military occupation ends, the suicide terrorism tends to stop.[5]

Pape's extensive study of suicide terrorism leads him to conclude that the phenomenon has little to do with Islamic fundamentalism. Indeed, the world leader in suicide attacks is a secular, Marxist group in Sri Lanka known as the Tamil Tigers. They invented the suicide vest.

"Suicide terrorism is mainly a response to foreign occupation, not Islamic fundamentalism," maintains Pape. "Since 1990, the United States has stationed tens of thousands of ground troops on the Arabian Peninsula, and that is the main mobilization appeal of Osama bin Laden and al-Qaeda. People who make the argument that it is a good thing to have them attacking us over there [rather than here] are missing that suicide terrorism is not a supply-limited phenomenon . . . [I]t is driven by the presence of foreign forces on the territory that the terrorists view as their homeland. The operation in Iraq has stimulated suicide terrorism . . . Before our invasion, Iraq never had a suicide-terrorist attack in its history. Never . . . Every year that the United States has stationed 150,000 combat troops in Iraq, suicide terrorism has doubled."

One of the reasons that it's sometimes hard for North Americans to see this is because, as mentioned in chapter 1, the story of U.S. interventions abroad is often cut from the main narrative, leaving only the terrorist response, which then appears unprovoked. So, in the eyes of many people, the original 9/11 attack appeared to come from nowhere. But this is only because we've been so uninformed about past U.S. attempts to impose military control over the Persian Gulf. The U.S. role in the region was candidly described by the neoconservative crowd, including Dick Cheney, Donald Rumsfeld, Paul Wolfowitz and Lewis Libby, who formed the Project for the New American Century (PNAC) in the late 1990s and then went on to run the Bush administration. In one of its key documents, *Rebuilding America's Defenses*, prepared in 2000, the PNAC unabashedly describes America's past military role and future aspirations for control of the region. "In the Persian Gulf, the presence of American forces, along with British and French units, has become a semi-permanent fact of life . . . Indeed, the United States has for decades sought to play a more permanent role in Gulf regional security. While the unresolved conflict with Iraq provides the immediate justification, the need for a substantial American force presence in the Gulf transcends the issue of the regime of Saddam Hussein."[6]

So, only a year before they actually gained power, here are some of the most powerful members of the soon-to-be Bush administration stating unabashedly that the desire to get rid of Saddam isn't just about Saddam or the "unresolved conflict with Iraq," but is about "the need for a substantial American force presence in the Gulf." In other words, it's about extending U.S. control over the region. Furthermore, as these neocons note, a permanent role in the Gulf has been a U.S. priority for decades, and U.S. forces have already become "a semi-permanent fact of life" in the region. All this would seem to be exactly the sort of foreign military presence that might well, according to Pape's analysis, spark a "terrorist" response.

One got little sense of this background and the aggressiveness of U.S. intentions, however, in a two-hour CNN documentary, "In the Footsteps of bin Laden," broadcast repeatedly in the weeks leading up to the fifth anniversary of 9/11, and reportedly seen by some ten million viewers. In the documentary, by senior CNN correspondent Christiane Amanpour, the story of what led to the 9/11 attacks is essentially reduced to the story of the personal transformation of Osama bin Laden from a very rich, young Saudi boy into a religious fanatic with a fervent hatred of America. There is little explanation of any motive for this hatred, other than zealotry and religion, despite the fact that bin Laden's many statements and writings clearly reveal a ferocious opposition to America's role as an occupying power and its unwavering support for Israel's occupation of Palestine. This omission is very interesting. Amanpour could have captured the utter brutality of bin Laden—his ruthlessness in killing almost three thousand civilians in the 9/11 attacks—without distorting his motives. By portraying him as a religious fanatic, Amanpour and CNN kept the spotlight diverted from the political nature of his motivation. This distortion helps prevent Americans from demanding any changes in U.S. foreign policy—the one thing that might actually reduce the risk of terrorist attacks against America.

Amanpour and countless other media correspondents and commentators have managed to make the U.S. role as a foreign occupying power largely disappear for North American audiences. This reinforces the notion that we Westerners are the victims in this clash with the Muslim world. Promoting the notion of our victimhood is no small feat, considering the fact that we have tens of thousands of troops in their part of the world, and they have none at all in ours. But then Western invading forces are presented positively to Western audiences, not as invaders but as "liberators." (Or if the "liberator" label seems too far-fetched, then they are presented at least as part of a well-meaning mission, intended to rid the world of some pernicious danger.)

The arrogance of this notion is stupefying. From time immemorial, invading armies have been hated in the countries they've invaded. It's only Western arrogance that leads us to imagine that our invasions would be received differently. *The Daily Show with Jon Stewart* captured the absurdity of this notion in August 2006 with a spoof on Condoleezza Rice's blithe dismissal of the suffering caused by the Israeli attack on Lebanon as just part of the "birth pangs of a new Middle East." In the spoof, an Arab commentator suggests that Middle Easterners willingly accept these birth pangs—just as Americans accepted 9/11 as the "birth pangs of a new America."

Violence and brutality somehow feel different when they're directed against you. What Western commentators dismiss as unintended "collateral damage" is experienced by those on the receiving end as the devastating deaths of family members. The British MP George Galloway, in a riveting TV interview in July 2006, berated a British television anchor for her insensitivity to the suffering of the Arab world, noting that she knew the name of every captured Israeli soldier, but not the name of the Palestinian family killed that summer by an Israeli gunboat on a Gaza beach.

But while our media have rendered the suffering of the Arab world invisible to us, it is highly visible to—and deeply felt by—the people in the region. So while Christiane Amanpour manages to sanitize the coercive role played by the U.S. and its allies in the Middle East, people living there see and experience it in powerful ways. In a seven-minute video of Israeli troops attacking crowds of unarmed Palestinians in July 2006, for instance, one sees a very young Palestinian boy—a six-year-old, it turns out—being carried away by an Israeli soldier. In the video, which was available on the YouTube Internet site, the little boy's face is contorted in fear as he reaches out over the soldier's shoulder for his mother, who chases desperately along behind, trying to free her son. Meanwhile other pleading, screaming, frantic Palestinian women, carrying their own young children, run after the Israeli soldier, also trying to free the captured boy, only to be pushed roughly out of the way by other Israeli soldiers. It is almost impossible to watch the video without gasping in horror and disbelief. There is something almost primeval about the forced separation of this young child from his mother by heavily armed soldiers. It captures the ultimate horror of occupation: the powerlessness of an occupied people against an all-powerful foreign army. This sort of video would never be shown on Western TV, but it fills the screens of TV sets throughout the Muslim world night after night.

Isn't this a more likely explanation for the rage that is surging through the Middle East?

If you attack your neighbour, destroy his house, trash his car, kill several members of his family and kidnap his six-year-old son, would it be logical to conclude that your neighbour is in a rage against you because he doesn't like how you dress and what movies you watch?

———

As Canada's troop casualties in Afghanistan mounted in the summer and fall of 2006, so did the calls for us to stay the course and "rally behind our troops." With each death, there were new pledges not to "cut and run." In early September, when four Canadians were killed in an attempt to retake a Taliban-controlled area in the Panjwai district, the media stepped in to prop up support for the mission. Touting the Canadian offensive as one of Canada's "biggest battles since the Second World War," the *Globe and Mail* ran a banner front-page headline: "Bloodied, but unbowed." The epic language suggested we were in the fight of our lives, that, in the face of immense suffering, we had to find the courage to go on. The media and the government were of one mind: much as we may feel our resolve waver at the sight of returning coffins and grieving relatives, *we must prevail*.

The only remaining question seemed to be the one that Lt.-Gen. Metz posed to his Canadian audience: do we have the will to fight?

But perhaps we should start with a more basic question: is this a war we should be fighting?

———

On a brilliantly sunny day in early February 2002, a few Afghan men were on a snowy mountain bluff in southeastern Afghanistan when they were blown to pieces by a U.S. Hellfire missile fired from a pilotless Predator drone.

A CIA team operating the drone from a remote location had picked up images of the men on the bluff, above a set of caves where a former Muslim guerilla camp had been located. (The site had been heavily bombed by U.S. aircraft the month before.) Suspicions arose. The men didn't appear to be local farmers. What was there to farm on this remote bluff? Besides, one of them was very tall, and the others appeared to be bending over— in an apparently deferential way. So there was a very tall man, surrounded by other men acting deferentially, not far from some caves where a guerilla camp had operated.

The CIA team had seen enough. Apparently thinking that the tall man could be Osama bin Laden, they released the Hellfire missile, instantly blowing away three men—and forever devastating the lives of their wives and children who lived in the nearby village of Lalazha, near the city of Khost.

The whole thing turned out to be an unfortunate mistake. The tall man wasn't bin Laden. He was Daraz Khan. At 5'11" he was a good five inches shorter than bin Laden, but then the Predator's images aren't perfect. And the men bending down probably weren't being deferential. Rather, it seems they were bending down to pick up scrap metal, which was why they had come to this remote location. They were poor villagers who had walked some fourteen kilometres to the site, which was strewn with the debris of the bombed-out camp, in the hope of collecting enough twisted metal scraps to earn perhaps a dollar and a half, to be split among the three of them. In the severe poverty of the Afghan mountains, that dollar and a half would justify the trip, making a difference in the diet of the families who depended on the three men.

The Pentagon justified its actions, explaining that the CIA team thought it might have had the al Qaeda leader in its sights.[7] A week later, Rear Admiral John D. Stufflebeem, the Pentagon's top military spokesperson, told a news conference that from the images, it appeared that there was "a meeting on a hillside" and that "the initial indications afterwards would seem to say that these are not peasant people up there farming." Another Pentagon spokesperson, Victoria Clarke, said: "We're convinced that it was an appropriate target" even though "we do not know yet exactly who it was."

In other words, the Pentagon was insisting it had made an honest mistake. U.S. officials spotted a meeting on a hillside, and unleashed a deadly missile on the chance that bin Laden might be one of the participants. No harm was meant to these innocent villagers; they just happened to get in the way of Washington in hot pursuit of its prey. Even though by a week later it was clear that the dead men did not include bin Laden, the Pentagon was satisfied that it had hit an "appropriate target," whoever the unidentified men were. By that, presumably, the spokesperson meant that it was legitimate for U.S. forces to drop the missile because they'd done it with good intentions.

The deaths of Khan and his friends didn't cause much of a stir in the West. Apparently it was understood that such unfortunate side effects of the "war on terror" are inevitable. Mistakes happen; it was all for a good cause. (And, of course, we in the West would understand and forgive if foreign troops came into our territory and mistakenly blew away several locals in their keenness to hunt down someone they had a score to settle with.)

The lack of Western reaction to the deaths is striking. Clearly, if Khan and his friends had been blown up in a terrorist hit on the London underground, their deaths would have provoked outrage in the West. But their killing by a U.S. missile is sloughed off as an honest mistake, even a *legitimate* mistake. (Who could blame those guys operating the drone? They thought there was an off chance they might have had Osama bin Laden in their sights!) All this is apparently consistent with the notion that the U.S. is morally justified in its use of force, even when innocent people are killed, because it doesn't intend to kill these people or it kills them only by mistake. As George W. Bush told the United Nations on November 10, 2001: "Unlike the enemy, we seek to minimize, not maximize the loss of innocent life." This distinction is frequently made by Washington and its supporters, in an effort to draw a moral distinction between acts of terrorism and violent acts carried out by the U.S. as part of its "war on terror"—even when both result in the killing of innocents.

But no such distinction exists in international law. Michael Mandel, a law professor at Osgoode Hall Law School in Toronto, argues that U.S. killings, such as those of Daraz Khan, were not only tragedies but the gravest of international crimes, because they were committed in the course of an illegal war—the U.S. invasion of Afghanistan, launched in October 2001.[8]

International law, as set out in the United Nations Charter, is very specific in defining scenarios under which war can legally be waged. As mentioned in chapter 1, there are basically only two scenarios that legitimize war. First, if a country is directly attacked, and there is no non-violent remedy, it can respond with military force in self-defence. The only other scenario—when the collective interest of international peace and security is at stake—requires the authorization of the UN Security Council. Mandel, author of *How America Gets Away with Murder*, notes that self-defence does not apply in the case of the U.S. attack on Afghanistan, since the U.S. launched wars against both Iraq and Afghanistan, even though it was not attacked by either country. Washington also failed to secure UN Security Council authorization. In the case of Iraq, Washington tried to get such authorization but failed, and so decided to proceed with its invasion anyway. In the case of Afghanistan, Washington never even tried for Security Council authorization.[9] Thus, says Mandel, both the Afghanistan and Iraq invasions were illegal under international law.

The illegality of the invasion of Iraq was more clear-cut and obvious, since no connection has ever been established between the 9/11 attack and Iraq. (Indeed, the illegality of the Iraq war has been widely noted, although not frequently acknowledged in the mainstream media.) But the war in Afghanistan has long been considered more complicated and nuanced, since the ruling Taliban apparently allowed the al Qaeda terrorists who carried out 9/11 to use Afghanistan as a base. It might seem then, that the U.S. could reasonably argue that it was attacking Afghanistan in self-defence, since Afghanistan had harboured a group that had attacked America.

The U.S. had used a similar argument in the 1980s to justify its attack on Nicaragua. In a case before the International Court of Justice, Washington argued that the Sandinista government of Nicaragua was harbouring insurgents from El Salvador, allowing them to use Nicaragua as a base to attack El Salvador, which was allied with the United States. Washington insisted that, in the interests of "collective self-defence (for itself and its ally El Salvador)," it was entitled to bomb Nicaragua and mine its waters. But the court rejected this argument, maintaining that the claim of self-defence applies only when a state attacks another state, not simply when it harbours the attacker.

No matter how compelling the U.S. case against bin Laden was, Washington did not have the right under international law to invade Afghanistan in order to pursue him. "One is not allowed to invade a country to effect an arrest," notes Mandel.[10]

The UN charter is in fact very specific about when self-defence can be invoked. Article 33, for instance, specifies that "the parties to any dispute shall, first of all, seek a solution by . . . peaceful means" such as "negotiation, enquiry, mediation, conciliation, arbitration, judicial settlement." In the case of Afghanistan, a negotiated solution would seem to have been a possibility. After all, Afghanistan was not the perpetrator of the attack, nor was there any evidence it was in on the attack; it had simply allowed al Qaeada to operate inside its territory. The solution, presumably, would have been to have Afghan (and perhaps Pakistani) authorities co-operate in handing over the al Qaeda operatives to some international authority for trial. Furthermore, the enormous power imbalance between the United States (the most powerful country in the world) and Afghanistan (one of the weakest countries in the world) would have given the U.S. enormous leverage, to say the least, in any negotiation. But Washington made no attempt to negotiate with the Taliban government of Afghanistan. Indeed, Washington actively rebuffed attempts by the Taliban to initiate negotiations.

Although little attention was paid to it at the time, and it's long been forgotten, in the weeks immediately after 9/11, the Taliban government tried to open negotiations with Washington, requesting that Washington hand over evidence of bin Laden's guilt. As Taliban leader Mullah Omar said on September 19, 2001: "We have told America that if it has any evidence of Osama bin Laden's guilt, it should be given to the Supreme Court of Afghanistan, so that we can take action in light of it . . . If the American government has some problems with the Islamic Emirate of Afghanistan they should be solved through negotiation."

The Taliban overture was immediately rejected by Washington. What right did a primeval, two-bit country have to demand proof from America?

But the Taliban had a point. As Mandel notes, they were simply following the rules of international law. Requesting evidence is the standard practice any nation follows when asked to extradite a criminal to another country. Mandel also insists that the U.S. had an obligation under article 33 of the UN charter to seek a non-military solution—something the Taliban were apparently keen to negotiate.

But Washington had no patience with the formalities of international law and hadn't the slightest intention of negotiating.

On September 20, Bush announced his demands: that the Taliban hand over bin Laden and all other al Qaeda members and supporters, close terrorist training camps and give the U.S. full access to them. "These demands are not open to any negotiation or discussion," he said.

On October 7, the U.S. bombing campaign began. Ten days later, the Taliban, now more desperate, became all the keener to negotiate. They dropped their demand for evidence, offering to hand over bin Laden for trial in a country other than the U.S.[11]

Now, one can easily scoff at these offers. Were the Taliban dealing honestly? Did they have the power to round up bin Laden and hand him over? Could a satisfactory third country be found? (Saudi Arabia would have been a possibility, since it had close ties with Washington and had maintained ties with the Taliban. Furthermore, bin Laden was a Saudi national. Presumably, once he was in Saudi custody, the Saudis would have been willing to extradite him to stand trial in the United States.) In any event, the point is that there were a number of possibilities, and the Taliban were apparently keen, indeed desperate, to negotiate. It was Washington that rejected all negotiations, refusing to operate within the parameters of international law. The Taliban even sought face-to-face talks with Secretary of State Colin Powell when he was in Islamabad in late October 2001, shortly after the bombing began, but the request was declined.[11]

Washington undoubtedly could have obtained approval from the Security Council to launch its invasion of Afghanistan, given the international outrage over the September 11 attacks. But the Bush administration didn't bother to get authorization, apparently because it wanted to do as it pleased, without any UN-imposed constraints. (Washington also wasn't interested in UN authorization limited to Afghanistan, since its real goal was regime change in Iraq.) Perhaps some might find America's desire for a free hand in Afghanistan understandable, given the viciousness of the 9/11 attack on America. But it's important to note that this approach has no legitimacy in international law. And international law is needed most of all in situations like this, when emotions are intense. It should be added that such intense emotions are hardly unique in international affairs. Do Americans assume that people in other countries don't also experience feelings of rage and desire for revenge when they are attacked or violated in some way?

Washington's refusal to abide by international law had enormous consequences. Ironically, in refusing to negotiate with the Taliban, Washington may have turned down a chance to actually get bin Laden. Of course, negotiations might have led to nothing. But it's possible that the Taliban would have been able and willing to seize the al Qaeda leader, and that they would have done so to save their own skins. If so, the world's most apparently dangerous terrorist might have been behind bars, or dead. So negotiating with the Taliban, as required under international law, might have actually produced a better result for America. Certainly the alternative—refusing to even try this lawful route—hasn't produced much success, by any standard.

Furthermore, thousands of Afghans died as a result of the illegal U.S. invasion. Estimates range from several thousand to twenty thousand dead in the first nine months, although the U.S. doesn't even bother to keep track of civilian deaths in Afghanistan (or Iraq). Daraz Khan and others like him not only are considered acceptable casualties of war but are barely even acknowledged as casualties at all.

This brings us back to the question of whether the deaths of these men—and thousands of others who died as a result of the U.S. attack on Afghanistan—aren't just as reprehensible as the deaths of the victims of terrorist attacks. Mandel argues that, under international law, Washington is fully culpable for these Afghan deaths and that, indeed, they represent not just crimes but "very serious crimes, in fact supreme international crimes."[12]

Mandel bases this assertion on the position taken by the Nuremberg Tribunal, set up by the allied powers after World War II to judge the Nazis. The Nuremberg judgments, which have been acclaimed throughout the West, concluded that starting a war of aggression—that is, an illegal war—is the supreme international crime. As the judges noted: "War is essentially an evil thing. Its consequences are not confined to the belligerent state alone, but affect the whole world. To initiate a war of aggression, therefore, is not only an international crime; it is the supreme international crime differing only from other war crimes in that it contains within itself the accumulated evil of the whole."

If we apply the reasoning of the Nuremberg Tribunal, the deaths of Daraz Khan and others come to be seen in a very different light. Since the U.S. invasion of Afghanistan was unlawful, it amounts to a war of aggression—the supreme international crime—and any deaths that result from it are war crimes committed by the perpetrator of the illegal war. Thus, the killing of Daraz Khan is just plain murder; that is, killing without a lawful excuse. The fact that he was killed by mistake is irrelevant. Of course, he wasn't actually killed by mistake. He was deliberately killed in what turned out to be a case of mistaken identity. But this is no excuse—any more than it is legal, under our criminal laws, to kill someone and then plead not guilty because you had intended to kill someone else instead. As Mandel notes, "The identity of the victim is irrelevant if you had no right to kill in the first place."[13]

So when the Pentagon's Victoria Clarke blithely declared Daraz Khan an "appropriate target," her position was similar to a murderer insisting that the person he killed was an "appropriate target" because that person may have looked like the person he was hoping to kill. One struggles to find some sanity—not to mention moral decency—in such a position.

Similarly, one searches for a way to understand the moral world of someone like Michael O'Hanlon of the Brookings

Institution, who described the U.S. bombing of Afghanistan as "a masterpiece of military creativity and finesse" that resulted in "relatively modest harm to innocents."[14] O'Hanlon estimated that the bombing caused about a thousand deaths, which he described as "a mercifully low number." Rather than being appalled at government officials for killing a thousand innocent people—imagine if those victims had been Americans living in Houston or Atlanta—he marvels at their creativity and finesse in waging war while "mercifully" killing only a thousand innocent people. Bravo!

This sort of logic—which permeates the mainstream commentary about the U.S. "war on terror"—springs from our failure to treat the lives of people in faraway places as equal in value to our own. It also springs from our failure to even take into consideration the pivotal issue of the legality of war. While the Nuremberg judges placed the issue of the legality of war at the very heart of their moral judgments, we have gone in exactly the opposite direction, barely acknowledging it as an issue at all. Mandel refers to the "great big hole in the modern practice of international criminal law: its refusal to distinguish between legal and illegal war-making, between aggression and self-defence."[15]

Once we acknowledge that Washington's invasion of Afghanistan was an unlawful war, waged outside the limits of international law, we are obliged to see it for what it was—the supreme international crime.

———

Since the U.S. invasion in 2001, national elections have been held in Afghanistan, and the elected government and the UN have approved the presence of NATO troops in the country. As a result, the ongoing war in Afghanistan is no longer—technically at least—an illegal war. Indeed, we're told it is a vital war to advance the cause of democracy. But the legitimacy of the war, and Canada's involvement in it, has always been murky, which explains why

Canadian MPs only narrowly supported extending our involvement to 2009 by a Parliamentary vote of 149–145.

Although Afghanistan is now technically a democracy, it is undeniable that Washington has largely called the shots since U.S forces overthrew the Taliban in November 2001. In June 2002, an assembly of Afghans, modelled on the traditional Afghan assembly or *loya jirga*, was convened to select a government, under the auspices of the United Nations. But the selection of Hamid Karzai to head the new government was essentially a deal worked out between Washington and the warlords of the Northern Alliance, whose horrific record of human rights violations easily matches that of the Taliban. As for Karzai, he was clearly Washington's man. He had had extensive experience dealing with U.S. intelligence agencies, and had also served as a consultant for the U.S. oil giant Unocal in the 1990s, when the company was developing plans to build a pipeline across Afghanistan to carry Caspian Sea oil to the Arabian Sea.

The Karzai government has since been confirmed in nationwide elections. But any assessment of the situation should acknowledge that these elections were held under the watchful eye of foreign troops. It's interesting to note, by comparison, that in March 2005, with Lebanese elections approaching, George W. Bush insisted that the elections would not be meaningful as long as Syrian troops remained in Lebanon. "All Syrian military forces and intelligence personnel must withdraw before Lebanon's elections for those elections to be free and fair," he declared. Strangely, few Western commentators questioned how meaningful the Afghan (or Iraqi) elections were, with U.S. troops occupying these countries.

For Canada, the legitimacy of our involvement in Afghanistan became particularly questionable in February 2006, when we took on a new role over there. Rather than just helping the Karzai government to maintain peace in Kabul and the area around the capital, Canadians became involved in a more aggressive mission in the southern part of the country, rooting out—and killing—Taliban insurgents, first as part of the U.S. force Operation Enduring Freedom and later as part of a NATO mission.

Among other things, this has meant that Canada has been part of a force that has killed Taliban fighters and also innocent Afghan civilians. In March 2006, Canadian troops shot dead an unarmed father of six who was travelling in a rickshaw that approached a Canadian military checkpoint near Kandahar. In October 2006, about a dozen villagers were killed and another dozen wounded in the Zhari district of Kandahar province when airstrikes by NATO helicopters ripped through three dried-mud homes while villagers slept. NATO officials said that they regretted any civilian casualties, and insisted such deaths were unintentional. They also disputed reports from locals that the casualties had been much higher. In one report, CBC Radio reporter Stephen Puddicombe noted how agitated the local people were "even if it is only eleven dead." Only eleven dead! Imagine the reaction if eleven Canadian soldiers had been killed, or if eleven civilians had been "unintentionally" killed in Canada.

Military authorities understood that winning over the Canadian public to the new, more aggressive role in southern Afghanistan could be tricky. Media help would be crucial. Accordingly, as Canadian troops took up positions in the south in the winter of 2006, a few Canadian reporters were selected to tag along with a Canadian Forces Civil-Military Co-operation unit as the unit made visits to small Afghan villages, extending a hand in friendship. There was much that looked promising in these visits, which were a key part of the strategy of triumphing over insurgents by winning the "hearts and minds" of the locals. In a report for CBC TV, Patrick Brown captured the good intentions of the Canadians and their apparent success in relating to the villagers.

But before the CBC even had a chance to air Brown's report, the same unit of Canadian soldiers, sitting down for another friendly encounter in the village of Shinkay, came under attack from an axe-wielding teen. Shouting "Allahu Akbar," the young man dropped the blade of his axe into the head of Lt. Trevor Greene. Canadian troops promptly pumped fourteen bullets into the teen, killing him on the spot, and soon found themselves in a gun battle with insurgent forces that had apparently been lying in wait in the hills just beyond the village.

The Canadian media reported with outrage the "raw brutality" of the axe attack. A soldier who'd witnessed the attack told the *Toronto Star* that the assailant had "poison in his eyes" as he raised the axe over Greene's head. It was said that the young man was "Taliban."

The attack is of course a gruesome and horrific tragedy, but it accomplishes little to heap scorn on the dead youth or dismiss him as a fanatic with poison in his eyes. No doubt he felt some sort of rage. But why?

One Kandahar-based freelance journalist, who interviewed some of the Shinkay villagers, has shed some light on this question. According to the journalist's report, reproduced by the Institute of War and Peace Reporting, the young attacker, Abdul Karim, was not connected to any political movement. The report quotes Tela Mohammad, a Shinkay elder, saying "Abdul Karim was not linked to the Taliban, nor did he know anything about any factions or groups." Another local resident, Haji Mohammad Esa, described Karim as a quiet boy, the son of a poor cobbler. "Karim was always alone. He didn't have much contact with the other villagers," said Esa. "We were all surprised when he suddenly attacked the soldier. But I think the main reason he did it was because he was angry at the foreign troops." These and other residents of Shah Wali Kot, where Shinkay is located, insisted that the local people do not make a distinction between Canadian and U.S. soldiers, and that the Canadians are starting to behave more like the Americans anyway. "We have gone to see the Canadians in Kandahar several times," said Esa. "We have asked them to have more respect for our culture and beliefs, but they don't."[16]

The axe attack and the following ambush highlighted the naivety that lies behind the Canadian mission, and the danger that lurks for Canada as it gets drawn deeper into the quagmire of Afghanistan, which has confounded foreign armies since the time of Alexander the Great. While Trevor Greene's unit no doubt came in peace, it came as part of a mission of war. This is the Three Block War in action. While the members of Greene's unit were hoping to establish a rapport with the local villagers, offering the carrot of humanitarian aid (while also gathering human intelligence), this was only one prong of the overall Canadian mission. The other two prongs involve Canadian troops killing and rounding up local insurgents and establishing military control over the area. So while Canadian soldiers may see themselves as helping Afghanistan, at least some Afghans apparently regard them as heavily armed occupiers who do not even respect local culture and beliefs.

———

The Afghan war is often justified as being a sort of humanitarian mission to help the people of Afghanistan. A key argument for propping up the Karzai government has been the notion that it has advanced the rights of Afghan women after the terrible anti-woman repression of the Taliban years. Indeed, the new government and its U.S. sponsors are often presented as champions of women's rights. In reality, however, there has been little meaningful progress for women under the Karzai regime. Even TV footage clearly shows that, outside Kabul, Afghan women are still covered in the traditional burka from head to toe. The patriarchal, anti-woman culture is deeply rooted in the country, and is embraced by the Northern Alliance as well as by the Taliban. This reality hasn't stopped Washington—and Ottawa—from suggesting there have been great improvements in the lot of Afghan women, recognizing this as a powerful way to sell Western audiences on the importance of the war.

So while there's been much celebration in the West about all we've done for the women of Afghanistan, the women themselves seem less impressed. Of course it's hard to know what most of them are thinking inside their cloistered world, but one indication has been the clear, strong voice of a group called the Revolutionary Association of the Women of Afghanistan. Based in Kabul, RAWA is a daring, outspoken group of activists who received wide attention in the West when they gathered evidence to expose the misogynist crimes of the Taliban. At great risk to their own safety, RAWA activists made a video of a public execution of an Afghan woman in the Kabul sports stadium in November 1999, and handed it over to CNN for broadcast. The graphic video helped draw world attention to the Taliban's brutality and earned Western respect for RAWA as a principled resistance group. RAWA has remained consistent to its principles and continues to oppose the Taliban. But it has also become a fierce opponent of the U.S. military presence in Afghanistan—an opposition that has received little attention in the Western media.

According to RAWA, anti-women fundamentalists have continued to dominate Afghanistan since the installation of the U.S.-backed Karzai regime. On its website, RAWA declared in the spring of 2006 that "still the Afghan women are hostage to the fundamentalists' claws . . . Murder, robbery, kidnapping and the rape of women and children has become the routine." While the North American media reported enthusiastically on the November 2005 Afghan election, RAWA dismissed it as a "disgusting mockery of an election" in which "even the ballot boxes remained in the hands of warlords, bandits and the U.S. agents before they were deposited at the polling centers." In a long article posted on its website, RAWA referred to those in the Karzai government as "westernized accomplices." It angrily dismissed the suggestion (made by a Republican congressional candidate who was in Kabul for the elections) that the Afghan people see the Americans as liberators. "How a nation 'sees as liberators' those who have blown to shreds not the terrorists but thousands of innocents? How can simple Afghans 'see Americans as liberators' while the 'liberators' are going to woo their men in the government and in the parliament to approve the establishment of U.S. bases on our soil for decades, which obviously goes contrary to the independence of the country?"

If the plight of desperate women were a key concern for Ottawa, we'd be fighting instead in Darfur or in the Congo, where the life and security of women and girls is more directly imperilled by lawless bands than it is in Afghanistan. (At a clinic in Goma in the eastern Congo, Dr. Kalumbe Mushabaa Ally primarily focuses on repairing vaginas damaged by repeated gang rapes.) Indeed, there's a huge irony in the Harper government's claiming to champion equality for women in Afghanistan even as it fights equality for women in Canada. In the fall of 2006, the Harper government actually removed the word "equality" from the list of goals of Status of Women Canada, ending decades of advocacy for female equality on the part of that federal agency.

Ironically, the position of women in Afghanistan may have been somewhat better back in the 1980s, after a moderately reformist government took power in the 1978 "April Revolution." Among the reforms were a ban on polygamy, programs promoting literacy and education for women and a constitutional guarantee of women's rights. For the first time in history, Afghan women were freed from wearing the burka. The government also expropriated the states of big landowners and cancelled debts for millions of peasants. The changes prompted an immediate backlash from patriarchal landowners who launched a powerful counter-offensive. When the Soviet army entered to prop up the besieged Afghan government, the United States sided with the patriarchs, who were cast in Western eyes as freedom fighters liberating their country from Soviet domination. (Among the forces of the patriarchs, known as the mujahedin, was Osama bin Laden.)

With the Soviet withdrawal in 1989, the victorious mujahedin forces took power and set up a reactionary Islamic state that, among other things, immediately began rolling back women's rights. In 1993, the Supreme Court of the Islamic State decreed women must be completely covered by the veil in public places, and banned the education of girls, except religious instruction by their male relatives. Thus, the assault on women's rights was well under way in the early 1990s, even before the Taliban took power in 1996. And that assault on women's rights has continued after the overthrow of the Taliban and the installation by Washington of a regime dominated by the Northern Alliance—which is mostly made up of fiercely Islamic, anti-women warlords, many of whom were mujahedin fighters in the 1980s. What is going on in Afghanistan is in many ways a long-running civil war between the two factions, both devotees of an extremely conservative brand of Islam, both intensely anti-women and both responsible for horrendous atrocities.

As RAWA puts it, the United States "drove the Taliban wolves through one door and unchained the rabid dogs of the NA [Northern Alliance] through another." It is this ongoing fight between the Taliban "wolves" and the "rabid dogs" of the Northern Alliance that Canada has entered—on the side of the rabid dogs.

Although the plight of Afghan women has been a major selling point for the war, there has also been a determined effort by the Canadian defence establishment to deftly move the focus away from soft, humanitarian considerations—like helping desperate women—to more geopolitical purposes, like fighting terrorists.

Thus, Jack Granatstein declares: "The war on terror is a reality and Canadians are targets, no matter how we try to convince ourselves that the world loves us. It doesn't."[17] The attempt is to make Canadians feel at risk of terrorist attacks, simply for being part of the Western world, and to erase the connection between terrorist attacks on the U.S. and the U.S. history of military intervention in that part of the world.

Of course, Canada could well be the victim of terrorism. Canadians were stunned by the arrests of seventeen young Canadian Muslims in June 2006, on charges of plotting terrorist attacks in Canada. It's difficult to know what to make of these alleged plots, which seem to have been at least partly encouraged by undercover government agents. Let's just note at this point that the charges have not yet been proven in court. It should also be noted that Canada's past insulation from terrorist attacks is almost certainly connected to the fact that we haven't provoked rage abroad as the U.S. has—or as Britain and Spain did with their support for the U.S. invasion of Iraq. Our insulation, of course, could change as we get more fully on board with the U.S. "war on terror." Granatstein's assertion that the world doesn't love Canada—whether true or not—could well become a self-fulfilling prophecy if we behave aggressively in the world or connect ourselves directly with the aggressive actions of others. In the summer of 2005, Canadian major general Andrew Leslie explained why the war in Afghanistan will be long—because, he said, "every time you kill an angry young man overseas, you're creating fifteen more who will come after you."[18] This might seem like a good reason *not* to go over there and kill angry young men.

Granatstein goes on to hint at what is more likely the real purpose of our venture in Afghanistan: to please the United States. "Our superpower neighbour, the nation to which 87 per cent of our exports go and on which our security depends, has been attacked and is still under threat, but somehow Canadians have not grasped that they are involved. We are." Similarly, Sean Maloney, a professor at the Royal Military College in Kingston, suggested in an article in *The Walrus* magazine that "the thinking [in Ottawa] may be that we will finally resolve the softwood lumber issue and keep our border open to trade by lessening America's burden in Afghanistan."[19]

Now hold it a minute. How did the softwood lumber issue and the fact that 87 per cent of our exports go to the U.S. creep into a discussion of our military involvement in Afghanistan? Is it concern about our trade balance that compels us into battle? This might come as a surprise to Canadian soldiers fighting over there, hyped up on a message of the life-and-death importance of their mission, on the need to help the desperate people of Afghanistan and rid the world of terrorists. Is it actually increased profit margins for the Canadian lumber industry that they're risking their lives for? This focus on the Canada–U.S. trading relationship also raises an interesting question: does the fact that Canada has extensive trade ties and common security arrangements with the U.S. oblige us to join in America's wars?

Advocates of closer economic and military ties with the U.S. have always denied that such ties infringe on our sovereignty. So why are these ties even being raised here? Do these ties restrict our freedom of action, oblige us to participate in American wars, or don't they? If they do, this would seem to be a compelling argument for loosening these ties, for developing more independent economic and military policies, in order to free ourselves of such obligations. If they don't, they shouldn't be part of a discussion about the purpose of our mission in Afghanistan.

The possibility that we are in Afghanistan to curry favour with Washington—to help make up for the fact that we sat out the Iraq war—is disturbing, and not just because it suggests a colonial mentality. It also suggests that, for the sake of enhancing our leverage in a trade relationship, we are willing to participate in a war to which we are not connected, and in which there is no evidence that we are making anything better in that country and very possibly making things worse. It suggests that in order to smooth relations with Washington, we are killing people in Afghanistan and handing others over to torture.

Much of the opposition to our involvement in Afghanistan has focused on the Canadian casualties. The media pose the question: is the price we're paying in Afghanistan too high? Of course, if our security were actually at stake or if there were some compelling purpose to our mission—as in the Second World War—no one would ask such a question. The question comes up, as it did for Americans during the Vietnam War and still does in connection with the war in Iraq, because we realize our security is not actually at stake, and we sense that there is no compelling purpose to this mission.

Of course, everyone knows that Canada doesn't have any aggressive designs on Afghanistan. We're over there helping Washington, providing it with a public show of our support for their "war on terror," and allowing it to move more American troops to the key battlefront in Iraq and possibly Iran.

We're not aggressors. We're just helping out the aggressors— in order to protect our trade balance.

The resistance of many prominent Canadians to the peacekeeper role is part of a larger resistance to the very notion of international law, and to the role of the United Nations as the world body that should be entrusted with ensuring peace and security around the globe. As we saw in chapter 1, former Canadian diplomat Allan Gotlieb has suggested that "Canadians liberate themselves from the belief that the UN is the sacred foundation of our foreign policy." The anti-UN message is also picked up and embellished by Jack Granatstein. "Unfortunately [the UN] doesn't work," writes Granatstein, "and there is no sign at all that the UN can be fixed. Canadians cannot pin their hopes for a better world on a flawed, crippled world body."[20]

This sort of blithe dismissal of the United Nations—as if it were an item one tosses aside with no more care than a broken toaster—is striking. And we should take a minute to examine exactly what these prominent individuals are up to.

First, it should be noted that the UN is not the failure that they make it out to be. In its sixty years, the United Nations has had an overwhelmingly positive impact, in setting humanitarian standards, in promoting human welfare, in contributing to global peace. In addition, it has been central to the emergence of a body of international law—including treaties that protect human rights, that ban torture and genocide, that limit nuclear weapons and that tackle global problems like ozone depletion and global warming.

On the peace front, most observers agree that early UN peacekeeping efforts were effective. More recently, neoconservative critics, like Michael Ignatieff, have tried to suggest that UN peacekeeping missions have become ineffective, or even disastrous, in the post–Cold War era. However, Canadian defence analysts Walter Dorn and Peter Langille see UN peacekeeping, even in the post–Cold War period, in a more positive light. Dorn, an associate professor at the Royal Military College of Canada, insists that "rather than abandoning the UN, Canada should contribute more peacekeepers to more missions, where they are much needed."[21] Langille, a political scientist at the University of Western Ontario, argues that overall—even after the Cold War— UN peacekeeping missions have been very successful. He notes that there have been four outright failures—Rwanda, Srebrenica (in Bosnia), Sierra Leone and East Timor. But he maintains that, in its thirty-five peacekeeping operations since the end of the Cold War, the UN has an 85 per cent success rate. "That's far better than the U.S. or NATO," says Langille.[22]

Furthermore, even where UN peacekeeping clearly failed, these failures can be more reasonably attributed to the refusal of member states of the Security Council to authorize sufficient military action. In Rwanda, for instance, we know that UN forces, led by Canadian general Romeo Dallaire, called out urgently for help and that UN Secretary-General Kofi Annan pressed the Security Council to respond. But key members, particularly the U.S. and France, declined to give their support. In many ways, this is reminiscent of what UN peacekeeping director Jean-Marie Guéhenno was describing when he talked about the failure of leading Western nations to give priority to some conflicts going on today in remote Third World nations. Is it reasonable to blame the United Nations as an institution for the failure of its member states, particularly those on the Security Council? Obviously, the UN can only be as strong and as effective in upholding world peace as its members allow it to be.

There is, however, a very serious danger that powerful members of the Security Council can manipulate the UN so that its authority is misdirected and even used to advance causes that violate the basic principles upon which it was established. For instance, throughout the 1990s and early 2000s, Washington was able to pressure the Security Council to maintain and enforce brutal UN sanctions against Iraq—sanctions that resulted in the deaths of more than a million Iraqis, according to former U.S. attorney general Ramsay Clark. Similarly, Washington was instrumental in creating a UN peacekeeping operation—to which Canada contributed troops—that propped up a ruthless right-wing regime in Haiti, after the United States had forced the democratically elected president, Jean-Bertrand Aristide, to leave the country in February 2004.

Still, despite the UN's serious shortcomings and possibilities for abuse—a subject we'll return to later—the UN has played a key role in advancing the cause of human betterment in the world. Its very existence reflects a collective desire to establish a set of principles that amount to a blueprint for the kind of world we aspire to create together. The fact that there is near universal agreement on these principles suggests that there is intrinsic merit in them, that they represent a kind of natural law with an inherent beauty to which human beings respond in some profound way. They represent what Nobel laureate John Polanyi has described as "the freely expressed will of humankind."[23]

In a thoughtful essay, Polanyi portrays the UN charter as "one of history's greatest acts of imagination." The very centrepiece of this act of the imagination is an attempt to find a way to end "the scourge of war." Conceived in response to the horror and human misery of the Second World War, the UN charter sets out its anti-war mission powerfully and explicitly in its opening words: "We the Peoples of the United Nations determined to save succeeding generations from the scourge of war, which twice in our lifetime has brought untold sorrow to mankind . . ." It then lays out a set of laws that seek to minimize the possibility of war by bringing the use of force by national governments under the control of the UN Security Council.

Of course, calling for an end to war and setting out how that end can be achieved doesn't mean there will be an end to war. But it establishes a principle—a principle that is endorsed by governments representing virtually all the world's people. Thus a marker is laid down. A world standard is set. The unauthorized use of force by national governments is unequivocally condemned. Wars of aggression—the cause of endless suffering and misery since the beginning of history—are designated henceforth unacceptable to the human community. Through the institution of the United Nations, the world has given eloquent voice to what is perhaps the deepest yearning in human beings—to live in peace.

Given the gravity of this quest for peace, it is striking that prominent Canadians like Granatstein and Gotlieb are so blithe in their dismissal of the UN. They would have us believe that their dissatisfaction with the UN springs from its ineffectiveness. One suspects that, on the contrary, their dissatisfaction springs from its very effectiveness. Although utterly lacking in military force, the UN has a legitimacy in the eyes of the world that bestows on it a moral power. It is precisely because the UN gives such a powerful moral voice to the human aspiration for peace that it presents an obstacle to those who want to make war. That was vividly illustrated in the case of the invasion of Iraq.

As we know from a number of published insider accounts, neoconservatives in the Bush administration were determined to invade Iraq. Sensing the UN would become a forum for resistance to the invasion, hawks in the administration had urged bypassing the world body altogether. In the end, the White House decided to take its chances at the UN, apparently under the assumption that enough members of the Security Council could be pressured and cajoled into accepting the flimsy American case for war. Secretary of State Colin Powell, who enjoyed the most international prestige in the administration, was put forward to make the U.S. case. Yet it became clear that Washington would not be able to muster the necessary votes. Despite enormous pressure from Washington, even some of the weaker nations holding temporary Security Council seats—including Angola, Cameroon, Guinea and Mexico—were expressing reluctance. Realizing it would lose the vote, Washington withdrew its resolution.

It was a pivotal moment for the world. The United States had failed—with the entire world watching—to win UN approval. Rebuffed and publicly humiliated, the Bush administration announced that the U.S. would invade Iraq anyway, with its "coalition of the willing." Rejecting the rule of law, Washington had decided to be a law unto itself. The next day, ten million people turned out in street protests around the world.

Many commentators have treated the Iraq war as a defeat for the UN, since the world body was exposed as powerless to stop the invasion. But this is the wrong measure to use. No power would be able to stop Washington from launching an invasion if it was determined to do so. The UN's power has never been a military one, but a moral one. And on this level, it succeeded. Despite enormous pressure and threats from Washington, the nations of the UN Security Council, even vulnerable nations holding temporary seats, stood their ground over Iraq. They didn't abandon their commitment to the UN's prohibition against aggressive war. They refused to knuckle under to American bullying. That might well rank as one of the UN's finest hours.

All this enraged right-wing hawks, who felt the need to diminish the UN's moral authority by trying to destroy its credibility. They focused extravagant attention on the UN "oil-for-food scandal," even after a top-level investigation by former Federal Reserve chairman Paul Volcker found minimal scandal and cleared UN Secretary-General Kofi Annan of any personal wrongdoing. (As UN misdeeds go, the oil-for-food scandal is utterly dwarfed by the much more serious scandal of the UN-imposed sanctions against Iraq—carried out at the insistence of the U.S.)

It is the UN refusal to accept American exceptionalism that lies at the root of the right's dissatisfaction with the UN. The United Nations provides a vehicle for challenging American exceptionalism and its corollary, a Pax Americana—a world peace enforced by U.S. military power.

Powerful forces inside the Canadian elite want to move Canada not only away from peacekeeping—as they've already succeeded in doing—but also away from an allegiance to the United Nations and the rule of law. They want us to accept the premises of American exceptionalism and the right of the U.S. to impose a Pax Americana on the world. Even as Washington runs roughshod over justice and international law, they want us to stand by helpfully, holding the bully's coat.

CHAPTER 3

ALL OPPOSED TO NUCLEAR DISARMAMENT, PLEASE STAND UP

One thing that American travellers rarely do is attach a U.S. flag to their luggage. By comparison, attaching a Canadian flag to one's luggage is a fairly common practice on the part of Canadians going abroad—and even on the part of some Americans hoping to pass for Canadians.

Countless polls have shown why avoiding the U.S. flag is a sensible idea for Americans. In one 2006 survey of public opinion in twenty countries, for instance, the country that the largest number of respondents considered "the greatest threat to global security" was the U.S.A., which beat out Iran, North Korea and China by wide margins.[1]

But how to explain that flicker of welcoming acceptance that seems to frequently greet those sporting a Canadian flag? My guess is that it has little to do with our past military glories, impressive as some of these may be. I suspect it has more to do with the way Canadians are perceived as usually pushing to make the world a better place and even, occasionally, succeeding.

In the world of weaponry, the land mine is a bargain. The device can be bought for as little as $3 (U.S.).[2] By laying a large number of these devices in fields and roadsides, an army can quickly turn a huge area into a danger zone. Anyone who happens to stumble on a land mine—a soldier, a farmer or a child playing in a field—can be instantly killed or maimed for life. Cheap, effective, easy to use, the land mine became immensely popular in conflicts that raged in the decades after World War II. As a result, an estimated 100 million land mines are currently deployed in some seventy countries around the world. And they kill or injure an estimated twenty-six thousand innocent civilians each year—more than the annual toll from conventional "terrorism," indeed, more than the total toll from all nuclear and chemical weapons over the last fifty-five years.[3]

Unlike most other weapons, however, land mines do most of their destruction after hostilities have ceased. They simply lie there in the ground, with the potential to kill, long after the fighting has stopped, rendering huge tracts of land effectively unusable. Since they are generally deployed in the underdeveloped parts of the world, where most of the conflicts are, they impose yet another roadblock on the path to development in some of the most desperately poor countries on earth—Cambodia, Mozambique, Angola, Somalia, Afghanistan, Vietnam, the Congo. Finding and removing them is extremely difficult. Only about eighty thousand to a hundred thousand are found and destroyed each year (and in the process, about eighteen to twenty mine clearers are typically killed). So, at the rate things are going, it will take more than a thousand years to clear all the mines already planted in the ground. In addition, another 150 million mines have already been manufactured, and are currently in storage.[4]

It's easy to understand, then, why a campaign to rid the world of these devices of personal terror was able to quickly gather worldwide momentum. In 1980, a UN protocol was established to regulate the use of land mines and prevent harm to civilians, but it had no policing mechanism and therefore virtually no impact. It wasn't until a few activist groups became involved in the early

1990s that the issue began to attract any serious attention. In 1991, Human Rights Watch and Physicians for Human Rights detailed the extent of the problem in Cambodia—a country with the world's highest rate of physically disabled people. Dismissing the UN protocol as utterly ineffective, the human rights group called for an unconditional ban on the manufacturing, sale or use of land mines.

It was a call that resonated with a number of international groups, including the Vietnam Veterans of America Foundation (VVAF). The issue struck home with the veterans group, in part because land mines had taken such a heavy toll among U.S. soldiers in Vietnam. Thousands of American soldiers died or were left permanently disabled after stepping on land mines laid by their own army; some estimates suggest that perhaps one third of the fifty-eight thousand U.S. deaths in Vietnam were caused by land mines.[5] The VVAF, which had been established by anti-war activist Bobby Mueller, a former Marine lieutenant, was also interested in trying to bring about American reconciliation with the Vietnamese and Cambodian people. On trips back to Southeast Asia, Mueller was struck by the sheer number of amputees. In 1991, the VVAF established a prosthetics clinic in Cambodia. Mueller also teamed up with a German medical group to begin organizing a campaign to ban land mines. Enlisting the help of Democratic senator Patrick Leahy and Congressman Lane Evans as well as other Washington-based groups, Mueller successfully pushed the United States to become the first country to impose a one-year moratorium on its own export of land mines.

In October 1992, VVAF, along with Medico International, Human Rights Watch, Physicians for Human Rights and a number of other non-governmental organizations (NGOs), met in New York and formally launched an international campaign to ban land mines. Jody Williams, from the VVAF, was appointed co-ordinator of what became known as the International Campaign to Ban Landmines. From the outset, the campaign managed to generate a fair amount of support and media attention. By the following year, the campaign drew some forty groups to its inaugural conference in London, and the next year, more than double that number showed up for its conference in Geneva. Eventually, the campaign became a coalition of some one thousand organizations operating in sixty countries.

The campaign's momentum got a huge boost in September 1994 when U.S. president Bill Clinton, addressing the UN General Assembly, pledged to fight for a worldwide ban on the use of land mines. This was indeed encouraging. Not only was Clinton arguably the most powerful man on earth, but the U.S. was one of the main sources of the problem. It was the largest producer of land mines—manufacturing some thirty-seven different models—and the largest user.[6] Following the U.S. lead, Belgium became the first country to ban the production, trade and stockpiling of land mines. Norway, Sweden and Austria quickly followed.

But the campaign soon ran into serious obstacles. Although some key U.S. generals supported it, including former Gulf War commander Norman Schwarzkopf, there was strong opposition from other quarters inside the Pentagon. Particularly strong was the opposition from those overseeing U.S. operations in Korea, where land mines were said to provide a buffer zone that prevented the huge North Korean army from staging a massive assault on the South. After a top-level U.S. military review came out strongly against a worldwide ban in 1996, Clinton watered down his support considerably. While insisting that the U.S. would take a leading role in international negotiations to bring about a ban, Washington announced in May that year that it was reserving the right to use so-called smart land mines (mines that self-destruct after a certain time period), and that any negotiations would include an exception for Korea. Such an exception would of course destroy any hope for a comprehensive ban, opening the door to a flood of demands for similar exceptions. Bobby Mueller declared the new U.S. position "a dagger through the heart of our international campaign to ban this weapon."

Meanwhile, that same month, negotiations that had been taking place under the auspices of the UN's Conference on Disarmament were also getting bogged down. Attempts to strengthen the 1980 protocol against land mines at a conference in Vienna in May 1996 produced little in the way of results. Strong opposition was coming, for instance, from India and China, with China reportedly expressing more resistance to giving up land mines than nuclear weapons. For that matter, none of the five permanent members of the Security Council—the U.S., Britain, France, Russia and China—was willing to support a total ban. It became clear that this powerful group simply wanted to tinker a bit with the existing protocol, adding a few new restrictions, making some additional references about the importance of protecting civilians, but avoiding any tough new rules or a mechanism for enforcing them. It was now evident that a significant split had opened up between the powerful countries on the one hand and, on the other hand, the international campaign of NGOs and a small group of small and middle-power countries that had developed a commitment to the issue. Jody Williams and those running the international campaign increasingly saw that the best way forward was to work on developing an alliance with these small and middle-power countries.

Canada was one of those middle-power countries committed to the issue. As early as 1994, Canadian foreign affairs minister André Ouellett had shown an interest, pushing internally to get the Defence Department to agree to a moratorium on the use of land mines by the Canadian Forces. He'd run into considerable resistance. The department would agree only to a moratorium on the *export* of land mines—a rather meaningless gesture since Canada didn't export land mines.[7] Ouellett decided to push the issue forward on his own, stating publicly that he believed Canada should destroy its stockpile of land mines and begin working towards a total ban. With the minister's blessing, a small group within Foreign Affairs began working with determination on the issue.

Lloyd Axworthy, who became foreign affairs minister in 1995, was even keener than Ouellett had been. A left-leaning Liberal, Axworthy had tried, as minister of human resources, to shield Canada's social programs from the deep spending cuts made in the name of deficit reduction. Axworthy was already interested in the land-mine problem when he took over Foreign Affairs. While in Opposition, he had developed an interest in the political conflicts in Central America. In visits to the region, he'd sensed the local fear of wandering much beyond the marked paths in the countryside. He'd even visited a small workshop on the outskirts of Managua where young land-mine victims made their own prosthetic devices out of wood. This was a file Axworthy was keen to take over.

Inside the foreign affairs department, the idea developed that it would be possible to get around the impasse in the UN negotiations by developing a separate track of negotiations. The problem with all UN disarmament negotiations was that they worked on a consensus basis. This meant that countries that wanted to block progress could easily do so, simply by withholding their consent. They didn't even have to be up front about their resistance. They could look as if they agreed with the main goal but just weren't satisfied with the terms being offered. This way, the whole process could become hopelessly bogged down. Axworthy, along with senior department officials Paul Heinbecker and Michael Pearson, decided that it was worth trying to set up a separate negotiating track, even though they realized that such a strategy—without the support of the big powers—had a high chance of failure. "It would be seen as an audacious, even impudent, step for Canada to take," Axworthy recalled, "since we would be breaking the rules of accepted international behaviour and running the risk of falling flat on our face. Yet in the absence of anything better, it was worth a look."[8]

By May 1996, the prospects for a land-mine treaty seemed dim in the aftermath of the failed UN conference in Vienna and Clinton's retreat on the issue. Canada immediately announced that it would host a conference—to be held in only a few months, in October—to plan a strategy for moving the campaign forward. And this conference would be different than the UN ones. The strategy was to develop a solid core of countries that were committed to developing a ban, and to put them together in the same negotiating room with the NGOs. The nations that weren't committed could come too, but they would be relegated to observer status. (This was the exact opposite of the UN conferences, where the resistant countries had a seat at the table, while the NGOs were relegated to observer status.) But separating out the resistant countries would have to be done carefully, so as not to alienate them further by making them feel discriminated against. Here, the Canadian planners came up with a clever idea: it would be up to each country to decide how to classify itself. If it wanted to sign a declaration stating its intention to support a full ban by 2000, then it would attend as a full delegate. Otherwise, it would attend as an observer.

The U.S. signed the declaration, but only after persuading Canada to withdraw the 2000 deadline. In other words, the rules would have to be bent to ensure Washington's participation. This bit of manoeuvring caused controversy. It compromised Canada somewhat in the eyes of the participants, and it also underlined how the U.S. had lost the leadership on the issue. No longer paving the way forward, Washington was now having to get permission— from Canada—to bend the rules in order to get admitted to the advanced team. Canada had, in a sense, taken over the leadership.

Fifty countries attended the Ottawa conference as full participants, with another twenty-four coming as observers. The full participants and the NGOs, all participating together, had little trouble agreeing on the need for a global ban on land mines. So the conference proceeded somewhat predictably. After several days of meeting, it was winding up on a Saturday afternoon, with delegates voting on a joint declaration and an action plan—all very nice but ultimately a meaningless gesture. No state would be committed to actually taking any action. The afternoon was wearing on. Some of the U.S. delegates had already left.

One person who was not just taking it all in stride was Lloyd Axworthy. Waiting outside the main conference room, he was more than a little nervous. He was thinking over what he planned to say, realizing that it would push things one significant step beyond what Canada had already done in redesigning the negotiating process. In the interest of trying to secure a global ban on land mines, he was about to put Canada at odds with the five permanent members of the UN Security Council. In other words, on this crucial issue he was about to challenge the authority of the world's greatest powers.

Axworthy is not known for charisma. Although he has an agreeable manner, he has a somewhat scholarly and plodding look about him. He's been dismissed by media commentators as dull and ineffectual. In their book *Double Vision*, influential journalists Edward Greenspon and Anthony Wilson-Smith describe the struggle that went on inside Cabinet in the early years of the Chrétien government between Human Resources Minister Axworthy and Finance Minister Paul Martin, as Martin went about his budget-cutting crusade. While Martin is portrayed in the book as strong and even heroic, Axworthy comes across as pale, confused, besieged, ineffective, stumbling, a "Liberal on his knees," as the chapter on him is titled. Axworthy's affable good intentions are simply swept aside by the dynamic Martin, who forcefully wrestles the deficit monster to the ground. As Greenspon and Wilson-Smith put it: "Martin, a powerful minister of finance with a head of steam and a will of iron, ate the human resources minister for breakfast."[9]

This sort of media fawning over Martin the deficit cutter was fairly common back in the 1990s. But how bold was it, really, for Martin to be tackling the deficit when he had the full backing of Canada's powerful business community for the task? On the other hand, Axworthy was going against the wishes of the business community in defending Canadian social programs, which business wanted to see cut. Similarly, in the land-mine case, Axworthy was going against the wishes of the world's most powerful countries. He knew he had the support of Prime Minister Jean Chrétien. And he'd also cleared his idea with UN secretary-general Boutros Boutros-Ghali. But his plan was contrary to the stated desires of the governments in Washington, London, Paris, Moscow and Beijing. Now, that requires some chutzpah.

Axworthy went to the podium and delivered the normal thank-yous. And then, taking a deep breath, he declared: "The challenge is to see a treaty signed no later than the end of 1997." That was three years sooner than the original 2000 deadline—a deadline that the U.S. had forced Canada to abandon as a condition of its participation in the conference. Axworthy had just quickened the pace dramatically. He'd set the bar higher than anyone had expected or even dared to hope for. "The challenge is to governments assembled here to put our rhetoric into action," Axworthy continued, as many in the audience gasped in disbelief. "The challenge is also to the International Campaign to ensure that governments around the world are prepared to work with us to ensure that a treaty is developed and signed next year." Axworthy announced that Canada would host a treaty-signing ceremony in Ottawa in December 1997—just fourteen months away—for a global land-mines ban. The NGO participants in the room leapt to their feet with applause. Many government representatives remained silently in their seats, apparently too stunned to know how to respond. Some delegates were visibly angry. Axworthy had thrown down the gauntlet, launching a bold strategy—which became known as the Ottawa Process—to get around the resistance of the world's most powerful players.

The Canadian move had taken almost everyone by surprise. "Canada had stepped outside the diplomatic process . . . It was really breath-taking," Jody Williams later recalled.[10] Even the countries strongly supporting a land-mines ban were initially shocked by what Williams calls "the Axworthy Challenge," since it put them in a position where they were pretty well obliged to follow through with quick action. "They had come to Ottawa to develop a road map to create a ban treaty and had signed a declaration of intent. What could they do?" asks Williams. "But once they recovered from that initial shock, the governments that really wanted to see a ban treaty as soon as possible rose to the challenge."

In the following months, it wasn't clear whether Canada's gambit was going to work. The U.S., France and Britain insisted that the proper place for negotiating a treaty on land mines was still the UN's Conference on Disarmament, in Geneva, and dismissed the "coalition of angels" involved in the Ottawa Process. They were deeply suspicious of the Ottawa Process—a process that, after all, they couldn't control. In January 1997, three months after Axworthy had set the process in motion, the Clinton White House announced that it would not take part. Instead, it would continue to work towards a global land-mines ban through the Conference on Disarmament.

There was, however, a core group of countries committed to the Ottawa Process from the outset—Austria, Belgium, Canada, Denmark, Ireland, Mexico, Norway and Swtizerland. And, even as the powerful nations resisted, the international campaign got a huge break. If there was anyone with enough global media clout to reach the public—over the heads of the world's most powerful politicians—it was Diana, Princess of Wales. The world's most photographed woman was enlisted in the struggle, and when she strolled through an Angolan minefield in January 1997, she brought the world's media in tow. Suddenly, land mines weren't just a story in the foreign sections of newspapers. With Diana, the story of land mines was catapulted onto prime-time TV and onto the front pages of newspapers, tabloids and glossy magazines. There was the princess, known for her glamorous evening dresses, suddenly wearing full protective gear and a visor, walking through mine-infested fields, and then visiting maimed children in a hospital. The media, generally indifferent to the suffering of poor, brown-skinned people in far-off places, felt obliged to at least offer a bit of an explanation about what the world's biggest celebrity was actually doing amongst such people.

For opponents of the international campaign, Diana's involvement was infuriating. Earl Howe, Britain's junior defence minister, described her as a "loose cannon" and defended his government's role in "helping to draw up a sensible worldwide compromise package." His wife, Lady Elizabeth, chimed in: "I think it's easy for the uninformed or the not very adequately informed to take it on an emotional level." British Tory backbencher Peter Viggers dismissed Diana as someone "not up to understanding an important, sophisticated argument." And in an article in the London *Spectator*, Bruce Anderson charged that Diana had "used Angola as a catwalk," and argued that "she should have called for more mine exports."[11]

As the year wore on, the Ottawa Process picked up momentum. Diana persisted in using some of the grimmest spots on earth for her continuing land-mine catwalk. And, even if the British elite found it offensive, the general public appeared to be quite captivated. The election of more left-leaning governments in Britain and France also made a huge difference to the campaign.

Within weeks of the election of the Labour government in Britain in May 1997, Foreign Secretary Robin Cook announced that the new government wanted to move faster towards a land-mine ban and said that it would join the Ottawa Process. France's new socialist government, led by Lionel Jospin, announced that it too would come on board. But with Axworthy's deadline looming, there was no time for the usual slow pace of diplomatic engagement and negotiation. In surprisingly rapid succession, a series of meetings were held around the world that spring, with more and more countries coming on board. By June, seventy-three nations had signed up for the Ottawa Process. At a crucial meeting late that month in Brussels, participants agreed to terms for a comprehensive ban to be confirmed at a conference to be held in Oslo in September, and then followed by the treaty signing in Ottawa in December—a fast-forward schedule that would meet Axworthy's deadline. Ninety-seven countries signed the Brussels declaration.

Washington refused to sign. The Clinton administration was divided over the issue. Clinton himself, as well as many Republicans and Democrats in both houses of Congress, seemed supportive of a comprehensive ban, but there was strong resistance from conservative hawks as well as from the Pentagon. The Joint Chiefs of Staff were united in their opposition to the Ottawa Process. George Stephanopoulos, a former top Clinton aide, attributed the president's refusal to act on the issue as "a surrender to the military."[13] Still, the White House was reluctant to bow out of the process completely. It announced its intention to attend the Oslo conference, even though it refused to agree to the terms of the Brussels declaration, and kept trying to use its clout to pressure the committed nations to agree to compromises. Washington was still pushing, for instance, for an exception for its "smart" mines, as well as for situations involving "national security"—a rather wide-open exception!—

and for Korea. (Interestingly, a former U.S. commander in South Korea, Lt. Gen. James Hollingsworth, acknowledged that "to be blunt, if we are relying on these weapons to defend the Korean peninsula we are in big trouble."[12]) Campaign co-ordinator Jody Williams denounced the American efforts, urging the nations in the Ottawa Process to stand firm and allow "no exceptions, no reservations, no loopholes."

The sudden, dramatic death of Diana at the end of August that year probably had a galvanizing effect on the international campaign. With the Oslo conference taking place just days later, even as world attention was hugely focused on her life and legacy, U.S. efforts to water down the scope and force of the land-mines treaty ran up against unusually strong resistance from the committed nations. For two weeks, the U.S. delegation pushed its case. Meanwhile, Clinton made personal phone calls to Jean Chrétien as well as to South African president Nelson Mandela, hoping to win their support for the U.S. position.

In fact, Canada was very keen to get Washington into the treaty. Axworthy recalls that the Canadian government tried to find some way to accommodate the American objections. "We wanted the Americans in, but not at the price of watering down the draft convention."[13] When Axworthy supported a U.S. request for a twenty-four-hour adjournment to allow for more consultations, Canada came under criticism from the NGOs for apparently bending to Washington. The adjournment was granted, and a new round of negotiations took place over the phone between Clinton and Chrétien, and also between Axworthy and U.S. secretary of state Madeleine Albright and National Security Council chairman Sandy Berger. It looked as if some sort of accommodation was going to be found. Berger phoned Axworthy at 11:00 p.m. to say that the United States would likely be in, only to phone back two hours later with the news that the president had finally decided that opposition to the treaty was simply too intense. Axworthy poured himself another drink—this time less celebratory—from the bottle of single malt he had cracked open at eleven.

The next day, chief U.S. delegate Eric Newsome announced to the conference that all efforts to reach a compromise had failed and that the U.S. was withdrawing. Within minutes of the U.S. withdrawal, the other countries voted to approve a total and immediate ban on land mines. The conference delegates spontaneously erupted in delirious applause.

The signing ceremony took place in Ottawa in early December 1997—right on schedule. Two thirds of the world's countries signed on within two days of the ceremony. The treaty was ratified the following September and became law in March 1999. Jody Williams and the International Campaign were jointly awarded the Nobel Peace Prize.

In many ways, the treaty was an extraordinary achievement. "It's a huge success," says Carleton University's Trevor Findlay. "Land mine manufacturers are out of business and enormous areas have been demined."[14] The International Campaign and Jody Williams had been the chief catalysts, but Canada's role was significant. Findlay notes that the treaty never would have come about if Canada had adopted the U.S. position. It had been Canada's determination to set its own course and its creative solution to the political impasse that had ultimately made the treaty a reality. Canada had succeeded in enabling a citizen-based grassroots movement to overcome the opposition of the five great powers that run the UN Security Council (and the world). By devising a mechanism for separate fast-track negotiations, outside the deadlocked UN disarmament talks, Canada had managed to bring about an international treaty in an astonishing fourteen months. Axworthy sees this as the successful use of "soft power." As he notes: "No one was threatened with bombing. No economic sanctions were imposed. No diplomatic muscles were flexed by the treaty's proponents. Yet a significant change was achieved in the face of stiff opposition."[15]

Using soft power, Canada also played a small but important leadership role on another front, perhaps the most vital front of all—nuclear disarmament. Once again, this involved Canada taking a stand that was opposed by Washington. But nuclear weapons and nuclear disarmament are highly sensitive issues that are of central concern to Washington, making Canada's willingness to chart an independent course all the more impressive—until that willingness suddenly collapsed.

———

With only hours to go before the 6:00 p.m. deadline on October 12, 2005, all eyes were on Paul Meyer, the Canadian ambassador.

There was a palpable excitement among the UN delegates in the room as Meyer rose to speak. While there's no shortage of resolutions presented to the UN, most are simply lofty statements about something that should happen but that everyone knows will not happen. But Meyer was poised to table a resolution that was a little different. Like other resolutions, it dealt with a seemingly intractable problem—in this case, the deadlock at the nuclear disarmament negotiations in Geneva—but it seemed to offer the promise of a solution, or at least a means of breaking the deadlock. Even among the jaded UN delegates, long accustomed to disappointment and inaction, this one was being watched with unusual anticipation. And it all came down to what Canada would do.

The stakes could not be higher, literally. At issue was the future of nuclear weapons, and therefore, ultimately, the future of the world. Theoretically, the demise of the Soviet Union in 1989 had changed the nuclear issue in the most profound way. The Soviet threat, which had been the justification for decades of building the massive U.S. nuclear arsenal, no longer existed. The U.S. had emerged as the world's uncontested nuclear superpower.

And yet, oddly, not much had changed. By the mid-1990s, negotiations on nuclear disarmament had virtually ground to a halt.

With the election of George W. Bush in 2000, a team of radical war hawks had taken control of the U.S. government. Under the Bush administration, Washington became downright obstructionist at the nuclear talks sponsored by the UN's Conference on Disarmament in Geneva. The U.S. behaviour showed that Washington had no interest in disarmament whatsoever, and instead regarded the Soviet demise as an opportunity to consolidate—and greatly extend—its nuclear advantage. Nowhere was this aggressive approach more evident than in the newest and most worrisome nuclear frontier: the spread of the arms race to outer space.

Ironically, decades earlier, it had been the United States that had pioneered efforts to keep nuclear weapons out of space. An initiative by the Eisenhower administration in the 1950s eventually led to a unanimous declaration by the UN General Assembly in 1963 that "the use of space shall be carried on for the benefit and in the interests of all mankind." As a follow-up, ninety-seven nations signed the Outer Space Treaty in 1967, banning weapons of mass destruction from space. Despite this early U.S. leadership on the issue, however, Washington later became the key opponent of attempts to put in place a more comprehensive ban. Under George W. Bush, this opposition had hardened, as the White House openly plowed ahead with plans for space-based weaponry.

The Bush administration had also undermined nuclear disarmament on other fronts, abrogating the Anti-Ballistic Missile Treaty and refusing to ratify the ban on nuclear testing. But the most significant battleground was over the future of the Nuclear Non-Proliferation Treaty (NPT). First signed in 1970, the NPT had for more than three decades been the bedrock of nuclear disarmament. It set out a formula under which nuclear nations were to work towards disarming, while non-nuclear nations were to agree to forgo nuclear weapons in exchange for access to nuclear-energy technology. But as the nations of the world gathered to review the treaty at the UN in May 2005, the U.S. revealed the extent of its obstructionist intent, withdrawing its previous support for even very general resolutions calling for a nuclear-free Middle East and reductions in worldwide nuclear arsenals. Washington even refused to allow these resolutions to be placed on the agenda for discussion. Taking an unrepentant hard line, the U.S. delegation made clear that it regarded the non-proliferation treaty—which for thirty-five years had been the standard of nuclear disarmament—to be a document of merely "historic" value.

That May 2005 UN gathering was regarded as such a disastrous setback that a number of organizations, including the U.S.-based group Mayors for Peace, began searching desperately for a way to get things back on track. The focus was on overcoming the deadlock in Geneva, which was supposed to function as the headquarters of nuclear weapons negotiations, but where there'd been no progress in almost ten years. The U.S. had been able to block progress because the Geneva talks worked on a system of consensus, which allowed a single country to grind the whole process to a halt. (Other countries also objected to various disarmament proposals, but the U.S. was the main and constant objector, the one country that appeared determined to derail the entire disarmament process.)

So, in the aftermath of the May 2005 fiasco in New York, there was a determination in some quarters not to allow the whole disarmament cause to simply be shunted back to Geneva, where it would just be put back on hold. If it could be kept at the UN, there would at least be a chance to move forward. At the UN General Assembly, every country has one vote, preventing any single country from unilaterally imposing its will. So the General Assembly could authorize UN committees to do the work that the committees in Geneva weren't doing—including actually negotiating treaties, such as a tougher treaty against weapons in space. This way, a set of parallel talks could be effectively put in place, forcing disarmament back onto the international agenda, despite Washington's foot-dragging in Geneva. The hope was that this would prod Washington to return to the table seriously in Geneva.

The plan, then, sought to use the UN General Assembly to kick-start the Geneva talks. The first and most difficult hurdle involved getting support for a resolution at what is known as the UN's "first committee," which deals with issues of international peace and security. If the first committee endorsed the resolution, it would then go before the General Assembly. Having received the endorsement of the first committee, it would almost certainly pass in the General Assembly, given the strong international support for disarmament. The difficulty was getting a country to come forward—in the face of strong U.S. opposition—to put a resolution on the agenda at the first committee.

Enter Canada.

The notion of Canada as an international weakling, so popular with our right-wing commentators, had little resonance in the corridors of the UN. On the contrary, Canada was seen as a wealthy, influential nation, well connected to the dominant Western powers through membership in the G8 as well as through NATO. But although Canada moved comfortably in these powerful circles, it had also developed a reputation as something of a friend of progressive international causes, such as banning land mines and pushing for nuclear disarmament.

Canada had been among the more innovative countries in trying to overcome the deadlock in Geneva, according to Theresa Hitchens of the Washington-based Center for Defense Information[16]. For instance, Canada played a key role in winning broad support for a 1998 initiative in which seven middle-power countries—including Brazil, Mexico and Sweden—attempted to break the disarmament deadlock. The group, known as the New Agenda Coalition, had had trouble at the outset winning support for its initiative, particularly from NATO countries, whose endorsement was considered crucial to any hope of overcoming U.S. resistance. Washington had made its opposition clear, and, in the first few years, Canada and all the other NATO countries simply fell into line behind it.

But that changed in 2002. Canada broke ranks with the U.S. and the rest of its NATO allies and actually voted for the New Agenda Coalition's resolution. In 2003, Canada supported the New Agenda resolution again—but this time seven other NATO countries followed Canada's lead. By 2005, fourteen NATO nations had come on board. But it was Canada that had led the way. "It took bravery for Canada to do this," says Douglas Roche, who had served as Canadian Ambassador for Disarmament decades earlier, in the 1980s. Roche credits former foreign affairs minister Bill Graham with the change in Canada's position, which helped push the disarmament cause within NATO. Although Canada and these NATO countries remain committed to the NATO Strategic Concept, which considers nuclear weapons "essential," they have at the same time endorsed the New Agenda Coalition resolution, which pushes in the opposite direction. Thus, disarmament has at least been given a foot in the door.[17]

So, in the aftermath of the disastrous meeting on the NPT in May 2005, it didn't come as a big surprise that Canada was once again playing a pivotal role in the initiative by groups like Mayors for Peace to do an end-run around the Geneva stalemate. Once again, a group of middle-power countries was assembled to support a resolution that was to be put to the UN first committee. Canada was involved from the outset—the only NATO country participating at this crucial, difficult early stage. Along with five other nations—Mexico, Sweden, Brazil, Kenya and New Zealand—

Canada had prepared a resolution that was to be presented to the first committee before the 6:00 p.m. deadline on October 12, 2005, in order to make it onto the General Assembly's agenda for that year. And Canada's ambassador for disarmament, Paul Meyer—a skilled negotiator devoted to the cause—was ready to stand up and table the resolution.

This time the stakes were much higher than with the New Agenda resolutions, because this time the resolution was about more than generalities. It was about actually setting in motion a set of parallel disarmament negotiations in New York, with the purpose of breaking the impasse in Geneva. Aaron Tovish, international campaign manager with Mayors for Peace, recalled that this had generated enormous excitement at the UN, and that a closed-door meeting, held a week before the resolution was to be tabled, was packed with delegates eager to learn more about it. "People said they'd never seen such interest," noted Tovish.[18]

But opposition from Washington was intense. A note had been sent to foreign capitals the week before denouncing the proposed resolution as "divisive" and likely to harm the Geneva process. Washington was applying particular pressure on Canada, according to Tovish, since Canada's participation was seen as key to the resolution going forward. "Canada was under a lot of pressure from the U.S.," he recalled. "[Washington] was using the argument: how can you be so out of line with NATO countries?"

Of course, Canada had shown itself willing to take the lead in moving NATO countries closer to disarmament with the New Agenda Coalition resolutions. And, in this case, there were signs that support was building, according to Peggy Mason, another former Canadian ambassador for disarmament.[19] Mason notes that the Netherlands and Norway, two other NATO countries, seemed likely to come on board. The new government of Norway had indicated, prior to its election the week earlier, that it would support the disarmament resolution.

But, with only hours to go before the deadline on October 12, Ottawa pulled the plug. In the hushed UN committee room, Ambassador Meyer stood up awkwardly to announce that Canada would not table the resolution it had been keenly promoting. The clearly disappointed ambassador referred pointedly to the "current blockage" at the Geneva talks "where the security interests of the many are being held hostage by the policies of a few." His frustration was clear, as he declared that if the Geneva process "turns in another sterile year in 2006, we will retain the option of reintroducing this initiative."

Tragically, the moment had been lost. A clever solution, which Canada had played a key role in developing, had been abandoned by Ottawa at the last minute because of pressure from Washington. Peggy Mason argues that Ottawa's retreat—which she insists would have only been done under orders from the Prime Minister's Office—was "outrageous," particularly since tabling the resolution would have only committed Canada to keeping the door open. "Tabling preserves *all* options—amending the proposal, voting on it in November, *not* voting on it or withdrawing it at a later date," she points out. By contrast, not tabling the resolution simply closed the door to any prospect of getting the issue onto the agenda that year. By caving in, the government of Paul Martin had quietly acquiesced to the U.S. desire to block all meaningful progress on nuclear disarmament for yet another year, allowing Washington to push forward with its plans for space-based weapons, with little public attention.

In allowing the UN disarmament resolution to die, the Martin government adhered to Allan Gotlieb's rule, referred to in chapter 1: avoid publicly differing with Washington. Even though we would prefer to keep weapons out of space, we accept the transcendent power of the U.S. to launch a new nuclear arms race. If we have any disagreements about this, we should whisper quietly in Washington's ear. And we shouldn't say anything more when our faint little whisper fails to push the Pentagon and the massive U.S. weapons industry off their course of endless expansion of the U.S. war arsenal.

It's hard not to feel that we missed an opportunity to use the small bit of leverage we have to actually make a difference on a matter of great significance to the world. There is no power on earth that can stop the U.S. government from moving the arms race into space if it is determined to do so. The only potential power is the power of public opinion. If world reaction helps show the American public that Washington's actions are needlessly aggressive, provocative and counter-productive to global peace, the government could fear an electoral backlash and be deterred from proceeding. It's a long shot, but it's really the only chance we have. Keeping the disarmament issue at the forefront of public awareness—and allowing Washington's obstructionism to be visible to the world audience—is thus vital.

Ironically, in this situation, Canada actually had a comparative advantage. Our status as a G8 country and NATO member meant that we could have added a particular heft to the group of middle-power countries trying to shine the flashlight on U.S. intransigence. We could have played a leadership role, as we had a few years earlier with the New Agenda Coalition. Instead, we stepped aside, allowing the opportunity to pass. Without Canada's key support, the UN disarmament resolution died, ushering in another year of deadlock on a matter of life-and-death importance to the world.

Canada's failure to stand up to the U.S. in this case is particularly galling given the fact that at the same time Paul Martin was taking a very loud and public stand against U.S. intransigence in the softwood lumber case. Martin was uncharacteristically tough talking in his public criticism of Washington for its failure to abide by pro-Canada rulings by NAFTA tribunals. But the softwood lumber issue was receiving huge coverage in the Canadian media, where even many right-wing commentators were joining in the criticism of Washington and urging Ottawa to play hardball with the Americans. And softwood lumber isn't as central an issue for the Bush White House as nuclear armaments and so-called national security. Given the high priority devoted to the softwood lumber issue in Canada, and the relatively low priority assigned to it by the White House, Martin felt emboldened. He managed to increase his approval ratings in Canada with some tough talk on softwood lumber—tough talk that was accompanied by no real action.

Meanwhile, far from the glare of TV cameras, Martin was quietly capitulating to Washington on something that was more important to the Bush administration: keeping disarmament out of the spotlight, so Washington could quietly pursue plans to build a new generation of nuclear weapons. From the point of view of his poll numbers that fall, Martin's two-tiered approach paid off. He rode the wave of anti-American sentiment in Canada over softwood lumber, punching big soft airy punches at the Bush administration, while surrendering to the White House over the disarmament resolution—which, if they'd known about it, Canadians would have overwhelmingly supported. (Imagine how many Canadians would oppose a resolution that simply sought to provide an international forum to advance the cause of restricting nuclear weapons. All opposed, please stand up.)

Canadian politicians know they can score points with the electorate by showcasing their determination to stand up to the U.S. The problem is preventing Ottawa from demurring to Washington when the cameras aren't rolling.

———

For the masked Palestinian men who had kidnapped a Western hostage in the Gaza Strip, this was bad news indeed. They had nabbed Adam Budzanowski in response to Israel's seizure of one of their comrades in March 2006. But, after blindfolding Budzanowski and dragging him to a grim basement hideout, the Palestinian militants emptied his pockets and found his passport. Their disappointment was palpable. They had assumed he was from an enemy nation—from the U.S. or at least Britain. But now they realized that what they actually had was a Canadian, which was about as satisfying as kidnapping a Norwegian or a Swede.

After grilling Budzanowski with questions about his hometown Toronto, which one of the captors knew well, the Palestinians were apparently satisfied that he wasn't an imposter. Having established that, their attitude changed. They handled him less roughly, and even started talking to him politely. Budzanowski says that they even told him: "We love Canada." One of his captors kept asking him to "say hello to Canada."[20] After thirty hours, Budzanowski was released unharmed.

Whether Budzanowski would be treated so well today is not clear. What is clear, however, is that Canada has managed for decades to be regarded favourably on both sides of the Arab–Israeli divide. This is a testimony to the skill of Canadian diplomacy, and to the Canadian attempt to behave fairly in what is clearly one of the most contentious and difficult disputes in the world.

It should be noted that Canada has never been a truly neutral player in the Middle East conflict. After the Second World War, Canada played a fairly significant role, through the United Nations, in creating the circumstances that enabled the establishment of the state of Israel in 1948. In doing so, Canada sided with Zionist interests inside the Jewish community, both in Canada and abroad, who were determined to establish a Jewish homeland in British-controlled Palestine, where the ancient land of Israel had once existed. This meant that Canada was rejecting the position taken by the Arab world, which fiercely resisted the Zionist plan on the grounds that the land of Palestine had been inhabited predominantly by Arabs for hundreds of years, and that allowing a Jewish state to be established on part of it amounted to theft of Arab territory.

Canada was initially reluctant to become involved. Before and during the Second World War, the Canadian government had rigidly refused to take in desperate Jewish refugees fleeing the Nazis. With revelations of the full extent of the horrors of the Holocaust at the end of the war, there was considerable guilt among at least some Canadians over Canada's refusal to open its doors, and a feeling that something should be done to assist Jewish survivors. This belated sympathy for the Jewish plight and for the notion of a Jewish homeland was tempered, however, by the rising political violence in Palestine, where Jewish extremists were staging violent attacks against British authorities in their campaign to establish a Jewish state. Canadians were deeply sympathetic to Britain, and there was anger in Canada over this anti-British violence, particularly the July 1946 bombing of Jerusalem's King David Hotel, where the British headquarters was located. Ninety-one people were killed and dozens injured in that blast, which was carried out by the Irgun gang under the leadership of Menachem Begin, who would later be elected prime minister of Israel.

Reluctant or not, Canada became involved in the dispute in 1947, when Britain handed the future of Palestine over to the United Nations to resolve. Canada's main interest originally was to avoid a rift developing over the issue between its two major allies, Britain and the U.S. Although Britain had originally supported the Zionist plan, allowing extensive Jewish immigration into Palestine after the war, its support had waned considerably as the situation became more contentious. Having handed the issue over to the UN, Britain adopted an officially neutral position. Washington, on the other hand, supported the Zionist cause, and therefore favoured the partitioning of heavily-Arab Palestine into two separate states, one Jewish and one Arab.

At Washington's instigation, Canada accepted a seat on a special UN committee to consider the issue. Travelling to Palestine in the summer of 1947, committee members held extensive meetings with Jewish representatives, while the Arab population boycotted the process. By the end of August, a three-member minority on the committee called for a single independent state to be created in Palestine. But a seven-member majority endorsed the idea of partition. The Canadian representative on the committee, Supreme Court Justice Ivan C. Rand—whom Ottawa had given a free hand to vote as he saw fit—had sided with the majority in favour of partition.

In fact, there was considerable debate within Canadian ranks over the Palestine issue, which was now put before all fifty-seven UN member nations. Canada's UN delegation included some strong opponents of the partition plan, including delegation head J. L. Ilsley, the federal minister of justice. Ilsley expressed concerns that the plan violated the rights of the Arab community to self-determination, which was, supposedly, a central principle of the United Nations. He also noted that it failed to uphold commitments made to the Arab population by the British during the First World War, when the Arabs had helped Britain fight Turkey in exchange for a promise of Arab independence in the Turkish-controlled region after the war.

Elizabeth MacCallum, another key member of Canada's UN delegation, also stressed the self-determination issue. As the Middle East expert inside Canada's department of external affairs, MacCallum questioned Canada's right "to insist on the partition of Palestine against the wishes of practically the whole Arab population and of at least a substantial minority of the Jews." She noted that the partition plan would "turn over 65 per cent of the territory to the Jews, who now own only 6 per cent of the land."

She suggested that the creation of a Jewish homeland in an Arab territory might amount to a violation of the UN charter, or at the very least, a dangerous precedent: "If [a] strong desire to settle in another community, to develop its land, and to take over the government of all or part of it, is now recognized by the United Nations as a valid cause for partitioning [a] country, a precedent will be set whose consequences may be easily foreseen."[21]

Others on the Canadian team vigorously supported the partition plan, however. Leon Maynard, also from External Affairs, dismissed concerns about legal obligations to the Arab community. He maintained that Arab leaders could be appeased through financial concessions and that, in any event, "it would be a mistake to entertain too many legal scruples about it."[22] More important was the support of Lester B. Pearson, then undersecretary of state for external affairs, who soon took over control of the Canadian delegation. Pearson had been deeply moved by the revelations of the Nazi death camps, and had become convinced of the need for a Jewish homeland.

A skilful mediator and diplomat, Pearson played an important role stick-handling the partition issue through the gauntlet of UN committees. He was particularly effective in steering a small working group—consisting of just the U.S., the U.S.S.R., Guatemala and Canada—that was established to work on the Palestine problem. Pearson thrived in such intimate settings, where personal persuasiveness could make an enormous difference. A front-page article in the *New York Times* in early November 1947, credited advances at the working group to the tireless efforts of Pearson. Later that month, a report in the *Manchester Guardian* also drew attention to his role: "Mr. Lester Pearson of Canada has been the creator of . . . successive compromises, and this capacity to watch a plan knocked down and then set up another should give him some special sort of status with the United Nations."[23]

While Pearson was committed to the creation of a Jewish homeland, he was also—unlike fellow Canadian delegate Leon

Maynard—concerned about protecting the rights of the Arab community. To this end, Pearson insisted on building safeguards into the UN plan to protect Arab interests, even at times over U.S. objections. At one point, for instance, the U.S. delegation balked at a Canadian amendment aimed at alleviating aspects of Palestinian problems that, according to the American delegation, "should not be over-emphasized." Pearson refused to bow to this U.S. pressure. "Pearson was adamant, and vigorous American public and private efforts to change his view met with little success," notes historian Anne Trowell Hillmer.[24] Pearson used his considerable negotiating skills to ensure the Canadian amendment survived.

Ultimately, Canada backed the partition plan reluctantly as, in many ways, the best of a bad choice of options. R. G. Riddell, a high-ranking member of the Canadian delegation, described the partition plan as "dangerous and provocative," but he argued that failure to adopt it would "play into the hands of Jewish extremists who are said to be prepared to seize the whole of Palestine by force."[25] This comment, by a key member of the Canadian delegation, suggests that Canadian support for partition may have been at least in part based on a fear that any other plan for Palestine would have led to greater violence by Jewish extremists, who had shown their willingness to resort to terrorism to get their way.

Back in Ottawa, there were also doubts about the partition option. But, in the end, when the issue came before the UN General Assembly for a vote in November 1947, Canada once again voted for partition. With the bare two-thirds acceptance required, the UN endorsed partition, thereby opening the door for the creation of a Jewish state in Palestine.

While Pearson had aimed to protect the rights of Palestinian Arabs, it should be noted that his safeguards proved utterly ineffective. Pearson had succeeded in including guarantees to ensure an orderly transition period—to be enforced by the UN—so that the two states could be established in a violence-free manner, protecting rights on both sides. But in reality these UN safeguards were ignored. Following the pro-partition vote at the UN in November 1947, Jewish extremists in Palestine carried out attacks against the Arab population, including the killing of 250 residents of the Arab town of Deir Yassin in April 1948, prompting the Arab population to flee in panic. These attacks, along with earlier attacks against the British, can be fairly described as "terrorist" attacks. It's interesting to note that the Jewish extremists claimed they were justified in killing people because their cause was just— an argument made by all terrorists. As Menachem Begin later wrote: "There is an unjust aggressive war which brings shame on those who wage it. And there is a just war of liberation which does honour to those who prosecute it. Both are accompanied by bloodshed and suffering, but it is the difference in purpose which establishes one as profane and the other as sacred."[26] Begin even pointed out with apparent pride that British newspapers and politicians had branded him "Terrorist Number One."[27]

Ignoring the UN rules and timetable for partition, the Zionists declared a Jewish state on May 14, 1948, on a somewhat larger piece of land than had been authorized by the UN. Within eleven minutes of the declaration, U.S. president Harry Truman recognized the new state, brushing aside concerns inside his own state department and effectively ending any possibility that the UN would enforce its own safeguards. The hundreds of thousands of Arabs who had fled their homes in Palestine became refugees—and have never been permitted to return.

While not always approving Israeli actions, Canada has remained committed to Israel's right to exist as a Jewish state, and has generally been supportive of Israel. In voting at the UN, for instance, Canada has tended to tilt towards Israel. Although not as rigid in its pro-Israel stance as the U.S., Canada has typically been more pro-Israel in its positions than the European countries.

Thus, Canada has often refused to go along with Arab resolutions condemning Israel for actions against the Palestinians or its Arab neighbours, sometimes voting against these resolutions or abstaining. In 1987, Canada was ranked by observers, including members of its own UN delegation, as second only to the U.S. in support for Israel.[28] (Canada's pro-Israel stance at the UN has become even more pronounced in recent years, particularly under the governments of Paul Martin and Stephen Harper.)

Despite strong support for Israel, Canada has also tried over the years to be at least somewhat even-handed in its approach to the Arab–Israeli conflict. In 1956, Canada played a significant role in the Suez crisis, in which Ottawa opposed aggressive military actions by Israel (and Britain and France)—a story to which we will return in the next chapter. Canada also came out strongly against Israel's invasion of Lebanon in 1982. Prime Minister Pierre Trudeau was one of the first Western leaders to condemn that invasion and call for a complete Israeli withdrawal.

Canada has also taken some interest in the Palestinian problem—a problem that Ottawa clearly contributed to by supporting partition and then not building sufficient safeguards into the partition arrangement. As a result, hundreds of thousands of Palestinians (and their descendants), who once lived in what is now Israel, are still living in terrible conditions in refugee camps in Lebanon, Jordan and the Gaza Strip. Millions more live under Israeli military occupation in the West Bank, the part of Palestine where the UN had originally envisioned an Arab state would be created as part of the partition plan.

In defence of Palestinian interests, Canada has, along with most of the world, refused to officially accept Israel's control over the West Bank, which Israel seized in the 1967 Arab–Israeli war along with Arab East Jerusalem. In keeping with this stance, Canada has officially refused to accept Israel's right to build Jewish settlements on this occupied land. In reality, though, Israel has gone ahead and built an extensive network of settlements throughout the West Bank and East Jerusalem, so that today some 400,000 Jewish settlers live in heavily armed compounds on this occupied Palestinian land. In recent years, Canada has also officially supported, along with most of the world, the notion that a sovereign Palestinian state should be created on this occupied Palestinian territory—a goal that is clearly made much more difficult by the presence of so many Jewish settlers determined to see the land permanently annexed to Israel.

Canada has also attempted to deal constructively with the Palestinian refugee problem. In the 1990s, Ottawa chaired international talks on the refugee problem under the Oslo peace accords. Canadian diplomats worked to alleviate suffering in the refugee camps and to raise financing from Middle Eastern leaders for a possible fund to compensate Palestinians living in the camps. Lloyd Axworthy argues that these Canadian efforts helped create a new approach to refugee rights—"the idea of recognizing Palestinians' right to return to territory now in Israel, but replacing actual resettlement with financial compensation and opportunities to settle elsewhere." Axworthy insists that Canada's good standing in the Middle East "gave us a real perch in the important run-up to efforts to resolve the issues in the late 1990s."[29]

But while Canada has offered some support for the Palestinians, it should be stated that Ottawa has failed to speak out clearly and strongly against ongoing Israeli encroachment on Palestinian land. In 1979, the minority Conservative government of Joe Clark actually co-operated with Israeli plans to assert control over Jerusalem, a city of enormous significance to Muslims, Jews and Christians and originally designated by the UN to be an international city. Acting on a campaign promise aimed at Jewish voters in Canada, Clark announced shortly after his election that his government would move the Canadian embassy from Tel Aviv to Jerusalem. The announcement sparked outrage in the Arab world, since it was seen as endorsing Israel's annexation of Jerusalem. It also proved highly contentious within Canada. There was opposition from some in the business community who considered the policy would seriously harm Canada's trade with the Arab world. There was also considerable resistance from the Canadian public. A Gallup poll taken in the summer of 1979 showed that a mere 15 per cent of Canadians supported moving the embassy to Jerusalem, while 70 per cent opposed such a move.

Faced with clear opposition, Clark backed off, and appointed respected former Conservative leader Robert Stanfield as ambassador-at-large to review the matter and, more broadly, to look at Canada's approach to the Arab–Israeli conflict. Stanfield travelled to the Middle East, where he met with Arab and Israeli leaders, and consulted widely with experts and interested parties within Canada. He concluded that moving the embassy to Jerusalem would be a mistake. In two reports, he argued that the primary issue for Canada wasn't the impact on our economic interests but rather the importance of Canada's playing a constructive role in creating a lasting peace in the Middle East. To this end, he argued that Canada had to be scrupulously even-handed: "To use effectively whatever influence we may have in the area to encourage moderation and compromise we must retain credibility with both sides as a fair minded inter-locutor," Stanfield wrote. "We could not do this if we were to move our Embassy to Jerusalem."[30] He also went on to assert that the Palestinian issue lay at the heart of the Arab–Israeli conflict, and that Canada should support the right of the Palestinians to a homeland.

Stanfield's ability to see the Palestinian issue as the root of the decades-old conflict is in sharp contrast to Stephen Harper, who, like George W. Bush, has defined the root of the problem as Islamic terror, without any reference to the ongoing occupation of Palestinian territory and the predictable violence that

that occupation fosters. As Harper has abandoned any pretense at even-handedness, siding clearly with Israel—cutting off aid to the democratically elected Palestinian government and refusing to condemn Israel's massive air assault on Lebanon in the summer of 2006—he has taken Canada in a radical new direction.

This change in direction, which began under Paul Martin, has become much more pronounced and significant under Harper, who has shown an unusual zeal for taking sides in the Israeli-Palestinian conflict. The Harper government jumped out in front of the rest of the world in cutting off aid to Hamas, and it has loudly trumpeted its hostility, with Foreign Minister Peter MacKay vowing that "not a red cent" would go to the "terrorist" government, and Harper branding Hamas "genocidal." Harper's break with traditional Canadian Middle East diplomacy has pleased domestic Jewish groups as well as the fiercely pro-Israel Christian right. It also mirrors Bush's break with previous U.S. administrations, which at least tried to keep an Arab-Israeli dialogue going. To a striking extent, Harper has followed Bush's broad strategy of turning the Middle East into another front in the "war on terror," demonizing the enemy and then refusing to even speak to him.

It is the image of Canada projected by Robert Stanfield, not the one put forward by Stephen Harper, that no doubt saved Adam Budzanowski from the Palestinian militants—and that also explains the flicker of welcome in the eyes of strangers around the world when they spot the Canadian flag.

CHAPTER 4

THE MOST DANGEROUS MAN IN THE ENGLISH-SPEAKING WORLD

In April 1965, at the height of the Vietnam War, Lester B. Pearson provoked the wrath of the White House. In a speech he delivered at Temple University in Philadelphia, the Canadian prime minister urged Washington to stop bombing Hanoi. Pearson chose his words carefully, noting that "the progressive application of military sanctions can encourage stubborn resistance, rather than a willingness to negotiate. Continued and stepped-up hostilities in Vietnam could lead to uncontrollable escalation."

Given the extent of the carnage caused by U.S. actions in Vietnam, Pearson's comments amounted to a rather mild rebuke. Mild or not, they enraged President Lyndon Johnson. The United States was at war, with the White House under siege at home. In the context, Pearson's statement ranks as one of the boldest criticisms of U.S. foreign policy ever publicly uttered by a Canadian prime minister—and right on U.S. soil. Certainly it is hard to imagine a Canadian prime minister speaking out like that today.

And Pearson didn't withdraw his remarks. Johnson asked Pearson to come to Camp David the next day. At their encounter, Johnson bluntly told Pearson his speech was "bad," and then proceeded to tell him why, barely allowing Pearson to get a word in edgewise. When Pearson was finally given a chance to respond, he tried—at least according to his own account—to explain what he had said and why, and that "the stepped-up bombing of North

Vietnam had not achieved the desired result. I also pointed out that public opinion in my country was profoundly disturbed by the implications of certain aspects of U.S. policy."[1]

Two years later, Johnson made an official visit to Canada, and Pearson again had a private chance to talk with the president at the prime minister's retreat on Harrington Lake. Pearson once again put the proposition to Johnson that he stop the bombing, to allow an opportunity to discuss a ceasefire and an eventual peace. Johnson again brushed aside the advice.

Pearson's urgings probably added to the president's sense of being overwhelmed by the extent of the opposition—both domestically and internationally—to U.S. actions in Vietnam. That opposition eventually led a besieged Johnson to decide not to seek re-election in 1968. So one could argue that Pearson's urgings may have, in some small way, contributed to ending the U.S. war effort in Vietnam. At the very least, one could say that Pearson gave voice to the deep discontent felt in his own country over the U.S. war, giving millions of Canadians an opportunity, through their prime minister, to speak "truth to power."

That's only part of the story, however. Pearson's protest over the bombing of Hanoi has to be seen in a larger context. His criticisms at Temple University were a small part of a speech in which he indicated overall Canadian support for what Washington was attempting to do in Vietnam. More seriously, Pearson's government was complicit in providing diplomatic support for the U.S. effort—support that helped Washington deceive the public about what it was up to. We'll return to that shortly.

Pearson was the dominant player in shaping Canada's new role in the world after the Second World War. Having emerged from its long sojourn in the shadow of the British empire, Canada suddenly found itself in the shadow of a new, and ultimately more formidable, empire right next door. How would Canada respond to this new situation? Pearson, probably more than any other postwar

Canadian leader, thought about what role Canada could play in the world and, due to his own particular skills, managed to create a role for Canada outside the U.S. sphere of influence—one that allowed Canada to occasionally have a beneficial impact on the world.

Other postwar Canadian prime ministers also showed bouts of independence in resisting some of the worst aspects of U.S. foreign policy. During the 1962 Cuban Missile Crisis, John Diefenbaker struck an independent course, to the great annoyance of Washington, when he delayed putting the Canadian fighter squadron on alert and urged the Kennedy administration to proceed with moderation and involve the UN. Later, Pierre Trudeau pursued his own course, sometimes irritating the Americans with his support for causes like North–South dialogue and East–West détente, and launching a personal, one-man peace initiative in a bid to reduce Cold War tensions. Jean Chrétien also showed some independence in connection with the U.S. invasion of Iraq. Chrétien did co-operate with Washington by sending Canadian warships to the Gulf but, crucially, he refused to contribute Canadian troops to the U.S. "coalition of the willing," thereby declining to provide Washington a veneer of legitimacy to its illegal invasion.

Thus, Pearson, as well as Diefenbaker, Trudeau and Chrétien, showed some capacity to take principled positions that conflicted with U.S. positions, to carve for Canada a role in the world outside the confines of the U.S. empire. They could be said to have shown a degree of independence and feistiness. In the end, however, it's important to avoid overemphasizing their autonomy. Like all of our postwar prime ministers, they ultimately acted within the framework of a global economic and military system dominated by the United States.

Pearson demonstrates more than any other the inherent tensions and contradictions of this new role.

Much to its own surprise and probably everyone else's, Canada emerged from the Second World War a relatively significant power, largely because of the collapse of so many other nations. With its economy buzzing from wartime stimulation, and many of the once-powerful industrialized nations in ruins, Canada found itself suddenly positioned to be an international player.

Right from the beginning, Canada was a keen advocate and supporter of the United Nations, playing an important role at the organization's founding conference in San Francisco in 1945. The UN, which had been largely designed by the administration of Franklin Roosevelt with heavy input from the private U.S.-based Council on Foreign Relations, had been intended to serve several purposes. It provided the architecture for a new international order aimed at reducing the likelihood of war, by tightly defining the circumstances under which an act of war would be tolerated by the world community. And, like other key postwar institutions, such as the International Monetary Fund and the World Bank, the UN was structured to allow the key Western powers, particularly the United States and Britain, to play a dominant role in the postwar era. To this end, the United States and Britain, along with their wartime allies France, Russia and China, were each given crucial veto power on the Security Council. Thus the UN was designed to be an instrument for implementing a new, peaceful world order—an order that would ultimately be supervised by the victorious powers, led by the United States and Britain.

Canada's strong support for the UN was not surprising. Ottawa was a dedicated ally and supporter of both Britain and the United States. Furthermore, the UN was a useful vehicle for a rising middle power like Canada. It allowed Canada to become involved in trying to shape world politics, rather than simply being part of an imperial alliance. Furthermore, the more internationalist approach that the UN represented was exactly in line with Canada's own perceived self-interest. Ottawa saw international peace as not only a good in itself but crucial to the country's own security. Canada had never started wars or engaged in wars on its own. But it kept getting dragged into wars caused by the imperial ambitions of other nations, losing more than 100,000 men in the Boer War and the two world wars. Keeping the peace was therefore a crucial goal for Canada in safeguarding its own needs.

Canada, which was renowned in the early postwar years for its excellent foreign service, quickly became an adroit and effective player at the UN, developing a reputation as an honest broker able to mediate complex situations. And no one was more central to this new role than Lester Pearson. Pearson had risen from modest roots as the son of a Methodist minister to become a history professor at the University of Toronto and later a diplomat in the Canadian External Affairs Department. He had been a member of the Canadian delegation to the founding UN conference, and from the beginning had been a keen supporter of the UN and its role as an enforcer of world peace. It was always Pearson's contention that the UN should have real military power at its disposal to carry out its peace-enforcing task. To achieve this, he urged the establishment of a special UN force that could be called upon in an emergency—a force that has never been created but that many still regard as an important step in the direction of world peace.

After being elected to the Canadian Parliament, Pearson became minister of external affairs in 1948 in the government of Louis St. Laurent. From the outset, Pearson was unusually prominent for an external affairs minister. He was particularly active at the UN, and was instrumental in Canada's growing prominence there. Canada came to be viewed as a model member state, and an effective mediator between other states. Pearson attributed Canada's prominence as a middle power at the UN partly to the significant role Canada had played at the UN founding conference and partly to Canada's close relationship with Britain and the United States, as well as to a number of Commonwealth countries. But there was also something about Canada's attitude, its keenness for the very approach of international co-operation that the UN embodied. As a result, Canada was routinely in demand to chair or sit on UN committees and to supply personnel for all sorts of UN operations. As Pearson wrote to a Cabinet colleague in 1956, "It seems that when there is a . . . critical situation, someone always comes to the Canadian delegation and suggests, 'You are the people to propose something.'" Or as Pearson later noted in his memoirs, "We did not seek any prominent or special role at the UN in those early years. But the role often sought us."[2]

Pearson's internationalism was in keeping with the mood of the times. Certainly in the aftermath of the wartime horrors carried out in the name of nationalism, there was a resurgence in Europe of internationalism and support for international institutions, particularly the UN. This spirit of internationalism was strong in the United States as well, but it was countered there by a sense of American power and a growing interest, particularly in Republican ranks, in asserting that power more forcefully in the world. Pearson's support for an internationalist approach, and his keenness to reduce Cold War tensions with Moscow and Peking, made him an irritant to many hard-line American anti-Communists, such as Col. Robert McCormick, the powerful U.S. newspaper baron. Pearson's refusal to co-operate with the anti-Communist witch hunts carried out by Senator Joseph McCarthy in the 1950s particularly provoked the American right, including McCormick. The depth of the colonel's wrath is clear in a March 1953 column he wrote in his Chicago *Tribune*, in which he denounced Pearson as "the most dangerous man in the English-speaking world."[3]

Pearson noted that his penchant for internationalism often made him "more popular in Oslo, say, than in Washington."[4] It was this interest in collective action—and his desire to maintain ties with Europe—that led him to be an early advocate of NATO. In recent years, NATO has been dominated by Washington. But it was actually Britain that first pushed for a European military alliance to ward off possible Soviet aggression. There were even fears at the outset that Washington would retreat back into isolationism and decline to participate. Pearson saw NATO as important for European and therefore Canadian security, and as a vehicle for maintaining Canadian links with Europe. As historian John English has noted, Pearson "believed that Canada's identity depended on the nourishment that flowed from its links to Europe and that without such links the economic and political sinews of Canadian nationhood would shrivel."[5] Pearson's desire to keep active ties to Europe even included the notion of drawing Europe into the collective security of North America, just as North America was involved in the collective security of Europe. (Washington had no use for this idea, however, preferring to keep the defence of North America more tightly under its own control.)

In supporting NATO, Canada was also promoting an internationalist vision of collective security, rather than simply tying itself and its security to Washington. R. J. Sutherland, a Canadian military strategist at the time, explained that part of the appeal of NATO in Ottawa was that it was seen as "an offset to excessive American influence." A former minister of national defence expressed the sentiment more graphically when he noted that "with fifteen people in bed you are less likely to get raped!"[6] Washington, however, was not keen to enter into a collective security arrangement on an equal footing with others, preferring instead to simply offer the group a presidential assurance that it would help out when needed. Pearson resisted this American approach, likening it to the Monroe Doctrine, under which Washington intervened selectively to "protect" weak and dependent Latin American countries. Pearson felt Washington's approach to NATO "smells of charity" and "would emphasize European weakness and dependence on the United States."[7]

Canada also wanted to shape NATO into more than simply a military alliance. It wanted NATO to be an institution that would promote co-operation on economic and social issues as well—a notion that in some ways anticipated the development of the European Union. The idea was to use NATO as a collective vehicle for encouraging progressive Western ideas and highlighting a positive free-market alternative to Communism. This way, Pearson explained, Canada's involvement would not "simply make us part of an American war machine against the Russians."[8] Canada succeeded in putting in place what became known as the "Canada clause," creating a non-military dimension to NATO. (As it turned out, NATO became almost exclusively a military alliance, and one dominated by Washington—two features that were not part of the original plan.)

With the outbreak of the Korean War in 1950, East–West tensions flared up. North Korea's invasion of South Korea was widely interpreted in Western capitals—including Ottawa—as aggression backed by China and the Soviet Union. The UN Security Council (with the Soviets temporarily absent) voted to intervene to defend South Korea, and Canada supported a UN-sanctioned force with troops and three Canadian destroyers. It soon became clear that at least some elements in the United States wanted to take advantage of the conflict to push things into a larger confrontation with China. General Douglas MacArthur, the famous Second World War U.S. military leader who was now commanding a UN-endorsed force in Korea, wanted to pursue the North Koreans back into their own territory and all the way up to the Chinese border. Pearson strongly opposed that idea, recognizing that MacArthur's real goal was to provoke a confrontation with China and eventually overthrow its new Communist government.

In November 1950, U.S. President Harry Truman threatened to use nuclear weapons in the conflict, saying that they had not been ruled out as a means to end the war. Pearson thought this was reckless and spoke out publicly against the use of the bomb: "Certainly its use for the second time against an Asian people would dangerously weaken the links that remain between the Western world and the peoples of the East."[9] He told the press that he assumed the president would consult other countries "before taking any decision to use the atomic bomb."[10] He also immediately sought clarification through diplomatic channels and began to work behind the scenes to gain international support for a ceasefire and, ultimately, for a resolution of the question of Communist Chinese participation at the UN.

Pearson described his own actions at the time as trying "to knock some sense into the more militant Americans."[11] In taking this position, Pearson risked alienating the Truman administration, and he was also at odds with some leading Canadian newspapers, which were clamouring for Ottawa to go along with Washington. He had the support of St. Laurent, who seemed to understand that, in the end, aggression by the West would fail. Cabinet documents show that St. Laurent expressed the view that "Asiatic peoples were ultimately going to take complete charge of their own affairs and territory, and would not tolerate outside domination and interference."[12]

It should be noted that Pearson, particularly in the early post-war years, subscribed to a rather simplistic Cold War view of Communism as an endlessly aggressive and expansionist power, and one that the West might have to check. "The crusading power of communism has been harnessed by a cold-blooded, calculating, victoriously powerful Slav empire," he said in 1948. "Our frontier is not even on the Rhine or rivers further east. It is wherever free men are struggling . . . It may run through our own cities, or it may be on the crest of the remotest mountain."[13] Still, both Pearson and

St. Laurent understood that American belligerence towards the Communist world could be counterproductive, and that some sort of accommodation was desirable. Pearson publicly described his goal during the Korean crisis as "an attempt through diplomacy to reach a modus vivendi with the Asian communist world."

Pearson even argued that it was a moral duty for Canada to challenge the United States when Washington adopted positions that were dangerous. While Pearson regarded the United States as an ally and the "leader of the free world," he recognized that the Americans could be reckless and provocative. In 1954, the fiercely anti-Communist U.S. secretary of state John Foster Dulles developed a NATO policy of "massive retaliation" under which Washington would retaliate with nuclear weapons if the Soviets made any aggressive moves against the West. Pearson responded by stressing that no such action should be taken without consulting other NATO countries, putting him in line with liberal opinion in the United States. A *New York Times* editorial noted that "what Mr. Pearson's statement has done is to stress again the importance of Canada in our security and the necessity of keeping her fully informed and winning her support."[14]

Pearson also opposed threatened U.S. intervention when China shelled two offshore islands in the Pacific in 1954. There was pressure from some quarters in the United States for Washington to attack China if the shelling was directed against the island of Formosa, where the former government of China had sought refuge after being driven out by the Communists. In Canada, some major newspapers were calling for Canada to get on board with the United States, but Pearson refused to, stating clearly that Canada disagreed with the United States on this crucial matter. He explained that he considered it would be "unutterable folly" to allow the fight over the islands to escalate into a major conflict. He also explained that, while it was not appropriate for Canada to criticize the United States on most matters, it was important that we do so, on vitally important matters like this.[15]

While the United States dug in ever deeper with its anti-Communist fervour, Pearson steered Canada into a more accommodating and open view of the world. In 1955, he became the first foreign minister of a NATO country to accept a Soviet invitation to visit Moscow. There he met extensively with Soviet leader Nikita Khrushchev, and returned convinced that a thaw in East–West tensions was possible and desirable. He also travelled to Egypt and held talks with the controversial Egyptian nationalist leader, Gamal Abdel Nasser, showing an openness towards the Arab world that was later to prove helpful in the resolution of the Suez crisis.

Pearson also charted a new course for Canada in developing an openness and supportiveness towards Third World countries struggling to emerge from colonialism. He developed a particularly strong relationship with Prime Minister Jawaharlal Nehru of India. In a series of lectures at Princeton in 1955, Pearson spoke in favour of the rising surge of anti-colonialism around the world. He described "the yearning and the effort of the people of the Islamic world, of India, and of South-east Asia," and talked of their movement as "exciting and . . . full of promise for the world." He went on to suggest that the West's "vision" had weakened during the first four decades of the twentieth century and that "the smug satisfaction with one's own superior righteousness" that pervaded Western colonial attitudes was no longer acceptable. Similarly, he told the U.S. National Council of Churches in 1954 that the West had to give up its "habit of authority," which had been fundamental to Western expansion since Columbus.[16]

Pearson showed his willingness to abandon the West's "habit of authority" when he proposed a compromise at the UN aimed at admitting as members a number of new nations that had previously been excluded. There was initially strong opposition to this

Canadian initiative, including from the United States, but eventually all sides agreed to the "Canadian compromise" under which membership was considerably expanded. The deal was to have a significant impact on the UN, as the traditionally dominant Western powers had to accommodate a new "Third World" grouping of countries that were not automatically pro-American or even pro-Western. Pearson had anticipated this effect, but had considered the expansion an important step towards making the UN more inclusive.[17]

It was a step away from the colonialism of the past, a sign that the West was prepared to consider accepting its former colonies as members of the international community. Then the following year, the imperial powers of the West seemed to slide back into their old imperial ways. Once again, a little guidance from Lester Pearson was apparently needed.

———

Pearson's distaste for colonialism played a role in what ended up being a significant diplomatic and foreign policy triumph: his handling of the 1956 Suez crisis, in which he helped defuse a confrontation that, among other things, pitted Britain and the United States against each other and threatened to lead to a major international war. The crisis originated in the postwar break-up of the fading British colonial empire. Britain had decided to end its military occupation of the Suez Canal Zone in 1955 and hand the crucial waterway over to Egypt. But the following year, Britain and the United States also abruptly withdrew promised financing to build the Aswan Dam across the Nile—a project that was central to Nasser's vision for the future development of Egypt.

The U.S. withdrawal from the project had been sparked by rising anger in Washington over Nasser's recognition of Communist China and his growing ties with Moscow, which had agreed to supply arms to Egypt (since the United States, and other NATO countries, including Canada, were supplying arms to Israel). The U.S. withdrawal from the dam project infuriated the Egyptian leader, who announced two days later that he was nationalizing the canal and would use the canal tolls to finance construction of the dam. The nationalization angered Britain particularly. British prime minister Anthony Eden spoke of the possibility of using force if the Egyptians proceeded. With the issue still before the United Nations, Israeli forces moved into Egypt as part of a secret plan Israel had worked out with Britain and France. The next day, Britain and France issued an ultimatum that both Israel and Egypt withdraw from the canal. When Egypt refused to comply, Britain and France began bombing the canal zone and positioned troops to seize the canal.

The crisis created a difficult situation for Canada, which had always supported Britain. But in this case, Britain seemed to be behaving in a needlessly aggressive, colonial fashion. Pearson noted that Egypt was not technically in violation of the Constantinople Convention of 1888, which ensured international access to the canal. After all, it had not refused to allow passage through the canal; it had simply decided to manage the passageway itself. In fact, Nasser had even stated that Egypt would pay fair compensation to stockholders of the Suez Canal Company, based on stock prices the day of the nationalization. So Egypt didn't really seem to be out of line. For many Canadians, it was wrenching to see Britain behave so badly, to carry on like an old-style colonial power. One British magazine described Canadian reaction as "almost tearful . . . like finding a beloved uncle arrested for rape."[18]

For Pearson, the key concern was bridging the divide between Britain and the United States. Washington had not been consulted and strongly opposed the military intervention. The Suez crisis was thus threatening to drive a wedge between Canada's two most important allies, and also splitting the Commonwealth, with member nations, particularly India, vehemently opposed to the neo-colonial actions of its mother country. Pearson worked behind the scenes at the UN to push for the creation of an emergency UN international police force to prevent the two sides from clashing. In the past, member countries had contributed troops to military missions that had received UN approval, such as the U.S.-led mission in Korea commanded by General MacArthur. But Pearson envisioned something different here—a specifically UN police force that would be responsible for safeguarding the peace while a political settlement could be worked out. It was an idea that Pearson had long nurtured, and the Suez situation seemed to call out for it.

On November 1, 1956, Pearson worked through the night manoeuvring both behind the scenes and in the UN council chamber. He managed to prevent motions condemning Britain and also to stall an American resolution demanding a ceasefire, until the ceasefire could be coupled with a resolution calling for the establishment of an international police force. In the next few days, Pearson worked intensely, using his extensive personal contacts developed over many years of careful diplomacy, to bring onside UN Secretary-General Dag Hammarskjöld, the Egyptians, the Americans, the British, the French and many others, including delegates from many of the new Afro-Asian countries whose admission to the UN he had helped bring about. Having prepared the ground through his diplomacy, Pearson put forward his resolution to the General Assembly on November 3, calling for the immediate establishment of an emergency police force to supervise a ceasefire. The resolution passed 57–0 (with 19 abstentions). In the following days, Britain and France, realizing their actions had been a terrible mistake and relieved to be spared condemnation from the General Assembly, withdrew their troops. The canal was reopened, and the UN Emergency Force flew in to enforce the peace. A confrontation in the Middle East—with the potential to spiral into a much broader conflict with consequences for Canada and the world—had been averted.

Back in Canada, the Conservative opposition accused the St. Laurent government—and Pearson in particular—of deserting Canada's two mother countries, Britain and France, in the Suez crisis. This was among the many charges that enabled the Conservatives to bring down the Liberal government in the 1957 federal election. Pearson ended up as a member of the Opposition, reduced from a fine ministerial suite on Parliament Hill to an austere basement office.

It was in these modest quarters that the phone rang on October 14, 1957. It was a Canadian Press reporter asking Pearson if he had any statement to make. But the days when the press hovered around Pearson in hopes of a statement had passed, and this seemed almost like a cruel joke. "On what?" he asked. The reporter explained that Pearson had been awarded the Nobel Peace Prize. Pearson corrected the reporter, explaining that he had been nominated but that many people are nominated each year. The reporter insisted that no, Pearson had won, and he read the telegram saying so over the phone.

At that moment, Pearson probably wasn't thinking of how Canada's reputation would forever be enhanced and how that would change the way Canadians see themselves and their country. At that moment, he simply sat back, looked around his bare little office and muttered, "Gosh."

But of course it was handling Canada's relationship with the United States, the newly emergent world superpower, that was the trickiest. What can be said of Pearson and his handling of our relations with Washington?

As noted, Pearson was, overall, supportive of the United States. In some of his writings, he sounds downright deferential to U.S. power. As he wrote in his memoirs, "One principle is that we should exhibit a sympathetic understanding of the heavy burden of international responsibility borne by the United States, not of her own imperial choosing, but caused in part by the unavoidable withdrawal of other states from certain of these responsibilities . . . Above all, as American difficulties increase, we should resist any temptation to become smug and superior: 'You are bigger but we are better.' Our own experience, as we wrestle with our own problems, gives us no ground for any such conviction."[19] Pearson also subscribed to many Cold War attitudes. In the name of preventing the spread of Communism, Pearson condoned and even clearly supported aggressive U.S. military action in Vietnam. In a letter to President Lyndon Johnson during the Vietnam War, Pearson wrote: "I want to assure you that my Government, and I in particular as its leader, want to give all possible support in the policy, difficult and thankless, you are following in Vietnam in aiding South Vietnam to resist aggression."[20]

Indeed, as external affairs minister and later as prime minister from 1963 to 1968, Pearson bears considerable blame for Canada's complicity in U.S. actions in Vietnam. The best-known example of Canada's co-operation with the U.S. over Vietnam was the role of Canadian diplomat Blair Seaborn in carrying threats from Washington to Hanoi in 1964, warning Hanoi of U.S. plans to bomb the city if North Vietnam didn't, in effect, surrender. This Canadian messenger role, which generated considerable controversy in Canada when it came to light through the publication of the Pentagon Papers in the *New York Times* in 1971, was rather harmless, compared to Canada's actual complicity in the U.S. war effort—a complicity that has received relatively little attention. The main vehicle for this complicity was Canada's involvement in the International Control Commission (ICC), which was set up to supervise the truce established in 1954 between the victorious Vietnamese resistance movement (the Viet Minh) and the departing French colonial power.

The details of the Vietnam War may seem like a bit of a diversion here, but the complicit role Canada played in assisting the aggressive U.S. war effort—which went on under both Liberal and Conservative governments—is worthy of attention. It's also a vivid early example of Canada holding the bully's coat.

The 1954 truce, established at a conference in Geneva, outlined a plan for general elections to be held throughout Vietnam two years later to elect a government to preside over a sovereign, united country. The Viet Minh—popular resistance fighters who had battled Japanese occupiers during the Second World War and then fought the French colonials after the war—were widely expected to win those elections. In the meantime, the Geneva conference had established a temporary military demarcation line between the north, the bastion of the Viet Minh, and the south, where the weak, pro-Western government was located in Saigon. The Geneva conference plan also prohibited the establishment of foreign military bases anywhere in the country, and created an international commission—the ICC—to monitor and supervise the truce. The ICC was to consist of Canada, Poland and India.

It was broadly assumed that India would act independently, while Poland would act as a puppet of the Soviets, who were supportive of the communistic Viet Minh. Canada, on the other hand, was regarded as being close to the United States, which quickly replaced the French as the dominant Western power supporting the fragile regime in Saigon. Ottawa adamantly rejected the insinuation that Canada was merely the Western counterpart of Poland, in other words, a choreboy for the Americans. Sadly, however, the record, which has been scrupulously examined by Canadian political scientist Victor Levant, suggests that the insinuation is not that far-fetched.

In a massive doctoral thesis and later in his book, *Quiet Complicity*, Levant traces how Canada used its role on the ICC to assist the Americans in their attempts to undermine the democratic process, which would have almost certainly led to a popularly elected Viet Minh government in a united Vietnam.[21] To prevent this from happening, Washington and the Saigon government consistently violated the terms for elections laid down by the 1954 Geneva conference, and Canada declined to identify these violations—even though the mandate of the ICC was to monitor and report such violations. Most important, Canada effectively provided cover for the United States as it established an ever-larger military presence to prop up the government in the south. Through its role on the ICC, Canada allowed the United States to fraudulently present its military build-up as a response to alleged North Vietnamese violations of the truce, when in fact it was the U.S. military presence that amounted to a gross violation of the truce. Levant cites a U.S. State Department background paper that discusses the different roles played by Canada, India and Poland within the ICC: "We can count on the continued Canadian efforts to serve Free World interests in the ICC. The main obstacle will continue to be the Indians who regard their role in an overly legalistic context; it is difficult for the Canadians to press vigorously for action for fear that the Indians will be offended and vote with the Poles on key issues."[22]

So, the State Department faulted the Indians for being "overly legalistic"—in other words, for insisting on following the actual terms set out in the truce agreement worked out at the Geneva conference. (Monitoring and supervising that truce was, let's not forget, what the ICC had been set up to do.) Canada, on the other hand, was regarded by the State Department as a willing accomplice in violating the terms of the truce, in the interest of advancing the interests of the "Free World" by blocking the election of the popular Viet Minh.

Canada's role in the ICC as an aid to Washington was extensive and important to the U.S. war effort. By early 1962, the United States had already established a military presence of four thousand U.S. troops in South Vietnam, in clear violation of the truce agreement. As Levant notes, "If Saigon and Washington wished to avoid censure for violating the Geneva Accords, they needed the legitimization of the International Control Commission itself."[23] Washington regarded this legitimization as crucial for keeping the American people onside. In a cable, U.S. diplomat Adlai Stevenson revealed his fears of a "hostile propaganda reaction in [the] U.S." if Washington was seen as breaking the terms of the Geneva truce. Stevenson suggested that the Soviets would make accusations to that effect, and if the Soviet accusations were supported by neutral countries in South Asia, it could "cause significant political damage." Accordingly, the Kennedy administration succeeded in pressuring India to replace its chief ICC representative—who was considered "overly legalistic" by the United States—with someone more willing to co-operate with Washington.

With India now in line, and Canada fully co-operative, the ICC produced a "special report" in June 1962 that essentially whitewashed Saigon's significant violations and portrayed the U.S. military build-up as a necessary response to Hanoi's "subversion" and "aggression." The evidence cited by the ICC to support these conclusions were nothing but unsubstantiated allegations made by the Saigon government. Meanwhile, Hanoi's complaints of violations by Saigon—which had been verified by ICC on-the-ground investigators—were dismissed in the report as mere allegations. The 1962 special report by the ICC became a crucial document, which was showcased by Washington on many occasions. That and later ICC reports in the following years allowed Washington to justify a military build-up that eventually reached 525,000 U.S. troops.

Gwynne Dyer notes in a foreword to Levant's book: "The fact is that Canada did have choices about its behaviour in Vietnam . . . and chose to behave badly." If Ottawa had insisted on playing an impartial role on the ICC, refusing to serve Washington's interests, there might have been some political or economic consequences for Canada. It's impossible to know. But as Dyer points out, doing what we did also had consequences—"the vast misery and suffering that Canada's complicity helped to perpetuate in Vietnam."

So, tragically, while Pearson showed courage at Temple University in publicly challenging the U.S. role in Vietnam, he seemed unwilling to use that courage to insist that Canada play the role of fair-minded observer on the ICC—where it really might have made a difference.

———

If the majority of Canadians came to embrace the peacekeeping legacy Pearson initiated, there were others who resisted it. One bastion of resistance, as we saw in chapter 2, was the Canadian military, particularly those running it or supervising it from inside the Department of National Defence. These senior members of the military establishment were cool not just to peacekeeping but to the internationalist role it represented, and were keen for Canada instead to focus on playing the role of trusted ally and military consort of the United States.

In many ways, this attraction to closer military ties to the United States came down to a longing for the kind of status, prestige and ample funding that the American military enjoys. As defence analyst Peter Langille notes, being part of U.S.-dominated alliances like NORAD and NATO gave Canada's military a feeling of "playing in the big leagues." While UN peacekeeping missions tended to be underfunded, ad-hoc ventures where soldiers ended up working alongside poorly trained and poorly equipped troops from Third World countries, NORAD and NATO offered military personnel an opportunity to rub shoulders with big-name U.S. generals, to be part of operations that were "world class." These U.S.-led alliances had the most sophisticated equipment and the most advanced training and offered the military equivalent of glamour and excitement.

Along with the pleasure of hobnobbing with the elite of the military world, there was a feeling of importance attached to what the U.S. military was doing, a notion that it was involved in nothing less than the "defence of the free world." This kept alive in Canadian military personnel the feeling of relevance and self-importance that they'd enjoyed during the two world wars. Military analysts Joseph Jockel and Joel Sokolsky explain that without NATO and NORAD, the Canadian forces would have had a hard time justifying significant military expenditures in a nuclear age. Thus, military leaders had a professional interest in maintaining Canada's role in big-power military alliances with the United States. "Historically, Canada has always fought alongside and against those of the great powers," note Jockel and Sokolsky. "This has been integral to Canada's military heritage. The post-war alliances allowed the military to continue this tradition."[24] The focus had simply shifted from fighting Britain's imperial enemies and Nazism to fighting Communism, which was now seen as the central threat to Western civilization.

Compared to this, notions of internationalism, of equality and understanding among nations, seemed secondary and even at times in conflict with the West-versus-Communism all-out struggle that was given centre stage. UN peacekeeping tended to be seen by those running the military as a distraction, as something that risked diverting attention and resources away from the military's real job. "The generals had never liked UN service and the political emphasis it received in Canada," notes historian Jack Granatstein. "To train for UN duties was to take time away from the important task of preparing to fight the Russians."[25] Thus there was a reluctance to channel the department's funds towards peacekeeping, or to give it institutional importance within the Canadian Forces or the Department of National Defence. Peacekeeping was something that was to be fitted in, to be accommodated where possible into the broader scheme of things, not to be given an importance and focus of its own.

This disdain for peacekeeping at the higher levels trickled down through the military ranks and came to permeate the Canadian military culture. "For the rank and file, peacekeeping was simply boring, a dull duty away from home among people whose culture was too different to enjoy," explains Granatstein. "The job was well done, but it was never liked." It's hard to know if the rank and file really found peacekeeping dull, as Granatstein suggests, or were simply absorbing the attitudes of their senior officers. Those interested in advancing within the military learned that completing courses and training at U.S. war colleges was usually considered more valuable experience than participating in peacekeeping missions.

The disconnect between the Canadian public's enthusiasm for peacekeeping and the military's disdain for it persisted, even when Canada's political leaders deliberately put emphasis on peacekeeping. Under Lester Pearson, peacekeeping was elevated to one of the top four priorities of the Canadian military. In a white paper on defence in 1964, Pearson's Liberal minority government specified peacekeeping as the fourth priority, right up there with basic priorities like defending Canada against attack. Pierre Trudeau also maintained it as the fourth priority in his government's 1971 white paper. But the military and the Department of National Defence were powerful bureaucracies with their own orientation and interests, and they were the ones that actually allocated funds from the defence budget and did the planning for defence operations. And since they never considered peacekeeping very important or appealing, it tended to be left to "last-minute" arrangements and minimal funding. So, despite its apparent importance as a Canadian defence priority, peacekeeping consumed less than 0.5 per cent of the defence budget in the early 1980s, according to one estimate.[26] When the government occasionally did override military planners and institute policies that actually gave an importance to peacekeeping, there was considerable resentment within the military establishment. The Pearson government's decision to unify the three branches of the military was seen in part as a move to facilitate peacekeeping, and this helped fuel resentment against unification. "If peacekeeping implied unification then the military wanted none of it," notes Granatstein.

In keeping with their disdain for peacekeeping, military leaders were also frustrated by the diminished role for conventional warfare in the postwar years. The existence of nuclear weapons changed the nature of war in a way that had profound implications for Canadian military personnel, whose status and considerable prestige in the nation had been derived from fighting conventional battles in two world wars. Now that sort of fighting seemed almost obsolete. With the prospect of human annihilation hanging in the balance, it was assumed that any conventional battles between the major powers would be short in duration, and would either be quickly resolved politically or proceed to ultimate destruction. This meant that there was little point in maintaining huge reserve armies and supply lines for long-drawn-out battles. The "short-war strategy" that emerged in the West and was adopted by Ottawa in the early postwar years meant a smaller military, and one that inevitably seemed less relevant and important to the country. None of this was very pleasing to those in the Canadian military. Nor was it good for the defence industries that had grown up in Canada during the wars and had built thriving businesses churning out military supplies for protracted battles.

Altogether, the early postwar years were very demoralizing for the Canadian military establishment. For those who considered themselves in the business of fighting wars, the prospect of no wars—or at least no wars involving actual fighting—was disheartening. With the Canadian public celebrating the spirit of internationalism and the UN, and a "short-war" strategy shaping a smaller, less well equipped force, Canada's military establishment felt neglected, marginalized and unappreciated. Granatstein captures the extent of that unhappiness in his book *Who Killed the Canadian Military?* In what sounds jarring to the non-military ear, Granatstein talks about the "harmful effect" of Pearson's Nobel Prize, filling Canadians as it did with positive notions of peacekeeping. "Because they fell in love with peacekeeping, Canadians began to fall out of love with the true purpose of the military—to be ready to fight wars." (This foreshadows Rick Hillier's even blunter assertion that the true purpose of the Canadian military is to be "able to kill people.") Granatstein, a keen advocate for the Canadian military, is apparently voicing the long-simmering resentment within military ranks over the lack of war-fighting when he contemptuously refers to peacekeeping as "do-goodism writ large" and dismisses Canadian expressions of support for peacekeeping as "prattling about peacekeeping."[27]

It wasn't until the late 1970s that the military establishment began to see some hope of a revival of a war-fighting orientation. At a NATO summit in 1978, member nations agreed to a target of increasing their military budgets by 3 per cent a year, ostensibly in response to an escalating Soviet threat. The "short-war" strategy of the previous three decades was giving way to a renewed interest in preparing for long-term conventional war, regardless of the threat of triggering nuclear war. While authorities justified the change on strategic grounds, it's interesting to note that some powerful multinational corporations stood to benefit financially in that a key part of the strategy involved building up the defence industries. All this promised to create a new opening for defence industries in Canada to push for a military build-up here as well.

With the election of Ronald Reagan in 1980, the climate improved still further, from the viewpoint of the Canadian defence establishment. Hyping the Soviet threat to the hilt, Reagan advocated a massive military build-up, even advancing the deluded notion that nuclear war was winnable and should not be shied away from. Gone was the notion of learning to live with enemies; the focus was now on arming for battle, on achieving "peace" through strength. This meant ever more weaponry, nuclear and non-nuclear. The dramatic increases in U.S. military budgets in the Reagan years fuelled aspirations north of the border in both the military and the defence industries. The title of a 1983 cover story in *Canadian Business* reflected that excitement: "Hail to the Hawks: Ronald Reagan's $200 billion-plus defence budget is good news for Canadian business."

Increasingly, a Canadian defence lobby began to emerge as a potent force in Canadian politics. Veterans groups and military institutes had long exerted pressure on behalf of the military, but these organizations became more active and effective in the 1980s. The most important of these is the Conference on Defence Associations (CDA), an umbrella group representing military and retired military personnel as well as business, academic and professional types with military interests. The CDA enjoys access at the highest levels, including direct access to the prime minister. While ostensibly an outside, non-governmental group, the CDA receives funding and organizational support from the Department of National Defence. In effect, then, the Defence Department is subsidizing a group to lobby the government to maintain the Defence Department's budget.[28]

In fact, the Department of National Defence subsidizes a number of apparently independent groups that advocate on behalf of the military, as defence analyst Peter Langille has documented.

Among these are the Canadian Institute of Strategic Studies—the group that organized the event featuring Lt.-Gen. Metz mentioned in chapter 2—as well as a number of institutes or strategic studies programs connected with our universities. As a result, most academic defence analysts in Canada are employed in positions subsidized by the Department of Defence, says Langille. Interestingly, the views of these analysts almost always reflect those of our Defence Department—possibly just a coincidence, but possibly part of a larger pattern in which government defence budgets have been used to help shape the public debate in a pro-military direction. So, for instance, David Rudd, director of the Canadian Institute of Strategic Studies, appears often in the media and speaks in favour of various things the military wants, including more military spending. No mention is made by the media of the fact that his institute receives funding from the Department of National Defence—the department that is hoping to get that increased military spending. So Rudd comes across to the public as an independent expert, and his advocacy sounds more credible than if it simply came from the Defence Department itself.

Key to the emergence of an effective defence lobby in Canada was the involvement of business. Canadian arms manufacturers had become a multi-billion-dollar industry with "a firm place for themselves among global arms dealers," according to a study prepared by the Ontario Legislative Research Services in 1983.[29] The industry had long worked closely with various departments of the federal government to promote international arms sales. But in the 1980s, business also began pushing for government help in developing a comprehensive industrial base geared towards military production, along the lines of what existed in the United States. An effective advocate for this strategy was the Business Council on National Issues (BCNI, later renamed the Canadian Council of Chief Executives). Established in 1976, the council of high-powered CEOs was a deliberate attempt to assert business interests more vigorously and to influence Canadian public policy in a more pro-business direction. From the outset, the Canadian defence industry was a crucial part of the BCNI, and in 1981 the BCNI created its Task Force on Foreign Policy and Defence to push for a Canadian military build-up. Six of the Canadian CEOs on the task force represented corporations with significant defence interests: CAE Industries, Control Data, EH Industries, Honeywell, ITT Industries and the SNC Group.[30]

The Canadian defence lobby also turned to the United States for help. Since the Second World War, the U.S. defence industry had been an overwhelmingly powerful force in U.S. politics, prompting Dwight Eisenhower to use his departing presidential address in 1960 to warn of the dangers of "undue influence" on the part of the "military-industrial complex." Certainly the United States offered Canadian military advocates a compelling example of how a defence industry can wield great influence in the corridors of power. Accordingly, the CDA set out to establish contacts in the U.S. defence industry in the early 1980s and quickly found a warm reception. Among other things, Pentagon officials briefed the Canadian military visitors on media strategies for selling the Canadian public on the need for increased military spending. Washington had long pushed for bigger Canadian military budgets—a goal it shared with the Canadian defence lobby—and the Pentagon welcomed an opportunity to make Canadian lobbyists more effective in pushing this agenda from within Canada. The American Defense Preparedness Association organized a Canadian chapter in 1983 and began working with Canadians on promoting contacts between government and the defence industry on both sides of the border.

In fact, the Canadian arms industry was already closely connected to the massive U.S. arms industry. That co-operation had begun in the Second World War and had been consolidated after the signing of the Defence Production Sharing Agreement of 1958, which essentially created cross-border free trade for weapons manufacturers. The agreement had been key to the development of a Canadian arms industry, since it allowed Canadian companies to bid on a wide range of Pentagon contracts. The Pentagon was pleased to award contracts to the Canadian industry, since a reciprocity clause in the agreement stipulated that the more Canadian military products the United States purchased, the more American military products Ottawa had to purchase. The effect of the clause was to bolster military spending and the military-industrial complex on both sides of the border.

There was also a natural fit between the industries of both nations, since many of the key Canadian companies were U.S.-owned. Among Canada's top ten military contractors, half were U.S.-controlled branch plants, such as General Dynamics Land Systems and General Motors Diesel Division. The high level of U.S. ownership in the Canadian arms industry has persisted since the mid-1980s, when the Canadian monitoring group Project Ploughshares began keeping records. Ken Epps, a researcher with the group, argues that even more important than the high level of foreign ownership is the heavy reliance of Canadian arms producers on the U.S. market.[31] Since 1985, the U.S. has represented two-thirds or more of Canadian arms exports.

This has had political implications as well, creating a constituency within the Canadian industry that has been highly supportive of America's military adventurism, and that has urged Ottawa to also be supportive. This was foreseen by the U.S. Defense Department, which specified in a 1960 directive that one of its reasons for supporting the Defence Production Sharing Agreement was to foster support for "closely integrated military planning between Canada and the United States." Thus the Canadian industry, combining its efforts with the Canadian military and military-funded academics and think tanks, has formed an effective lobby in favour of Canadian government support for and involvement in America's wars.

The high degree of foreign ownership in the Canadian arms industry had been a bit of a sore point for the Trudeau government, which in the late 1970s had been interested in increasing Canadian ownership in a number of key sectors, including defence and energy. These sectors were believed to offer unique opportunities for developing a strong Canadian economy—energy because of its significance as the engine of the industrial world, and defence because of its reliance on advanced technology leading to innovation and highly paid jobs. In reality, the possibility of an independent Canadian defence industry had effectively been killed with the cancellation of the Avro Arrow program by the Diefenbaker government in 1959. The superb design of the Canadian-developed supersonic fighter had been well recognized, but the key potential purchasers—the U.S. and NATO allies—had defence industries of their own to keep in business. The Arrow's abrupt termination stirred nationalist sentiments across the country—sentiments that continued to reverberate in the Trudeau era and beyond. It was partly in response to these sentiments that in 1980 the Trudeau Cabinet proposed a new industrial strategy aimed at using defence spending to encourage a Canadian-owned defence industry. But, unlike the Trudeau government's detailed plan to Canadianize the oil patch through the National Energy Program, there was no equivalent development of a plan to Canadianize the defence industries. They continued to be largely American owned, and mostly focused on producing component parts for weapons systems produced by the major U.S. defence contractors.

The election of Brian Mulroney's Conservative government in 1984 was a refreshing and energizing tonic for the Canadian defence lobby. Mulroney openly courted Washington and was responsive to interests—on both sides of the border—that wanted to see Canada develop a stronger military. Right from the beginning, the Mulroney government showed its interest in strengthening the military and encouraging the emergence of a strong industrial defence sector, operating within the larger context of the U.S. military-industrial complex. Whereas the Trudeau government had toyed with the idea of trying to develop an independent Canadian defence industry, the Mulroney government fully accepted Canada's branch plant role in the U.S. military-industrial complex, and saw that as the basis for a lucrative, Pentagon-driven arms sector in Canada.

To this end, the Mulroney government quickly set up the Defence Industrial Preparedness Task Force (DIPTF). The very language of "defence industrial preparedness" echoed U.S. military themes of the time. The task force, which was established within the Defence Department in Ottawa, was instructed to collaborate with the U.S. Defense Department "in studying ways and means of enhancing the integration of the North American Defence Industrial base."[32] To no one's surprise, then, the task force, after collaborating with U.S. defence officials, concluded that there was a great need for government-business co-operation "within a single market Canadian–U.S. continentalist framework." That U.S.–Canada collaboration eventually led to the signing of a charter in 1987, formalizing U.S.–Canada co-operation on defence preparations and establishing an organization to oversee that co-operation, the North American Defence Industrial Base.

The Mulroney government worked towards not only closer Canada–U.S. defence ties but also closer business-government collaboration on the defence front. Responding to a BCNI request for such close collaboration, Defence Minister Erik Nielsen replied that "it may well be to Canada's advantage to have a parallel group such as [U.S. Defense Secretary Caspar] Weinberger's Defense Policy Advisory Group."[33] So, following the U.S. example, the Mulroney government established the Defence Industrial Preparedness Advisory Committee, an exclusive group consisting of a small number of CEOs and others who met with the defence minister to discuss a range of policy issues. This signalled the Mulroney government's interest in listening to the defence industry, not just on how to develop and encourage the growth of arms manufacturing in Canada but also on the shape of Canada's military and foreign policy.

In fact, the advisory committee was just one way that the military lobby was able to get its voice heard loud and clear within the Mulroney government. More important were the informal contacts, and the way key players moved around between top jobs in government, industry and the military, creating a set of close personal connections and a fading of the distinction between the roles of those pushing an agenda of military expansion and those having to make decisions about that agenda. In the United States, we've seen this phenomenon played out in recent years at the very highest levels, with Dick Cheney going from the top job at the Pentagon to Halliburton CEO to U.S. vice-president and key promoter of the war in Iraq, where Halliburton has enjoyed multi-billion-dollar contracts. Although no one has cut as striking a figure as the vice-president in his seamless moving around within the U.S. military-industrial complex, Canada has seen its own share of nimble movement within our own little complex.

Gen. Paul Manson, for instance, had a long career in the Canadian military during which he headed up a procurement program for fighter aircraft and later became the country's top military man during the Mulroney years, as chief of defence staff for the Canadian Forces from 1986 to 1989. After his retirement, General Manson moved into the executive suites of some of Canada's top military contractors, including Unisys Systems, Paramax, Loral Canada and Lockheed Martin Canada, where his familiarity with the military's procurement process no doubt came in handy. In 1992, while he was president of Paramax, Manson helped his company win a $5.8-billion contract for military helicopters—from the

Mulroney government, whose officials Manson knew well from his years as the nation's chief military leader.

But perhaps no Canadian has moved more dexterously at high levels within military, business and government circles than Derek H. Burney. Burney developed high-level government connections when he served as Mulroney's chief of staff from 1987 to 1989, and as a key architect of the Mulroney government's top priority—the Canada–U.S. Free Trade Agreement. After that, Burney developed political connections in the United States, where he served as Canada's ambassador until 1993. Although Burney's background was in government, not in the weapons industry, Canada's leading defence contractor, CAE, recognized the importance of his contacts and hired him to head up the company from 1999 to 2004. From his post at CAE and also his role as a prominent member of the Business Council on National Issues, Burney became an outspoken lobbyist for higher military spending. A Pentagon agency promoting George W. Bush's missile defence system also understood the usefulness of Burney's Ottawa connections when it awarded CAE a contract from a special Pentagon fund that had been set up, according to the magazine *Defense News*, to "lure foreign firms with U.S. military dollars and hope the contractors sway their governments to get on board."[34]

Burney became a leading advocate of Canadian participation in the dangerous and technologically far-fetched missile defence scheme and appeared to have won over the Liberal government until public opposition forced Ottawa to retreat. Burney's continuing influence in Ottawa is reflected in the fact that in 2006 he headed the transition team for the new Harper government, which, among other things, selected retired general and defence industry lobbyist Gordon O'Connor as the new minister of defence. The in-house military-industrial tradition continues. (Certainly the web of connections remains tight. Rick Hillier served on the staff of Lt.-Gen. Patrick O'Donnell, before O'Donnell retired. Now

O'Donnell is a lobbyist for Lockheed Martin, a key competitor for a lucrative contract to provide aircraft to the Canadian military, now headed by Hillier.)

It's hardly surprising, then, that, with high-level business input at the very top political levels, the Mulroney government veered significantly away from the defence policy of previous Canadian governments and adopted a hawkish policy more closely resembling Washington's. In its 1987 white paper on defence, the Mulroney government struck a distinctly different tone than the white papers of the Pearson and Trudeau eras, and one that was music to the ears of the defence lobby. To begin with, the Mulroney paper emphasized the danger of the Soviet threat and the need for greater military readiness in the face of it. This signalled a move away from the "short-war" strategy and an acceptance of the notion of preparing for a long war, complete with an ongoing industrial mobilization for war. To this end, the paper committed the government to a fifteen-year plan for steady increases in military spending and a dramatic threefold increase in the nation's reserve forces. Along with the greater manpower, there would also be a lot of new military hardware, including new investment in aerospace, more tanks for Canada's NATO brigade and, most significantly, a new fleet of nuclear-powered submarines, with a hefty price tag of $8 billion. The white paper pledged the government would "implement this program vigorously."

The defence lobby was delighted, and swung into action to mobilize public support for the new agenda. The Canadian Institute of Strategic Studies and the Defence Department both organized teams of speakers to get the message out to the public that the Soviets posed a dire threat and that the strategy outlined in the Mulroney government's white paper was the response that was needed. Within military circles, it was well understood that winning over the public to a more overtly militaristic agenda wouldn't be easy. "Success will depend on concerted action by government, business associations and defence-related associations and institutes to ensure that the necessary public and political initiatives are undertaken . . . ," argued Brig.-Gen. George Bell. "But we must realize that this is only phase one of what will be a long and difficult campaign."[35] Even as they settled in for a long battle to win over a resistant public, the defence lobby savoured the victory of how far it had already managed to move the federal agenda. As Brig.-Gen. W. J. Yost later put it, "Doing away with the short-war policy was a long struggle that took a lot of effort and over ten years."[36]

All this suggests the rise of a mini Canadian military-industrial complex. The Canadian defence industry is actually relatively small. There are some 1,500 companies involved to some extent in arms production, mostly in building components for U.S. weapons systems. A handful of these companies—including CAE, General Dynamics and Bombardier—dominate the industry and get the lion's share of Canada's military contracts. Altogether, the industry generates revenues in the range of $7 billion a year. But its influence is multiplied well beyond this by its close co-operation with the Canadian military, as well as with prominent military-funded think tanks. The result is an influential bloc promoting ever-greater government spending on the military.

The development of a strong defence sector can have important consequences, creating a dynamic for an ever-expanding military. If the number of companies—and citizens—involved in weapons production and the military is significant, they become a potent force politically, pushing for ever more military expansion. Once the nation's economic growth becomes closely tied to military spending, that creates a pressure for ever more military spending, to keep the economy buoyant. This economic dynamic, sometimes called "military Keynesianism," means that the nation's economic well-being becomes integrally connected to high levels of military spending. When this happens, military spending takes on a life of its own, disconnected from the country's actual military needs. What happens if the military threat to the nation declines? The military budget won't necessarily decline, because that would threaten the interests of a sizable sector of the economy—a sector that will use its considerable political clout to prevent a spending reduction.

The ultimate danger of this dynamic is that the combined power of the defence industry and the military establishment will create a bias favouring not just a diversion of the country's resources towards the military but ultimately pressure for taking the country to war. These powerful interests have a vested interest in promoting the notion that the country is in danger of being attacked. Without a serious prospect of being attacked, what is the justification for massive public expenditure on armaments and the military? So there is a need to hype the threat posed by foreign enemies. Part of the message of the defence lobby—echoed by a generally co-operative media—is the ominous nature of the enemies out there, whether Soviet or radical Islamic. If the public is constantly revved up about the threatening nature of these enemies, it becomes more willing to consider doing battle against them. With a public willing to go to war and powerful interests that benefit financially from the waging of war, the stage seems to be set for, well, war.

This was presumably one of the dangers that Eisenhower had in mind when he warned the American public about allowing the military-industrial complex to gain too much influence. Certainly the tendency of the U.S. military-industrial complex to push the United States towards war has proved to be a grave danger to the world. The development of a mini military-industrial complex in Canada clearly poses less danger to the world. Still, the danger is significant, to the world and to Canada as a nation. Already our military-industrial complex has played a role—a largely invisible role—in pushing us to join in Washington's reckless military ventures, out of some notion that we too are threatened by America's enemies.

Even back in the 1980s, the Canadian defence lobbyists understood well the importance of hyping the enemy as part of a campaign to put Canada on a war-mobilization footing. The Conference of Defence Associations developed the notion of the "Total Defence of Canada"—the idea that the Soviet threat was so great it required the mobilization of the entire economy in constant readiness for war. As Col. H. A. J. Hutchinson told the association's annual meeting in 1985: "I would say that the Total Defence of Canada requires much more than just the support of the Canadian Armed Forces, it involves the organization of our total economy, our industrial base, towards a single objective—the defence of this country." The colonel, a former chairman of the association, went on to insist that the Total Defence of Canada required a commitment that "can only be made if the Canadian people perceive that it is necessary and that, in fact, it is the only course of action open to them."[37] To believe that it is the only course open requires the public to believe the danger the nation faces is indeed great.

With the help of the Mulroney government, a Canadian defence lobby had become a powerful player on the Canadian political scene by the late 1980s, with the potential to bring about changes that would alter the nature of the country, its economy and its relationship to the world. But almost no one foresaw a development on the horizon that stood in the way of all these changes.

The seriousness of the reforms launched by Mikhail Gorbachev's policies of glasnost and perestroika had not properly been appreciated by the West. As political agitation swept through Eastern Europe in response and the Berlin Wall was torn down in 1989, the massive Soviet empire—against which the West had been mobilizing its war machinery for decades—effectively disappeared. The West was suddenly bereft of an enemy. In Canada, the Department of National Defence stated the situation bluntly in late 1989: "No one seriously believes that the current Soviet leadership has any intention of attacking Western Europe or North America."[38]

What, then, was the need for a massive military build-up? For those who had painstakingly developed a case for redesigning Canada as a war economy—for rousing the nation to mount a "Total Defence of Canada"—the future suddenly looked very different. The whole strategy was about to unravel. The threat of peace had intruded, laying waste the best-laid plans for war.

CHAPTER 5

THE THREAT OF PEACE

The collapse of the Soviet Union seemed to catch the world off guard. For more than forty years, the globe had been divided into East and West, ostensibly separated by ideological differences too deep to bridge. Then, almost inexplicably, the whole edifice on the far side of the divide collapsed. It was said that capitalism had triumphed. Perhaps. But mostly, the enemy of capitalism, if that's what it was, had simply disappeared. The possibility of all-out war against the Soviet empire, of world annihilation—something an entire generation had been weaned on—just vanished, the threat disappearing as mysteriously as it had appeared in the late 1940s.

Inside the United Nations and in like-minded quarters around the world, there was a guarded optimism that the paralysis that had locked the world rigidly into two opposing camps had ended. The postwar dream of a peaceful world order, centred on a potent United Nations, seemed at last once again a possibility.

That optimism led in January 1992 to an unusual meeting of heads of state of members of the UN Security Council, which concluded the meeting with an invitation to UN Secretary-General Boutros Boutros-Ghali to draw up a proposal for putting peace front-and-centre on the world agenda. It was a task that a UN secretary-general dreams of, and five months later, in June 1992, Boutros-Ghali produced *An Agenda for Peace*, an ambitious document that set out ways to use the UN to promote preventive diplomacy, peacekeeping, peace-making and peace-building activities. Presenting his report to the world body, Boutros-Ghali, an Egyptian diplomat with an impressive academic background in international law, pointed to the rareness of the opportunity that had suddenly unfolded: "The nations and peoples of the United Nations are fortunate in a way that those of the League of Nations were not. We have been given a second chance to create the world of our Charter that they were denied. With the cold war ended we have drawn back from the brink of a confrontation that threatened the world and, too often, paralysed our Organization."

Like a suddenly cured cancer victim, the world surveyed the new possibilities with wide, somewhat disbelieving eyes.

Since the build-up of Soviet and American nuclear arsenals after the Second World War, any sane person could see the folly of the world's preparing the means of its own destruction. In 1955, Albert Einstein, inventor of the atomic bomb, teamed up with Bertrand Russell and other pre-eminent intellectuals and scientists and declared: "Here, then, is the problem which we present to you, stark and dreadful and inescapable: Shall we put an end to the human race; or shall mankind renounce war?"

With war between the two superpowers certain to bring about mutual destruction, any potential benefit in initiating a war had disappeared. The only possible justification for the massive apparatus of death both sides kept amassing was deterrence. As long as the enemy had a devastating stockpile of nuclear warheads, it was necessary to have one too, to deter the enemy from using his. On the other hand, if both sides disarmed, the world could do without all this destructive firepower. But how to get there?

In the early years of the nuclear arms race, proposals for nuclear disarmament had emerged from a number of quarters, but the most influential plan was put forward by two prominent

Americans, Wall Street lawyer Grenville Clark and Harvard Law professor Louis B. Sohn. The Clark-Sohn plan, developed in 1958 and refined in 1960, 1966 and 1973, was a comprehensive plan to redesign the United Nations so that it could actually achieve what it had theoretically been designed to do: eliminate war. The premise of the plan was that world peace could be achieved only through the development of world law, along with global institutions—including a UN court and a UN police force—with the power to apply and enforce that world law. In great detail, Clark and Sohn set out how this could be accomplished. The first requirement was complete disarmament, with effective controls.

In 1959, the year after the Clark-Sohn plan appeared, both the British and the Soviet governments separately brought comprehensive disarmament proposals to the UN. The Soviet proposal laid out a particularly detailed plan for action, calling for the elimination of all armed forces and armaments in three stages over a four-year period. This led to the establishment in March 1960 of the Ten-Nation Disarmament Committee (TNDC), set up by a group of nations, including the Soviet Union and the United States, in association with the United Nations. The task of this committee—which included five Eastern bloc countries and five Western bloc countries (including Canada)—was to negotiate nothing less than a general and complete disarmament.

By September 1961, the U.S. and Soviet governments issued a joint statement, referred to as the McCloy-Zorin Accords, setting out the principles for a far-reaching disarmament so that "war is no longer an instrument of settling international problems." Five days later, President John F. Kennedy, in an address to the UN General Assembly, called for negotiations to continue "without interruption until an entire program for general and complete disarmament has not only been agreed but has been actually achieved." Kennedy also called for the creation of world law to outlaw war and weaponry, with strong UN-based enforcement mechanisms.

Of course, we know that none of this happened. No such disarmament took place, nor was any comprehensive world law established to prevent war nor a powerful UN police force created to enforce such a law. Instead, in the wake of the 1962 Cuban Missile Crisis, the arms race simply heated up.

Achieving full disarmament would clearly require an enormous level of trust. Even assuming that there had been genuine interest in comprehensive disarmament in both the U.S. and Soviet leadership—a huge assumption—the necessary trust seemed impossible to create between the two hyper-armed superpowers. Which is why the sudden collapse of one of those superpowers in 1989 seemed to offer an intriguing opening to an all-but-abandoned cause—a cause that offered such hope for world betterment. If ever there was a moment to be seized, this was it.

Such a moment rarely comes along. And one can only hope that when it does, there will be those in positions of power who will rise to the challenge, on behalf of the human race. In this particular case, the opportunity to do so fell, above all, to two men who, as it happened, viewed the concept of "disarmament through world law" with ferocious contempt.

If the end of the Cold War had unleashed a guarded optimism around the world about a renaissance for the UN and all it stood for, a very different set of possibilities was being eyed by those inside the Republican administration of George H. W. Bush.

The Republican right had long resented the very internationalism that the United Nations represented. The influential Washington-based Heritage Foundation, for instance, had for years maintained a special section with the sole purpose of compiling and publicizing material aimed at discrediting the UN. As noted earlier, U.S. conservatives considered the UN premise of collective power and responsibility a potential restriction on the use of U.S. military power. In addition, they profoundly resented the UN's focus on issues like poverty and development. These were issues that had been brought forward aggressively by Third World nations who saw in the UN a rare venue for putting their grievances in front of a world audience. As the UN General Assembly increasingly came to reflect the concerns of these disempowered nations—who had no voice in world bodies like the IMF, the World Bank and the G7—the American right had grown increasingly disenchanted and even hostile towards the UN. In other words, not only did the UN represent a potential check on the exercise of U.S. power but it had become a forum for grievances about inequality and disempowerment and environmental degradation—grievances that always seemed to be levelled primarily against America. The right resented this attack. In its view, the United States was rich and powerful and the world's biggest consumer of world resources because it deserved to be, and Third World attempts to change the system to accommodate the needs of the poor were an unfair assault on legitimate, well-earned U.S. supremacy.

Certainly the UN had changed dramatically from the world body that had been created in the wake of the Second World War. In its early days, the UN consisted of only fifty-one member nations, mostly the West and Latin America, and they looked supportively to the United States for leadership. Since it had begun opening up to new members—an initiative orchestrated in part by Canada in the mid-1950s—the UN General Assembly had grown steadily. By the early 1990s, more than one hundred new members had overwhelmed the original fifty-one, dramatically changing the character of the world body. Many of the new members were desperately poor former European colonies in Africa and Asia with distinctly different world attitudes and interests than the West, and often resentful towards the West, particularly the United States and Britain.

This anti-Western sentiment deeply irked the American right. The CATO Institute, a libertarian Washington-based think tank, complained that the General Assembly had become "dominated by non-Western states whose elites seldom shared the political culture of the democratic West." While the institute highlighted the undemocratic nature of many of these regimes, its real concern was more likely that their voting patterns were of a "distinctly anti-American cast." Meanwhile, the West was expected to foot the bill. "In 1992, for example, the United States was assessed 25 per cent of the general UN operating budget, while 79 member-states each paid 0.01 per cent of the budget," the CATO Institute complained.[1] What the institute didn't bother pointing out was that, while the United States was just one country, it had far greater resources than all the new UN members combined.

With intense anti-UN pressure from the powerful American right, Washington had been less than co-operative with the world body even under Democratic administrations, and certainly under Republican ones. By the early 1990s, Washington had withheld UN dues worth more than half a billion dollars, leaving the organization perennially strapped for funds. And, even as the UN geared up for a more prominent role in the post–Cold War era, Washington was busy trying to limit its scope. One tactic for doing this was getting anti-UN types appointed to key positions in the organization. To this end, the administration of George H. W. Bush put pressure on Boutros-Ghali to appoint Richard Thornburgh, an abrasive former attorney general under Bush and Reagan, to the crucial post of under-secretary-general of the UN. The Bush administration even dangled the prospect of the U.S. paying its back dues to the UN if Thornburgh got the job. Once he did, however, no back dues were forthcoming.

Thornburgh used his UN post to strike from within at UN programs that had long been in the crosshairs of the U.S. right. He quickly, for instance, shut down the UN's Center on Transnational Corporations (CTC), which had been a particular irritant to corporate America. Established in 1974 in response to demands from the developing countries for a new international economic order, the TNC had become an important source of data and analysis about the growing power of transnational corporations, releasing reports that drew rare worldwide attention to the growing reality of global corporate power. TNC documents showed that, in just a few decades after World War II, transnational corporations had become a formidable force, rivalling the more obvious and transparent power wielded by governments. By 1985, for instance, the 350 largest transnational corporations—about half headquartered in the United States—had combined sales far larger than the combined GNP of all the developing countries, including China.[2]

This sort of information began to spark moves within the United Nations for regulations to govern these transnational giants. The goal was to be able to restrain irresponsible corporate behaviour, such as Nestlé's aggressive promotion of infant formula as a substitute for breast milk in poverty-stricken countries. By the late 1970s, the UN's Economic and Social Council had orchestrated negotiations between the corporate world and the developing countries, with the CTC providing key data. The negotiations remained deadlocked through the 1980s and into the early '90s. Then, with the Earth Summit approaching, the CTC was ordered to break the impasse and prepare recommendations for a code of conduct, to be presented for signing at the summit. It was at that point that the newly appointed Thornburgh killed the CTC—before George H. W. Bush was placed in the embarrassing position of rejecting such a code at the Earth Summit.

But if the American right was offended by the UN's increasingly ambitious agenda for social progress, it was even more hostile to the UN's desire to treat the end of the Cold War as an opening to a new era of peace and internationalism. There was only one kind of peace and internationalism that interested the Republican war hawks—an American-enforced one. And Boutros-Ghali's *An Agenda for Peace*, with its vision of a renaissance for the United Nations, was attempting to take the world in exactly the opposite direction. The right had no use for Boutros-Ghali, who was regarded as insufficiently pro-Washington and far too wedded to principles of international law.

Within the administration, the task of shaping a post–Cold War policy fell principally into the hands of Paul Wolfowitz, undersecretary for defence policy, and his boss, Defense Secretary Dick Cheney. Wolfowitz, an arms expert, was a hard-line anti-Soviet who had worked in the administrations of Richard Nixon and Gerald Ford. Unabashedly opposed to détente with the Soviets, Wolfowitz had pushed instead for a strategy of U.S. supremacy through superior weaponry. He had struggled within the bureaucracy against the influence of Henry Kissinger, whom Wolfowitz considered too trusting of the Soviets.

Cheney had also worked in the Nixon White House, teaming up with Donald Rumsfeld to undermine federal anti-poverty programs. When Cheney was appointed defence secretary in 1991, he put Wolfowitz in charge of mapping out a post–Cold War strategy, knowing that Wolfowitz would advocate a considerably more aggressive U.S. posture. So, in the spring of 1992—even as Boutros-Ghali was drafting *An Agenda for Peace*—Wolfowitz was drafting the "Defense Planning Guidance." The contrast between the two documents couldn't have been starker. While Boutros-Ghali saw an opportunity for seriously advancing the internationalism that had been a key principle in the founding of the UN, Wolfowitz unabashedly called for what amounted to U.S. world domination, enforced by unchallenged U.S. military power.

Wolfowitz's forty-six-page draft, prepared for Cheney, was a blueprint for Washington's maintaining control of a world in which it was the only superpower and in which potential competitors were deterred from "even aspiring to a larger regional or global role." All nations—even Western allies—were to be discouraged from becoming rivals to U.S. power, militarily and economically. To prevent the rise of any serious competitors, the Wolfowitz paper argued that Washington "must sufficiently account for the interests of the advanced industrial nations to discourage them from challenging our leadership or seeking to overturn the established political and economic order."[3] In its first paragraph, the paper identified the "less visible victory" implicit in the end of the Cold War as being the "integration of Germany and Japan into a U.S.-led system of collective security and the creation of a democratic 'zone of peace.'"

Central to Wolfowitz's strategy was the notion that the United States should prevent other nations from building nuclear arsenals. Noting that the now-collapsed Soviet regime was "the only power in the world with the capability of destroying the United States," Wolfowitz wanted to expand the U.S. nuclear arsenal while preventing other nations—particularly potentially hostile nations like Iraq and North Korea—from joining the nuclear league. To head off such a development, pre-emption might be necessary. The United States could respond, for instance, to a *potential* attack of nuclear, chemical or biological weapons by "punishing the attackers or threatening punishment of aggressors through a variety of means." One method, the paper suggested, would be attacking plants inside enemy countries where such weapons might be produced.

What is striking in the Wolfowitz paper is the clear intention that decisions about the fate of the world be left solely up to Washington. Even as much of the world was contemplating a renaissance for the United Nations, Wolfowitz apparently saw no significant role for an organization that represented the world's nations. This lack of interest in the UN is particularly striking given that Wolfowitz wrote his paper only a year after the first Gulf War, in which the U.S. military led a coalition that had received the sanction of the UN. So it wasn't that the world body was posing any obstacles to the exercise of U.S. power. But it is clear that Wolfowitz didn't want to be hampered by the need for UN approval. If such approval was available, fine. But if not, then the United States would proceed without the UN.

To the extent that other nations are involved, Wolfowitz sees them in a clearly subordinate role, co-operating in U.S-led coalitions. In this way, the UN, with its deliberately shared decision-making process and multiple veto powers, is simply replaced with a more co-operative group of nations, operating under U.S. influence and control. "We should expect future coalitions to be ad hoc assemblies, often not lasting beyond the crisis being confronted, and in many cases carrying only general agreement over the objectives to be accomplished," the paper states. But what is important, it argues, is "the sense that the world order is ultimately backed by the U.S." and that "the United States should be postured to act independently when collective action cannot be orchestrated."

While the United States is portrayed as a benevolent power, the Wolfowitz paper reveals a clear intention that the U.S. rule the world by force or the threat of force—an intention that might seem less benevolent to those outside the U.S. defence establishment. Not surprisingly, there was negative fallout in world capitals and even in the U.S. Congress when a leaked draft of the paper was published in the *New York Times*. The administration of Bush Sr. retreated somewhat, insisting that the paper wasn't official policy. In the next few months, the paper was toned down, before being officially released, at almost the same time as Boutros-Ghali's *An Agenda for Peace*.

With the Democrats taking control of the White House later that year, Wolfowitz and his boss, Cheney, were both soon gone from the Pentagon. But, as later became clear, the ferocious contempt for international law and disarmament revealed in the paper—like the two men responsible for it—were not about to go away.

———

As a long-time promoter of the UN and its peace initiatives, Canada was only too pleased to offer its support for Boutros-Ghali's *An Agenda for Peace*. Indeed, in the early months of 1992, Canada had contributed to the preparation of the report, coordinating with the Nordic countries, as well as Australia and New Zealand, in preparing recommendations for the secretary-general to include, many of which made it into his report. With the report's release, there was considerable enthusiasm for it at high levels within the Canadian government.[4] In both the Senate and the House of Commons, committees began reviewing the document with an eye to reshaping Canadian defence policy to adapt to the new UN peace approach. Among the public, there was also support. Canadians had traditionally veered towards peaceful solutions and approaches, and were certainly content to embrace peace with new enthusiasm now that it was said to be on the international agenda in a new and meaningful way.

It was a different story, however, inside Canada's Department of National Defence and the Canadian Forces. With the end of the Cold War, a siege mentality had set in inside these two bastions of military power. The apparent opening to peace inevitably threatened to make the military seem even more peripheral than usual to the lives of Canadians. And if the concept of a "peace dividend" had nothing but positive connotations to the Canadian public, it smacked of cutbacks and a declining sense of relevance to those whose careers had been built around preparing for war.

"The military was in the dumps," recalled Louise Frechette, who served as deputy minister of defence from 1995 to 1998. "It was licking its wounds, trying to cope with enormous budget cuts." In fact, all departments were suffering from budget cuts, as the Liberals tried to grapple with the federal deficit. But those in the defence establishment felt particularly embittered. "They felt they had been targeted more than others," said Frechette, "They had been cut for many years before the Martin budget [of 1995]." They also felt increasingly isolated. Their support system of think tanks, defence industry associations and pro-military institutions was still operating, but seemed to attract less attention in the new "peace" era. Frechette recalled that it seemed as if the military's main defenders were a handful of pro-military professors—people like Jack Granatstein and David Bercuson.[5]

What was at stake was the military's ability to remain a force able to engage in full-combat warfare—in other words, to remain in the big leagues of U.S. and NATO forces, rather than being reshaped so as to better serve the interests of UN peacekeeping. "For the military, NATO is always important," said Frechette. "It's the standard you have to achieve, in terms of the kind of equipment you buy and the capability you achieve. It's central to the design of the Canadian Forces. We're part of this defensive alliance. We're part of this club. We have to play our part." But NATO had been conceived to defend Europe against a Soviet invasion, and had been nurtured for years despite the lack of evidence that the Soviets had intentions of invading Western Europe. With the collapse of the Soviet Union, the maintenance of a huge army in Europe seemed suddenly exposed as pointless. For the Canadian military—with its focus heavily trained on NATO—this came perilously close to calling into question much of what it was doing and wanted to continue doing.

Certainly, there were signs that things were going to change in ways that the military establishment found threatening. There appeared to be considerable interest, both inside and outside the country, in an expanded role for the UN and peacekeeping. In August 1992, U.S. presidential candidate Bill Clinton, signalling his divergence from the unilateralist approach that Wolfowitz and Cheney had advanced under the Bush administration, indicated he would support a UN rapid-deployment force—a force long considered essential to the UN's ability to be an effective peace-keeper. That pledge was repeated by his secretary of state, Warren Christopher, in February 1993, shortly after the new Democratic administration took office. There were similar expressions of support for a revitalized UN from other major powers, notably Russia and France. French president François Mitterand offered to make available to the UN one thousand French soldiers on forty-eight hours' notice, with another thousand available within a week.

In addition to the growing international support for the UN and the promotion of peace, there was the tightening fiscal situation in Canada to back up the case for military cutbacks. With the business community and mainstream press howling over Canada's mounting deficits, public debate was peppered with the language of austerity and cutbacks, and all public programs seemed to be viewed with suspicion, as sources of crippling debt. The military was particularly vulnerable. After all, if vital programs like health care, education and basic social supports were being forced to do a lot more with a lot less, it seemed increasingly hard to justify billions going towards military spending, when the only ostensible enemy in sight had just folded its tent.

A group of Canadian non-governmental organizations tried to capitalize on the new support for peace by setting up the Citizens' Inquiry into Peace and Security. The inquiry travelled across the country, attracting sizable crowds to public hearings, trying to draw attention to the unusual opportunity Canada had for freshly thinking through its military options, and to urge Canadians not to leave the key decisions, as in the past, in the hands of the military and defence establishment. In particular, the inquiry sought to draw attention to the UN *Agenda for Peace*, and the possibility of revamping Canadian military priorities in line with a more UN-oriented peacekeeping agenda.

Peace activists tried to capitalize on the new mood by pushing a novel idea: converting Canadian Forces Base Cornwallis in Nova Scotia into a peacekeeping training centre. This sort of conversion would be essential on a broad scale if there were really going to be any move towards peace and disarmament. The proposal was a clever idea. Rather than simply mothballing a redundant military base—and in the process jeopardizing the economic vitality of the area and provoking a local backlash—the government could convert the base into a badly needed centre for upgrading the peacekeeping skills of Canadian troops going out on UN missions. The base could even be used for co-ordinating and preparing multinational troops for a UN rapid-deployment force. It could also serve as a centre aimed at educating the public on peace issues, and promoting support for Boutros-Ghali's *An Agenda for Peace*.

The Cornwallis conversion project, proposed by two Ph.D. students in peace studies, Peter Langille and Erika Simpson, quickly attracted wider support from community groups, academics, UN officials and politicians, even attracting interest at the national level. The Liberal party adopted a resolution in 1992 supporting the Cornwallis conversion project, and just before the 1993 federal election, Liberal leader Jean Chrétien highlighted this support, arguing that "the time for such a centre has come."

The increasing public support for Canada to contribute actively to a UN peacekeeping agenda was reflected in the pre-election platforms of both the Liberals and the New Democrats. The NDP strongly endorsed the UN *Agenda for Peace*. More importantly from a political point of view, the Liberals also highlighted peacekeeping in their *Foreign Policy Handbook*, released in

May 1993. Endorsing a more central role for the UN, the Liberal document argued for "a military force structure for United Nations peacekeeping, monitoring, verification and peace enforcement operations" and for a Canadian defence policy geared towards UN peacekeeping. And, in what seemed like a provocative challenge to the way the defence establishment often undermined government priorities it didn't share, the document promised that a Liberal government would "ensure that defence planners meet these commitments."

The push for revamping Canadian defence strategy towards the UN even got backing from some prominent Canadian academics, politicians, media commentators and business leaders. With a grant from the Walter and Duncan Gordon Charitable Foundation, Janice Stein, a professor of international relations at the University of Toronto, put together a high-profile group that included Robert Stanfield, Maurice Strong, John Polanyi, Sylvia Ostry, Gérard Pelletier, Ivan Head, Knowlton Nash and Ann Medina. Dubbed the Canada 21 Council, this unusual ad hoc group of well-connected and influential Canadians lent their prestige to strengthening the Canadian commitment to UN peacekeeping. "We are deservedly proud of our distinguished record in peacekeeping," they wrote in their report. "Our contribution to peacekeeping has given us influence at the United Nations and in other international institutions far beyond our place in the hierarchy of states. Beyond our contribution to common security, we believe that Canadian interests are advanced by our participation in peacekeeping."[6]

But the Canada 21 Council wasn't simply endorsing Canada's past UN peacekeeping role. It made clear that it was advocating change, that it saw the end of the Cold War as an opportunity to push Canadian defence policy in a new, more peace-oriented direction. It rejected the status quo, insisting that it would be wrong to simply maintain a defence policy "virtually indistinguishable from that of ten, twenty or thirty years ago." Drawing on studies it commissioned, it argued that Canada avoid involvement in combat operations involving heavy armour and air power. And it took direct aim at a basic, long-standing premise of Canadian defence policy— that Canada should maintain an all-purpose army ready to fight full-scale wars. "Unless policy is changed quite radically, the result will be that Canada will have simply a miniature model of a traditional 'general purpose' military force—one with just a little bit of everything, but not enough of anything to be effective in any conceivable situation," the council's report argued.

This sort of challenge to the status quo was even coming from some within the military establishment. In the fall of 1993, two influential defence analysts wrote articles in Canadian academic journals urging an approach that bore some resemblance to that advocated by the Canada 21 Council. Col. David Harries, director of the defence department's Centre for National Securities Studies, wrote an article in *Canadian Defence Quarterly* calling for a major rethinking of military operations and doctrine. "The way ahead . . .—certainly for middle or less powers—seems to be to concentrate on a limited number of strengths, on 'niche' capabilities—rather than continue to claim some non-existent 'general-purpose' ability."[7] Another challenge came from defence analyst Allan Sens. Writing in *Canadian Foreign Policy*, Sens questioned the wisdom of maintaining an all-purpose combat force, warning that Canada's military strength could end up being "a mile wide and an inch deep." Sens went on to argue that in the post–Cold War world, "future Canadian governments may be more, rather than less, disposed to peacekeeping operations and contingency missions as a means of asserting an international multilateral role for Canada."[8]

This notion that Canada should specialize in a niche—and that that niche should be UN peacekeeping—certainly fit comfortably with the reality of Canadian budgetary constraints, as well as with the notion that global realities allowed Canada to finally move towards a more peace-oriented defence strategy. But this struck at the heart of the Canadian military's vision of itself, raising the prospect of being turned into an adjunct to a UN police force. So, while public pressure grew for the Canadian military to adopt a more UN-centred approach, the Canadian defence establishment hunkered down to resist any such change. Gen. John de Chastelain, chief of defence staff, showed the military's resistance in an article he wrote in *Canadian Defence Quarterly* in June 1992. While acknowledging the significance of the end of the Cold War, de Chastelain apparently envisioned only minimal change in defence policy. Whereas Canada had long stationed general-purpose, combat-ready troops in Europe, de Chastelain now said the shift would be towards "the concept of general-purpose combat-capable armed forces, *stationed in Canada for the most part*, ready to deploy anywhere in the world in Canada's interests" (italics added).[9] So a change as momentous as the end of the Cold War meant nothing more than that Canada would move its full-purpose armed troops back to Canada—not that there'd be any adjustments in overall military strategy to help the UN step forward and fulfill its function of creating a less war-prone world. Peter Langille, one of the advocates of the Cornwallis conversion project and now a political scientist, dismissed de Chastelain's approach as "smoke and mirrors, attempting to give the impression that the CF were readily adapting to the new environment."

The resistance to change was deeply rooted in the psyche of the Canadian military establishment, whose members appeared to be largely indifferent to the desires of the Canadian people, or their elected representatives. This determination that the military—not the civilian side—make the decisions on key matters is reflected in a report by Brigadier-General Lalonde. In a review of peacekeeping for the military's Force Mobile Command, Lalonde concluded that "we must resist distorting our raison d'être by organizing for UN duties." What if the public or political leaders want to move the military in that direction? Doesn't matter, according to Lalonde. "The provision of a general purpose combat capability will remain the raison d'être of the Canadian Forces for the foreseeable future *no matter how the defence priorities are written up or whatever popular of political support is or is not generated*" (italics added).[10]

The defence establishment showed its determination to preserve the status quo—despite public support for change—in its resistance to the proposal to transform the Cornwallis base into a peacekeeping centre. The transformation could have been a focal point in the new Liberal government's embrace of the UN peace agenda, highlighting its commitment to UN peacekeeping and its willingness to get out front in providing substantive and badly needed support. But the initiative ran counter to the military's own vision of its role in the post–Cold War era. Recognizing that there was considerable public support for the conversion project, the defence establishment didn't simply reject the idea entirely but rather proposed taking it over and reshaping it. Accordingly, the Canadian Institute of Strategic Studies (CISS), one of the leading defence lobbies, came up with a counter-proposal for a peacekeeping centre that would be a watered-down version of the dedicated training centre originally proposed.

In the end, the newly elected Liberal government opted for the CISS proposal. In 1994, it announced that Cornwallis would become a peacekeeping centre, named after Lester B. Pearson, but it would offer no actual training of peacekeepers—the whole point of the original proposal. Rather, there would be some modest courses for the trainers of peacekeepers and some general study of peacekeeping—all very theoretical, when what the UN badly needed was real training for real peacekeepers, or what could be called "boots on the ground" courses for peacekeepers.

More worrisome, Ottawa announced that the new peacekeeping centre would be privatized, and its operation and funding handed over to CISS—an organization closely associated with the military establishment. (In 2001, the centre severed ties with CISS, and was designated an independent, non-profit organization.)

The three-year battle over Cornwallis had taught those inside the military establishment some lessons, just in time for the bigger battle of shaping the new government's overall defence agenda. The Liberals had promised a full and open review of defence policy during the election campaign of 1993, and it was difficult to know how serious they might be about this, especially with strong public support for a more peace-oriented approach. Inside the Defence Department, top officials were determined that the review not get out of control and become a forum for pushing for real changes in defence policy. Deputy Defence Minister Robert Fowler, for instance, was concerned that public support might build for the key concept of developing a UN army, as suggested by Boutros-Ghali's *An Agenda for Peace*. Recalling how public support for the Cornwallis conversion had mushroomed and become a serious problem for the military establishment, Fowler wanted more vigilance this time to prevent the idea of a UN army from gathering any momentum. In a handwritten memo to an assistant deputy minister, Fowler wrote: "Much as the Cornwallis Peacekeeping Academy got out of hand because we didn't stomp on it hard enough, loud enough and soon enough, this one [a UN army] will acquire legs very quickly. Please prepare a forceful brief which the CDS [Chief of Defence Staff] and I will sign off to both Ministers (cc. PCO) ASAP."[11]

Fowler's concerns were apparently heeded. When the Liberals launched their defence review in early 1994, it was structured in a way that almost ensured there would be no meaningful challenges to the status quo. The parliamentary committee set up to conduct the review relied heavily on advice from generals and others in the defence establishment. Langille notes that none of these advisers would be likely to challenge the defence establishment or advocate the UN peacekeeping alternative. Liberal senator Colin Kenny, the committee co-chair, seemed frustrated by the process, sensing that the committee wasn't getting the full picture of the options available. As he told one witness appearing before the committee: "We've had some terrific briefings from the military brass . . . We have had the most impressive sales pitch in favour of the status quo that you can imagine. What advice would you suggest for this committee in terms of questions or an approach to ensure that the senior military officers who appeared before us give this committee real options and the real consequences of those options?"[12]

Kenny even questioned the military's insistence that it remain a "general-purpose, balanced" force. "Why is it such a firm part of the pitch?" he asked after he heard this line repeated by witness after witness from the Defence Department. Typically, the general-purpose force was justified as necessary for the defence of Canada. But one witness before the committee offered a different explanation that may shed light on another possible motive. In revealing testimony, retired colonel Douglas Bland explained that the commitment to a "general-purpose, balanced" force was part of an internal consensus within the Department of National Defence—a consensus that served the interests of all those within the department. "If you say 'balanced' then everybody is happy they will have their turn at the equipment window. Everybody will be able to service their preferred interest . . . The general-purpose balanced force is an attempt to service everybody's interests within the department."[13] Needless to say, servicing "everybody's interests within the department" sounds like it's more about serving the interests of defence and military bureaucrats than about serving the defence needs of Canada.

The defence review certainly took on the feel of a closed club, with defence bureaucrats and military personnel providing assistance to the committee as it conducted its investigation. Not surprisingly, these officials were quick to give the thumbs-down to ideas that departed from the department's "internal consensus." They seemed especially keen to discredit the report of the Canada 21 Council, perhaps because they feared its potential influence, since many of its members enjoyed strong ties to the Liberal party. Suggestions that some of these individuals might be helpful for the parliamentary review process—in raising, for instance, just the sort of issues that Colin Kenny complained were absent from the discussions—were strongly dismissed by Defence Department officials. Instead, the Defence officials proposed experts funded by the department's Military and Strategic Studies Program, many of whom had links to the defence industry or defence lobby groups.

Any lingering hope that the review might result in some fresh thinking ended when Liberal Defence Minister David Collenette came out clearly on the side of the defence establishment. Speaking to a defence lobby group in May 1994, Collenette said that shifting more emphasis to peacekeeping would risk leaving Canada with a military that couldn't fight. He suggested that the whole national debate had become too "dovish" and urged the defence lobby groups to get actively involved in helping him counter the claims of the doves. Of course, the defence lobbies already were heavily involved, aggressively countering the claims of the "doves" before the parliamentary committee, where their voices alone were being heard, but they were happy to heed the minister's invitation to get still more involved. By the following month, a group calling itself the Committee of 13—made up of generals, academics and defence industry officials—came forward to refute the peace-oriented ideas of the Canada 21 Council and reaffirm the traditional all-out combat approach preferred by the military establishment.

In the end, the strong resistance of the defence community managed to head off any meaningful change in Canadian military policy, despite the enormous opportunity opened up by the end of the Cold War. In its 1994 Defence White Paper, the Liberal government made some overtures in the direction of peace. It announced some significant cuts in overall military spending, in keeping with the new government's obsession with deficit reduction and government cutbacks in all areas, and it spoke of the importance of the UN and peacekeeping, and even pledged an expansion of troops available for UN missions. But it backed off from any sort of fundamental overhaul that would have introduced the kind of significant changes aimed at actually making the Canadian military more useful to a UN force. There was only one reference in the white paper to *An Agenda for Peace*, and no willingness to confront the defence establishment's insistence on maintaining a general-purpose army and its resistance to developing a UN rapid-deployment police force. Not surprisingly, General de Chastelain welcomed the white paper, noting that the troops were relieved that "they are to remain a fighting force and not some sort of Gendarme." The Liberals had essentially retreated from their bold pre-election talk about bringing defence planners into line. Rather, it was the Liberals who appeared to have been brought into line, or "house-trained," as Langille puts it. "The new Liberal government clearly wanted no part of a public confrontation with the Canadian Forces or the defence establishment."[14]

The end of the Cold War didn't bring about peace, but it did bring about an increase in peacekeeping missions. In his *An Agenda for Peace*, Boutros-Ghali had called for an ambitious expansion of UN peacekeeping, introducing new, somewhat ambiguous concepts like peace-making and peace-building. This proposed change coincided with a change in the nature of the conflicts that seemed to require UN intervention. In the Cold War era, peacekeeping had been largely about preventing national armies from fighting each other, often as proxies for the super-powers, by inserting neutral UN troops to act as a buffer between them, as in the Suez crisis in 1956 or in Cyprus, beginning in 1964. But the conflicts of the 1990s were increasingly rooted in power struggles within a country, such as civil wars based on ethnic or tribal strife. As the UN waded into these conflicts with a renewed zeal and belief in its potential to create peace, it encountered situations considerably more complicated and problematic than it had generally faced in its earlier efforts.

Past conflicts had involved violence and discord, but these new conflicts were particularly highly charged, abounding in ethnic rivalries and hatreds, making the job of UN peacekeepers extremely difficult. In Rwanda, peacekeepers were unable to stop a genocide that quickly took the lives of some 800,000 people. In the former Yugoslavia, a UN protection force also seemed unable to stop widespread violence and civilian slaughter. The difficulty faced by the UN was highlighted when UN peacekeepers in Bosnia were taken hostage in 1995.

These difficulties led to the conviction that peacekeeping had to become more robust, with better-armed troops able to engage in battle. They also led some to conclude that NATO was better suited to the task. Under the 1995 Dayton Peace Accords, NATO replaced the UN in providing peacekeeping troops in Bosnia, with UN authorization. Three years later, NATO "peacekeepers" carried out a destructive and bloody air campaign against Serbian nationalists in Kosovo, this time without UN authorization. Increasingly, the line between peacekeeping and war making was becoming blurred. This blurring has continued in Afghanistan, a NATO force, endorsed by the UN, is presented as a peacekeeping and nation-building mission, but it also bombs enemy targets and actively seeks out and engages in warfare with insurgents.

All this has created real confusion about what constitutes peacekeeping, and whether what is presented as peacekeeping has much to do with peace any more. It also raises the question of whether peacekeeping—carried out either by the UN or by NATO with UN authorization—is even a beneficial activity, or is simply a cloak for Western powers to pursue their own agendas with a veneer of international legitimacy.

Let's start by admitting that these are extremely difficult questions. Certainly, the UN has been used to further the interests of Western powers. This can be seen in Haiti, where, as noted earlier, a UN peacekeeping force helped prop up a brutal regime put in place by Washington, immediately after Washington had removed the democratically elected government of Jean-Bertrand Aristide in February 2004. The role of the UN in this blatantly undemocratic "regime change"—supported by Canada—raises important questions, partly because Canadian officials seemed to regard these actions as justifiable under the principle of "responsibility to protect," a doctrine promoted by Canada and endorsed by world leaders at the UN General Assembly in 2005.

Under this doctrine, the nations of the world, acting through the UN, are considered to have a responsibility to intervene to protect civilian populations at risk of suffering severe human rights abuses such as genocide or ethnic cleansing at the hands of their own governments. The notion of the world acting collectively to protect helpless people in desperate situations has an obvious appeal. But it is also fraught with problems. It undermines a key UN principle—the sovereignty of each nation—by allowing nations to collectively violate the sovereignty of another nation, in the name of preventing it from carrying out severe abuses. But which abuses will be deemed worthy of intervention? What other factors may motivate the interveners? This "responsibility to protect" doctrine, for instance, could have been invoked to justify the overthrow of Saddam Hussein. And, indeed, among the key supporters of the doctrine (along with Lloyd Axworthy) has been Michael Ignatieff, who supported the invasion of Iraq as a necessary action to unseat a brutal dictator.

Disturbingly, Canada appears to have relied on the notion of "responsibility to protect" to justify the removal of Aristide's democratically-elected government. Canada's role in the events in Haiti is somewhat murky. Ottawa hosted a meeting in January 2003, which included representatives of the U.S., France, La Francophonie and the European Union, to discuss the future of Haiti. No officials from the Aristide government were invited, and there is some evidence that the participants agreed on the idea of removing Aristide from office, although this has been denied by Denis Paradis, who was then Canada's secretary of state for Latin America and the Francophonie.[15] But whether or not Canada was involved in any advance planning of Aristide's overthrow, Ottawa certainly went along with Washington's regime change. Paradis has justified the removal of Aristide on the grounds of the "responsibility to protect" vulnerable Haitians. "If you've been to Haiti you've seen the poor conditions in which Haitians are living and anyway from what I've seen personally there, I think that if there is one place where the principles of this 'responsibility to protect' would apply around the world, it's Haiti ..." Paradis told an interviewer in September 2004. "[I]sn't the role of the international community to make sure that the people can survive in a country, can have an economic well-being?"[16]

Paradis even seemed to be suggesting that the "responsibility to protect" can be stretched to the point that it covers not just preventing genocide and ethnic cleansing but also ensuring the economic well-being of citizens. This would leave the door wide open to interventions by Western countries on the grounds that impoverished Third World nations need to open up their economies to foreign investment and free trade in order to improve their prospects for economic development. In fact, this approach to economic development, dubbed the "Washington consensus," is highly controversial. Critics like Nobel prize-winning economist Joseph Stiglitz have noted that while the approach serves the interests of advanced capitalist countries looking for markets, there's little evidence of its success in lifting nations out of poverty.

Certainly, this illustrates the danger of the UN being used to advance powerful Western interests in the guise of preventing humanitarian disasters. It is the possibility for this sort of abuse that has led some international legal experts, such as Toronto lawyer David Jacobs, to argue against UN interventions that violate national sovereignty. Jacobs insists that, given the clout of the U.S. and Britain on the Security Council, the UN ends up intervening "exclusively in countries where the U.S. or Britain wants regime change." Human rights abuses in those countries are then selectively focused on by Western governments and the media—and sometimes fraudulently misrepresented. "At the end of the day, what does foreign intervention do?" he asks. "It creates a new government made up of forces friendly to the U.S." Similarly, Jacobs rejects the legitimacy of international tribunals prosecuting war criminals, arguing that they're put in place by the West to serve Western interests. "Until we can envisage George W. Bush or Tony Blair being brought in front of these tribunals, then they're really political institutions that aren't going to bring about justice."[17]

The danger of the UN's being used as a tool of the West is real, but so is the danger of losing the UN. It is, after all, the closest thing we have to a legitimate world body, and it is under fierce attack these days from those on the right who seek to deny its legitimacy and to replace it with NATO, with U.S.-orchestrated "coalitions of the willing" or with unadorned U.S. power. These are far worse alternatives. The UN provides at least some potential restraint in the name of law, as we saw with its refusal to endorse Washington's Iraq invasion.

Furthermore, there is evidence that the upsurge in UN peace-keeping in the post–Cold War period has been effective. According to the *Human Security Report 2005*, produced by the Liu Institute for Global Issues at the University of British Columbia, there has been a significant, but largely unreported, decline in the number of wars, genocides and international crises over the last decade or so. The report, which received funding from the governments of Canada, the U.K., Norway, Sweden, and Switzerland as well as the Rockefeller Foundation, concludes that there has been a 40 per cent decline in all armed conflicts since the early 1990s, and an 80 per cent decline in the most deadly civil conflicts. The report attributes this decline largely to increased international activism through the United Nations, as well as "literally thousands of NGOs that have both complemented UN activities and played independent prevention and peace-building roles of their own."[18]

Graeme MacQueen, former director of McMaster University's Centre for Peace Studies, argues that rather than giving up on the UN, we should put serious effort into reforming it.[19] The goal would be to make it more genuinely representative, not just by bringing more nations into decision making on the Security Council but also by including some neutral players—perhaps NGOs like the Red Cross or Amnesty International.

MacQueen argues that it would also be beneficial to begin transforming peacekeeping into something that more closely resembles policing. Policing is about upholding the law and reducing the destructiveness of conflict, whereas military action is about dominating one's opponent, usually to advance a particular interest. Political scientist Robert C. Johansen has elaborated on this difference: "Armies seek victory; police tranquility. Police do not seek to establish a victor's justice through unconditional surrender to one side or another, but to restore peace so that the political mechanisms representing both sides can work to bring justice another day."[20]

MacQueen notes that to transform UN peacekeepers into more of an international police force would require special training. The Canadian military has insisted that the best training for peacekeepers is normal military training. But military training teaches aggression and coercion, since it is about overpowering an enemy. Police training teaches how to use minimal force effectively, since it is about defusing potential conflict. "If there's a hostage in a house, you don't drop a bomb on the house. Military systems regularly do the equivalent of dropping a bomb on the house," says MacQueen.

Police also operate within the bounds of the rule of law, which gives their actions legitimacy in the eyes of the community. Similarly, peacekeeping should be carried out within the bounds of international law, notes MacQueen. If UN peacekeeping missions fail to do so, if they appear to be acting in the interests of a nation or group of nations, they lose all legitimacy. In such situations, MacQueen argues, they become more like mafia organizations, operating under their own code of conduct, offering those on their side "protection" against bad guys while using violence to subdue the bad guys and perhaps take control of their resources.

Transforming UN peacekeeping into a genuine international police force could be a crucial step towards more fundamental, far-reaching reforms aimed at seriously reducing the possibility of war.

In a modern democratic state, we all surrender the right to commit personal acts of violence. We accept that we are governed by laws and that those laws are applied by the courts and enforced by the police. This system could be adapted at the international level, as proposed by Grenville Clark and Louis B. Sohn in 1958, with the UN's International Court the ultimate legal arbiter and a UN army the police force. This would strip power from nations to use force as they please, in the same way that our domestic laws strip power from individuals to use violence as they please. The international model is really no more far-fetched than the national one. The right to commit *personal* violence is arguably just as basic—if not more basic—to the individual than the right of his or her nation to wage war. In both cases, a sacrifice of rights is required. But in both cases, such a sacrifice creates a much, much bigger benefit—the ability to live free from violent attack and the fear of violent attack. Few people would prefer to live in societies that rely on the law of the jungle rather than the law of the courts. Living in a world governed by the law of the jungle, or by mafia-like armies, is no more appealing and no more logical.

Let me quickly say, before I'm simply dismissed as a naive dreamer, that I have no illusions about this sort of transformation happening any time soon. I am well aware of the immensity of the political obstacles that stand in the way. Still, it strikes me that there is value in considering these ideas, as part of a process of establishing goals to which we aspire. Goals can serve as guideposts. Even though I don't expect to ever see these ambitious goals realized, I believe it helps to have them glimmering in the distance. Knowing where we ultimately want to go helps us figure out which path to take. It allows us to see the importance, for instance, of pushing for actions that strengthen the international legal order, and the importance of resisting actions—often advocated in the name of "realism"—that weaken it.

So despite the confusion that has developed over the UN and its peacekeeping role, it is worth striving to try to meaningfully reform and transform these institutions. UN peacekeeping can play a vital role in strengthening the international legal order, which may be key to eventually achieving more far-reaching changes. As Johansen notes: "UN peacekeeping can be a central dynamic in the transition to a warless world because it reminds us of the difference between police enforcement and military activity. It shows the possibility of global nonpartisanship in contrast to the partisanship of national uses of armed force."

When provoked, a gentleman didn't have to spend a lot of time in previous centuries thinking through the problem of how to respond. If his honour had been offended—if say, someone had questioned his integrity, or the virtue of his betrothed, or the extent of his bravery on the battlefield—he knew he had little choice but to challenge the offender to a duel. The stakes would be high; both men would have swords or pistols capable of killing the other. And the public, as well as family and friends, would come out to watch. Despite the potentially tragic consequences, the duel was an accepted part of social interaction. After all, humans have natural aggressive instincts, so what could be more natural than that two men, locked into an apparently irresolvable conflict, would resort to personal violence? It's all just part of the human condition. Or so it must have seemed, as the loved ones of the defeated gentleman watched him lie dying on the ground.

Looking back, the duel seems hopelessly quaint and primitive, an idea long ago shelved. It's not that humans have evolved so that petty insults no longer sting us or provoke our anger. It's just that, in the modern world, we've rejected the format of the duel as a way to resolve our disputes. Now, if someone insults us, we can sue that person for slander or libel. Or if a neighbour makes plans to build an extension on his house that will block our sunlight, we can try to stop him at a municipal bylaw hearing. If we were instead to show up at the offender's house with a weapon in hand, we'd be regarded as not only dangerous but weird and loopy.

Of course, violent personal behaviour still exists in pockets of our societies—in gangs and other outlawed forms. But our mainstream culture has fully adapted to solving disputes through the legal system. What once seemed no doubt utterly natural—that two men would resolve a dispute by recourse to personal violence—now seems completely out of place in Western society, part of a culture that exists only on the margins. This represents an apparently enormous change in human behaviour. What accounts for it?

Perhaps human nature has evolved, becoming more gentle and compassionate? Tempting as it may be to believe this contention, there doesn't seem to be much evidence to back it up. Duelling, which began in Europe in the mid-sixteenth century, was a common practice among upper-class men in parts of Europe and America, lingering even in some areas into the early twentieth century, when it finally disappeared. And yet, one would be hard put to make a case that humans somehow became more gentle and compassionate in the late nineteenth century. The twentieth century was perhaps the bloodiest century ever. One doesn't have to resort to statistics or laboratory studies to review the evidence around us in the modern world; humans appear to be still just as capable of aggression, violence and cruelty.

But if humans don't appear to have fundamentally changed, other things have. To begin with, our modern laws prevent duelling. If two men were to attempt to square off against each other with swords (or knives or guns) on a sidewalk or in a public park, someone would quickly call the police, and they would find themselves arrested and facing charges. But the prohibition against this sort of behaviour goes beyond the fact that we have laws against it. On another level, it has simply lost its cache, its social acceptability, its legitimacy. To behave that way is to identify oneself as a hoodlum, misfit or mental case. A normal person with a grievance doesn't even bother to weigh the advantages and disadvantages of being charged for criminal activities if he engages in some sort of duel. He's simply absorbed the notion, from all his experiences in life, that the duel isn't an acceptable form of behaviour. At some level, he is blocked from behaving that way because he knows if he did, his friends, family and acquaintances would regard him as, well, ridiculous. In fact, the duel has slipped so far outside normal practice these days that it likely wouldn't even occur to him that he could solve his grievance through a duel. The notion of a duel has become, as political philosopher Anatol Rapoport would put it, "an obsolete habit of thought."[21]

So the disappearance of duelling from our modern culture probably has as much to do with our public disapproval of the practice as it does with laws actually banning it. What allowed duelling to exist for so long was the fact that it enjoyed some sort of public legitimacy, that it was accepted as a way to demonstrate one's "honour." So, for instance, as Alexander Hamilton prepared himself mentally the night before his famous duel with U.S. vice-president Aaron Burr in 1804, he felt he was conforming to an accepted social tradition. He even felt—strange as it may seem to us today—*obliged* to take part. As his diary makes clear, he was actually reluctant to take part for a number of logical and compelling reasons: he felt no ill will towards Burr, he opposed duelling on moral and religious grounds (and by this point, duelling was illegal under the laws of New Jersey, where the duel was to take place) and he realized his duel posed a great risk to the financial well-being of his wife and children. "I shall hazard much and possibly gain little," he wrote. Still, he felt the need to take part, because, he wrote, defending oneself in a duel was what "men of the world denominate honor." Therefore, if he declined, he would be the object of derision and contempt by those whose opinion mattered to him. So, with all logic and feeling against it, Hamilton made his fateful decision to bow to "public prejudice in this particular."[22]

The peculiar set of social attitudes that drove Hamilton to enter into his duel have disappeared and been replaced with a set of social attitudes that would cause a similarly positioned person today to react very differently, without resort to violence. Thus, through social disapproval and legal prohibition, modern societies have rendered obsolete an institution that, for centuries, seemed just plain natural—an expression of the apparently basic human appetite for violence.

Of course, the duel was a particular institution. More broadly, we agree as members of society to give up our right to commit personal violence of any kind. We surrender that power to the state, as part of an implicit pact in which every other member of society does the same. The state then has a monopoly on violence, and we collectively—through our democratic voting power—determine the laws we will all live by. Only the police are given the right to use violence, and only to enforce the laws we've collectively agreed upon. By giving up the right to protect ourselves through violence, we achieve something even more precious—the right to live our lives free of violence.

Few today would lament this trade-off, any more than they would regret the passing of the duel. Modern living seems much more comfortable and congenial without violence in our midst. Indeed, the thought of any nation permitting such violence among its citizens—or unable to stop it, as in the case of nations where warlords are able to function—strikes us as evidence of a more primitive culture, something our society has evolved beyond.

Yet oddly we seem to see nothing absurd about continuing to accept an institution of violence *between* nations, namely the institution of war. As the Prussian strategist Carl von Clausewitz observed in his classic 1832 book, *On War*, "War is nothing but a duel on a larger scale." Compared to the duel, war is of course a far more lethal institution, indeed one with the potential today to obliterate not just a few proud gentlemen but the entire human race. How odd, then, that we continue to find war acceptable, making it a central part of the way we organize our societies, even though it's an institution no more "natural" than the duel.

————

Of course, war is generally regarded not as an institution but rather as the inevitable clash that results from deep-rooted human aggression. In other words, it's regarded as not something we chose to accept or reject but rather simply something that happens. This prevailing view doesn't imply that war can't be averted; obviously it sometimes can be, through diplomacy or political strategies. But the prevailing view does see war as a sort of normal and inevitable part of human behaviour. So while it's good to work at minimizing the chances of any given war, there's an unspoken assumption that war, in some form, will always be with us. Any notion of "ridding the world of war" is seen as hopelessly naive, rooted in some misguided notion that human nature can be reshaped into some nobler form.

Aggression does appear to be something that occurs naturally in humans, just as many other behaviours—laughing, crying, loving, hating, working, mating, communicating, making friends, helping others, co-operating with others—seem natural. So war may well be an expression of the aggressive part of human nature. The question is: Is it an *inevitable* expression of that aggressive side? Duelling—something that appeared to be basic and natural—simply disappeared over time; today duelling would be considered a silly anachronism, if anyone bothered to think about it. Could it be that war, like duelling, is an institution, rather than an inevitable expression of human nature? As an institution, war requires some form of social approval and support. Is it possible that ultimately such social approval and support could be withdrawn? In other words, is it possible that humans could choose to reject war?

Rapoport, who belongs to a school of thought known as peace studies, sees war in precisely this way, as an institution that continues to exist only because we continue to give it legitimacy. Rapoport points to other human institutions and practices that have failed to survive over time—slavery, absolute hereditary monarchy, binding the feet of young girls, gladiatorial combat. Political scientist John Mueller adds a few other practices that also became defunct once our society began to regard them as uncivilized and even repulsive: human sacrifice, the burning of heretics, bearbaiting, freak shows, Jim Crow laws, family feuding, public and intentionally painful executions, public flogging, execution for minor crimes, deforming corseting, laughing at the insane.[23] And yet all these practices were at one time considered acceptable, with some of them deeply ingrained in the social fabric.

Slavery, for instance, certainly offends our modern sensibilities about intrinsic human rights. And yet what could seem more basic to human nature than the desire to control and take advantage of others—a desire ultimately achieved in actually owning another human being? Hence, one could imagine an argument in which slavery would be defended as simply an extension of basic human traits, such as aggression, selfishness and the desire for dominance, and the rejection of slavery would be characterized as naive idealism.

Slavery might in some ways be considered a closer analogy to war than duelling, in that slavery, like war, involved a significant infrastructure that many profited from—slave-trading and slave-shipping companies and manufacturers of slavery equipment, like chains and restraints of various sorts. Furthermore, like war, slavery was an institution that existed in many parts of the world, and as far back as the dawn of civilization. Slavery also conferred important financial benefits upon the slave-owning class, which typically was the dominant social group with considerable, if not absolute, political power. So any campaign to do away with slavery—like doing away with war—would seem to face formidable obstacles.

What's striking, though, is how quickly slavery largely disappeared from the world. If we look at the span of human history, we see that slavery existed for thousands of years, and then effectively disappeared rather suddenly in recent centuries. The Swedes were ahead of the pack—who would have guessed?—abolishing slavery in 1335. After that landmark, nothing much happened until the late eighteenth century. Then, starting with Portugal, which abolished slavery in 1761, a wave of abolitions swept through many parts of the world, particularly Europe and the Americas: England and Wales (1772), Haiti (1776), Upper Canada (1793), France (1802), Argentina (1813), Chile (1823), Mexico (1829), Denmark (1848), Russia (1861), the Netherlands (1863), the United States (1865), Cuba (1880), Brazil (1888). By the late nineteenth century, abolition spread farther afield, including Korea (1894), Zanzibar (1897), China (1910), Burma (1929), Ethiopia (1936), Tibet (1959), Saudi Arabia (1962) and Mauritania (1980).

How did this happen? One might guess that society abandoned slavery simply because it became economically unviable, as some have argued. And it's true that Adam Smith, the eighteenth-century economist who came up with the theory of modern capitalism, argued that free labour was more efficient than slavery. Still, slavery apparently remained viable and profitable as an economic institution, and it was certainly financially rewarding to slaveholders, many of whom depended upon slavery for their financial well-being and who might have been unable to make a profitable transition to a slave-free world. The historian Stanley Engerman has noted that in "the history of slave emancipation in the Americas, it is difficult to find any cases of slavery declining economically prior to the imposition of emancipation." Similarly, the historian Seymour Drescher notes that even as nations started abolishing slavery in the late eighteenth and early nineteenth centuries, the Atlantic slave trade "was entering what was probably the most dynamic and profitable period in its existence."[24]

Nor is there any evidence of slave owners en masse having a sudden change of heart and freeing their slaves, although there were individual cases of this. Rather, the determining factor in ending slavery appears to have been the rise of strong abolition movements in a number of countries, particularly Britain and the United States. Such movements had the effect of changing the way people viewed this age-old institution. What had been regarded for centuries as an acceptable, natural form of human behaviour came to be seen as uncivilized, immoral and repugnant. As Mueller puts it: "Slavery became controversial, then peculiar and then obsolete."[25]

Rational argument certainly played a role in this process. The abolitionist movement and those responding to it were influenced by the ideas of the Enlightenment, ideas about human rights and freedoms. Adam Smith's arguments about the greater efficiency of free labour no doubt underscored the inappropriateness—and lack of economic necessity—of slavery. So rational argument was marshalled, along with appeals to human compassion, in order to fundamentally alter the way a vast number of people regarded this particular institution. The abolitionist movement worked on a number of levels, spreading its ideas through intellectual debate and literary appeals, as well as through political action that resulted in laws abolishing various aspects of slavery, such as the slave trade. In other words, concerted and determined effort, based on rational arguments as well as emotional appeals, succeeded in stripping slavery of its legitimacy in the eyes of the public. Once the public no longer found it acceptable, slavery ceased to be viable, no matter how much certain powerful figures wanted to hold on to it.

Would the abolition of war, then, also be possible? This intriguing question is raised by Rapoport and others like Graeme MacQueen. It's important to note that the possibility of an end to war doesn't rest on the notion that humans would change in some fundamental way, becoming perhaps more peaceful or loving creatures. After all, duelling and slavery have passed into history without human nature becoming any more compassionate, or even improving in any detectable way.

The possibility of abolishing war also doesn't rest on the notion that the "warrior class"—those in the political, corporate and military establishments connected to war—would be converted to an anti-war stance. It's assumed that these people are unlikely to change, given their financial ties to the industry of war or perhaps simply because they've absorbed the values and arguments of a society long accepting of war's inevitability. Ultimately the views of the people in these elites—despite their enormous power—may not matter, however, just as the views of slave owners didn't matter once slavery had become peculiar, uncivilized and unacceptable in the eyes of the public.

If it seems inconceivable that war could ever be made to seem peculiar, consider the amazing transformation that has taken place in Europe in the last few decades. For centuries, Europeans were almost constantly at war with each other, from the age of barbarism that followed the collapse of the Roman Empire to the tumultuous world wars of the twentieth century. And yet, in recent decades, the inclination among European nations to wage war against each other has effectively disappeared. How to explain such a profound and sudden change, other than to see it springing from a kind of collective revulsion towards war—a revulsion that arose in the wake of the horrors of World War II? Given the scope and senselessness of that bloodbath, in which tens of millions of people died and much of the continent was destroyed, Europeans came to simply reject war as a means of solving their differences. To this end, European nations, with the support of their populations, came together and created the European Union, as a way of emphasizing their commonly held goals and as a forum for working together to jointly advance their prosperity. One could say that war among European nations lost its legitimacy. Today, anyone in Germany, France or Italy advocating war against another European nation would be regarded as unbalanced, unsophisticated, even ridiculous.

It's interesting to consider what role may have been played in bringing about this transformation by the establishment of the European Union, an institution aimed at breaking down patterns that in the past had led to war. In other words, was the ultimate result of de-legitimizing war among European nations advanced by the interim step of creating this new institution? Could a similar approach work in a campaign to de-legitimize war in general? Rather than focusing on trying to bring about a de-legitimization of war—a rather huge and difficult concept to convey—a campaign could set interim goals that would advance that ultimate goal. For instance, a campaign could set the interim goal of pushing national governments to pass laws banning participation in the arms trade, just as the anti-slavery movement focused on banning the slave trade as an interim step to the ultimate goal of banning the entire institution of slavery.

Rapoport reminds us that it's not even necessary to convert the general public to the philosophy of pacifism; it's simply necessary to undermine war's acceptability. Thus, the task is to destroy something, which is generally easier to accomplish than to build something. The strategy is simply to make the waging of war seem peculiar, uncivilized, even revolting. "The abolitionist doesn't bank on radical changes in people's deepest feelings" notes Rapoport, in an article he co-wrote with Leonard Johnson, a retired Canadian general turned peace activist. "His is the traditional task of the revolutionary—to undermine and ultimately destroy the legitimacy of an institution, in this case one that is already feared and held responsible for misery and destruction by many and is seen by many as a threat to the survival of humanity."[26]

Indeed, the ever-increasing destructive power of war would seem to provide a solid rational and emotional basis to the war-abolitionist cause. It's interesting to note, for instance, how much more lethal the weaponry of war has become over time, with a particularly sharp increase in lethality since the mid-nineteenth century. Military historian Trevor Dupuy has drawn up an index to provide a rough measure of "lethality"—or killing power—of weapons through human history. For the first million or so years, the destructive power of weapons was relatively minimal. Throughout ancient and medieval times, the available weapons— the longbow, the crossbow, the early cannon—all score below 50 on Dupuy's "lethality index." This starts to change only in the mid-1800s, and by the late 1800s, rifles are scoring above 150 on the index. Then things really take off. By 1903, the Springfield rifle measures 495 in lethality. In the First World War, the lethality of machine guns comes in at 3,463; in the Second World War at 4,973. Meanwhile, the lethality of a Second World War fighter-bomber measures 1,245,789 on Dupuy's index. This is in turn utterly dwarfed by the lethality of the first nuclear bomb, which measures a staggering 49,086,000. By 1952, the hydrogen bomb scores 695,385,000 on the lethality index. Since then, the lethality of nuclear weapons has continued to grow in leaps and bounds.

The lethality of nuclear weapons is such that a nuclear war is simply irrational. Of course, nuclear war has always been understood to be irrational. But, as discussed earlier, the one apparently reasonable justification for it—the need for deterrence against the nuclear weapons of another power—was removed by the collapse of the Soviet Union, making it possible for Washington to begin the process of worldwide nuclear disarmament without jeopardizing American safety. We know that Washington has chosen to reject this path, and we can see in the documents produced by the Bush administration that the reasons for this rejection appear to be rooted in Washington's desire to consolidate U.S. control over the world.

But while a desire to control the world may be stronger in top administration officials than a desire to live in peace, this sort of megalomania is not shared by the American public. Polls consistently show overwhelming popular support among Americans for nuclear disarmament—even though the issue is not remotely on the actual political agenda. Ordinary Americans, like ordinary people throughout the world, intuitively understand that it makes no sense to support a policy capable of destroying humankind. We don't even need to think through the issue in some sort of cost-benefit analysis—the pros and cons of nuclear holocaust. It is intuitively obvious that there are only cons. John Mueller uses the example of a person in a hurry trying to decide how best to get from the fifth floor of a building to street level. The person could walk down the stairs—or jump out the window. Faced with such a decision, the person doesn't have to do a set of calculations to realize that the advantage of jumping—getting there faster— would be more than cancelled out by the disadvantage of ending up hopelessly crippled or dead.

And yet, astonishingly, we continue to prepare for the option of jumping out the window. We continue to accept the legitimacy of war, partly because this vital subject somehow, unbelievably, escapes the spotlight of public scrutiny. The war planners are not obliged to make an argument defending nuclear war. Rather, the issue is simply not directly discussed. There are debates, to be sure, about related issues—whether a particular missile system would be effective or affordable, whether the Nuclear Non- Proliferation Treaty should be renewed and extended, whether certain countries should be punished for violating the treaty. But there is no real, serious debate about whether there is any possible justification for continuing to hold on to this ultimate weaponry of war.

This avoidance is possible because the institution of war, even in the nuclear age, has become adapted and integrated seamlessly into our lives, thus becoming effectively invisible as a system of mass destruction. Its normalcy has made it seem strangely harmless. The apparatus of war has become so pervasive—the arms industry, the army and defence bureaucracy, the scientific community researching new weapons systems—that it is possible to work in a small corner of it and yet feel completely disconnected from the overall project of war. A machinist in an arms manufacturing company, a lab technician in a chemical plant or a personnel supervisor in a branch of the Pentagon is likely no more aggressive or bloodthirsty than any other member of society. And their participation in the war machine likely causes them no particular concern nor causes others to shun them. They are simply doing a job—a job that meshes invisibly with all the other jobs out there in the modern world.

Some, particularly in the United States, are deluded into thinking that maintaining the machinery of war is integral to our prosperity. This view clearly overlooks the fact that the massive human and financial investment that goes into the arms industry could instead be invested in something else—something with far greater usefulness to our lives. It is ironic to note that the arms industry produces products that have no purpose other than destruction. The very best scenario that can be hoped for is that its products will never be put to use. By allowing our economic activity to be tied to the business of armaments and war, we have created a mirage of prosperity—a prosperity based on the production of something that is actually of no value, or worse, something that will destroy us all.

And so it is that we all go about our lives, allowing the legitimacy of an ultimately insane institution to simply go unchallenged, and leaving the power to destroy the world in the hands of a small and largely unknown elite, led by characters like George W. Bush and Dick Cheney—an elite that, for all we know, might decide that the best way to get to the ground floor is to jump out the window.

Rapoport and Johnson compare our society to the cells of the body of someone in the process of committing suicide. All the cells keep operating normally, each doing its own job, allowing the body to keep on functioning, even as the person writes a suicide note, puts the gun in his mouth and prepares to pull the trigger. "The cells in the meantime (i.e. all of us) go about their business, having nothing to do with suicide," they note. "Yet all of these 'normal' activities add up to collective suicide."

And we think *duelling* has outlived its usefulness?

If there was one message that our political and corporate leaders drummed into us in the 1990s, it was that globalization was changing the world. The comforting security of the past—knowing you had a job for life, a pension waiting at the end of your career and that if you or your loved ones somehow stumbled, there would be a social welfare net to catch you—all this was being swept aside by the gale-force winds of change. In the new interconnected world of computers and instant global telecommunications, the borders of national sovereignty had to give way to the borderless world of free trade, where there would be no security. "If you don't think globally, you deserve to be unemployed and you will be," warned globalization guru Peter Drucker, capturing the spirit of the new age.

The changes involved would be immense. We were told we had no choice but to accept far-reaching "free trade" deals that stripped national government of their sovereign powers to protect their economies and their workers. If we protested that we didn't like the new world being offered, we were told that it wasn't possible to hold on to the past. "A feudal mindset has no place in a global economy," David G. Vice, chairman of the Canadian Manufacturers' Association, declared at a Toronto conference on globalization in March 1990. Those resisting change were dismissed by *Maclean's* columnist Diane Francis as "latter-day King Canutes trying in vain to order an end to the tides."

But when it came to war, there would be no room for bold new thinking. There would certainly be no willingness to consider giving up sovereignty over our national right to wage war—the way we were told we must give up sovereignty over our national economy and our social programs.

When it came to war, a feudal mindset would be just fine.

CHAPTER 6

BACK FROM THE ABYSS

As U.S. defense secretary, Donald Rumsfeld was easily one of the most powerful men in the world. So everything he said, everything he did and everywhere he went was thoroughly recorded by the media. A coterie of reporters followed him to every foreign destination, even when he made lightning in-and-out visits to Iraq. Yet there were plans to slip the defense secretary in and out of Canada in September 2006 without anyone being the wiser.

In the end, Rumsfeld did not make it to his scheduled appearance on September 13, 2006, to deliver a keynote address to a top-secret gathering of North American political, military and business leaders, held at the stately Banff Springs Hotel. But Rumsfeld's scheduled address in the hotel's Cascade Ballroom—he was a confirmed participant on confidential conference documents—indicated the importance of the meeting. Among the attendees were such high-level U.S. figures as Admiral Tim Keating, commander of U.S. Northern Command; former CIA director James Woolsey; former Secretary of Energy and Defense James Schlesinger; as well as former secretary of state and Bush family confidant George Schultz. Among the high-level Canadian attendees were Defence Minister Gordon O'Connor, Public Safety Minister Stockwell Day and Chief of Defence Staff Gen. Rick Hillier, as well as prominent business leaders such as Suncor Energy CEO Richard George, TransCanada Corporation CEO

Harold Kvisle and business lobbysists Tom d'Aquino and Roger Gibbons. The meeting, organized by the Canadian Council of Chief Executives and the Canada West Foundation, was to focus on a North American energy strategy and North American integration and security co-operation.[1]

The secrecy surrounding the meeting was extraordinary. Despite the presence of top public officials, no notification was given to the media, and when local rumours of the event eventually prompted a few media inquiries, almost nothing about the meeting or its participants was divulged. John Larson, who acted as a spokesperson for the gathering, which called itself the North American Forum, refused to confirm who had attended or to release details of what was discussed. "The participants joined the conference essentially knowing that it would be a private function," he said.

A private function? In what sense could this be considered a private function when it involved top-level government officials and business leaders from the United States, Canada and Mexico, and when the topics discussed included some of the most important and contentious issues of our time? Do these powerful government and business leaders consider these vital public-policy questions simply a private matter, to be worked out quietly amongst themselves?

In many ways, the meeting is the ultimate expression of the treachery—I realize that's a strong word, but I can't think of a more appropriate one—of our business and political elite. The essence of what was going on in Banff was that key members of our elite were meeting with business and political leaders from the United States to discuss ways to further a far-reaching agenda that is at odds with the Canadian public interest. Two of the key themes of the meeting, which are clear from the meeting's unpublished agenda, revolve around North American energy security and Canada–U.S. military and security co-operation. Both of these are U.S. priorities, not Canadian.

Take the issue of energy security. As noted in chapter 1, it is Canada that is in the more favourable position in terms of energy resources, and it is thus in the interests of the United States—not of Canada—to have an integrated energy market that ensures both nations have "energy security." Despite consuming about a quarter of all the oil produced in the world each year, the United States has only 3 per cent of the world's oil reserves, and is therefore highly dependent on foreign suppliers, and growing more dependent each year. While the bulk of the world's oil is in the Middle East—where, as Dick Cheney once said, "the prize ultimately lies"[2]—much of the solution to the U.S. energy dilemma lies right here in Canada. We're already America's top supplier of oil and gas, and certainly its most reliable source. As political uncertainty makes U.S. access to oil from other key suppliers like Venezuela and even Saudi Arabia less certain, Canada's importance grows by leaps and bounds.

So getting Canada to agree to the goal of ensuring U.S. energy security is a significant coup for Washington. One question perhaps puts the issue in perspective. If the tables were reversed and the U.S. had greater energy reserves than Canada, is it likely that Washington would sign a treaty guaranteeing Canadians access to U.S. energy resources, even if that meant energy shortages for Americans? If we can't honestly answer that question in the affirmative, then surely we should stop making deals with the United States to achieve "North American energy security," and start focusing instead on something that has received far too little attention: *Canadian* energy security.

Similarly, on the military and security front, it is clearly Washington's agenda—not Canada's—to be waging aggressive wars in the name of fighting "terror." If Washington had not invaded Afghanistan in a lawless pursuit of Osama bin Laden and the Taliban, would Canada be there? It is hard to imagine that we would be. Canada has no history of intervention that has made us an object of hatred in that part of the world—at least, not until now. By joining the Bush administration's "war on terror," the Harper government is not only helping provide political cover for Washington's aggressive and increasingly unpopular behaviour, but also endangering Canada's hard-earned reputation in the world as a fair player and promoter of international law. Ottawa's reckless actions may even be putting Canadians at an elevated risk of terrorist attack on our home soil, as we become more closely identified with a superpower widely hated throughout the inflamed Muslim world.

Canada has also bent over backwards to accommodate the U.S. desire to create a "Fortress North America" in the wake of 9/11. This has involved massive new Canadian spending, not just on the military but also on all agencies involved in policing, border security and domestic anti-terrorism surveillance, thereby diverting funds that could have been spent on health care, education and other programs important to Canadians. Despite the fact that the terrorist risk was virtually non-existent here before we wedded ourselves so closely to Washington, Canada has developed a whole new security infrastructure to satisfy the Americans. This has involved, among other things, broadening the Official Secrets Act and passing a sweeping Anti-Terrorism Act, which allows for easier electronic surveillance and ministerial power to define terrorist groups. In addition, immigration laws have been used to imprison, without charges, five Muslim men suspected of terrorist links. By December 2006, the five had spent a total of 273 months in Canadian jails, much of it in solitary confinement.

There has also been an elaborate redesigning of Canada's political structures to put greater emphasis on security and our relationship with the United States. This has involved strengthening the security and defence committees and secretariats inside the Prime Minister's Office and the Privy Council Office, and creating a Ministry of Public Safety and Emergency Preparedness to act in co-ordination with the U.S. Department of Homeland Security, as well as a number of initiatives aimed at enhancing screening at the border. All this has diverted resources and attention from other priorities, has imposed limits on civil rights—severe limits in the case of the five Muslim men—and has had the effect of making Canada a more heavily monitored and security-obsessed society.

So, while the Canadian public interest in energy, military and security matters cries out for an independent Canadian course, members of our business, political and military elite huddled at a Banff hotel with their U.S. business and military allies to work towards forwarding the U.S. agenda on these fronts. If there is doubt about the willingness of our elite to compromise the Canadian public interest, one telling clue is the dark veil of secrecy that shrouded the Banff meeting. If our Canadian leaders had been discussing something in the public interest—how to save Canada's environment, how to improve our national infrastructure, how to strengthen our public health care and education programs—would there have been any need for such secrecy? Would they have even wanted secrecy? If these people were doing something—anything—that benefited the Canadian public, would they be sneaking furtively into the Banff Springs Hotel, like lovers meeting for a forbidden tryst?

Evidently, holding the bully's coat—like cheating on a spouse—is something people prefer to do in private.

———

Even as business elites on both sides of the border worked on promoting a North American energy strategy, the centrepiece of that strategy—the development of Alberta's oil sands—blocked Canada from developing any sort of responsible policy on global warming.

By the fall of 2006, Canada's irresponsibility on that front was becoming increasingly visible to the world, as Canada aligned itself with the United States and Australia in refusing to even try to move forward on Kyoto. The Europeans tried repeatedly to bring Canada back onside, but Canada rebuffed their advances. The Harper government actually cancelled a Canada–EU summit that was scheduled to be held in Finland in late November. The key topic the Europeans wanted to discuss: global warming. Harper decided a few weeks before the meeting that he was too busy, even though he was making time to attend a NATO summit to be held the following week. Frustrated by this unusually unco-operative Canadian government, French prime minister Dominique de Villepin proposed that the European Union impose a carbon tax on goods from countries like Canada that refused to do their part in tackling global warming.

Canada was suddenly taking on a prominent new role in the world—as a leading obstructionist in worldwide efforts to fight climate change. And once again, our elite commentators were on hand to sell this negligent agenda to the Canadian public. From their prominent perches in the *Globe and Mail*, the closest thing Canada has to a national newspaper, Rex Murphy and Margaret Wente took up a lot of space trying to undermine the public's confidence in the science of global warming. In fact, there are few things on which the scientific community has spoken more clearly. The Intergovernmental Panel on Climate Change (IPCC), set up by the United Nations and the World Meteorological Organization to canvass thousands of scientists around the world on the issue, has produced reports that clearly set out the seriousness of the global warming problem and the role of human fossil fuel consumption in contributing to it. "There is no debate among any statured scientist of what is happening," says Harvard's James McCarthy, who has been involved in the IPCC process.[3] But Rex Murphy isn't convinced. "The science is not complete. The models are not perfect," he scoffed. "In my view, it cannot be emphasized sufficiently that the climate change movement is at least as much a subcategory of rhetoric—the art of persuasion—as it is a branch of science."[4] Everyone is entitled to an opinion, but why is so much space given in our media to this sort of supercilious contrarianism, which gives the government and business community a bit of cover as they plow ahead recklessly with the oil sands development?

Certainly, Canada's footprint in the looming climate change disaster is unmistakable. While most of the European countries have succeeded in cutting emissions, Canada's emissions have actually risen over the past decade, leaving us with one of the highest levels in the world. The French produce an average of 6.8 tons of carbon dioxide per person a year, while the British produce 9.5 tons and the Germans 10.2 tons. Meanwhile, Canadians produce twice as much as the Europeans—19.05 tons per Canadian per year. We are only slightly better than the Americans, who produce 20 tons per person per year. Meanwhile, opponents of Kyoto often point to the rising energy consumption of China, which was not included in the first Kyoto round of reductions, as a justification for not cutting back our own emissions. But China, which produces only 2.7 tons per person per year, has a long way to go before it approaches the level of irresponsibility found in the industrial world. To put this all in perspective, the sustainable level of carbon dioxide per person per year in the world has been estimated to be 1.2 tons.[5]

Canada not only has been a serious and heavy emitter but, under the Harper government, has actively tried to sabotage the Kyoto process. As chair of the Bonn conference in May 2006, Canadian environment minister Rona Ambrose seriously undermined the prospects for future progress by opposing a tougher set of worldwide targets after the first Kyoto round expires in 2012. Ambrose insisted that a country's targets should reflect its national circumstances, such as its economy and energy resources. What a convenient doctrine for an energy-rich country like Canada! Ambrose also insisted that we shouldn't "point fingers at one another and suggest that one initiative is somehow better than another initiative." So if some countries choose to tackle the problem by cutting back emissions while others choose to, say, simply consult with industry about possible cutbacks in the future, we shouldn't resort to finger-pointing. The irresponsibility of this position is stunning. The only hope of averting what is likely to be a planetary disaster lies in a collective solution in which all the world's nations do their part and also hold each other to account. But instead of contributing seriously to this process, Canada's environment minister lectured the world as if she were instructing Grade 1 students on how to clean up their workstations: just do your best, and don't worry about what your classmates are doing.

The negligence of the Harper government's position is heightened by the fact that ultimately, as British author George Monbiot notes, it is the developing world that will pay the highest price for our failure to address global warming. As if the world weren't unfair enough, global warming is going to make it a lot more unfair. While it is almost exclusively the industrial world that has caused the global warming problem, the heaviest burden of droughts, hurricanes and floods is expected to fall on regions inhabited by the world's poorest people, who are also, of course, the ones least able to protect themselves.

So as the desperate of the world face the prospect of broiling, drowning or starving to death, Canada will be watching from a relatively protected, privileged spot on the sidelines, doing its best to make sure nobody points the finger our way.

———

It should be noted that Canada's disastrous role in efforts to address global warming is, unfortunately, not out of keeping with our inadequate efforts in other key areas, including our stunningly low level of foreign aid. At just 0.3 per cent of GDP, our aid falls far short of the UN goal of 0.7 per cent—a level most European countries have committed to reaching.

One of the most glaring examples of Canada's irresponsible environmental behaviour in the world has been our opposition to adding asbestos to an international treaty, the Rotterdam Convention, which restricts trade in toxic substances. But Canada continues to be one of the world's leading exporters of asbestos, with more than 90 per cent of these exports going to developing countries, where standards tend to be lower or poorly enforced. "Canada is knowingly exporting a product that will result in thousands of deaths from mesothelioma, asbestosis and lung cancer in Asia, Africa and South America," charges Canadian environmental lawyer David R. Boyd.[6]

All twenty-five members of the European Union and Australia support adding asbestos to the Rotterdam Convention, in the interests of restricting its sale and use throughout the world. But Canada continues to lobby hard against such a move, anxious to protect a lucrative niche selling a highly toxic carcinogen to the world's poor.

Canada has also distinguished itself as an obstructionist to global efforts to prevent one of the most destructive forms of fishing, called bottom trawling, which destroys crucial habitat for fish. As in the case of global warming, Canada was once a leader in developing laws to protect the marine environment, having been one of the instigators of the wide-ranging Law of the Sea Convention in the 1970s. But in recent years Canada has joined with just a handful of other nations in opposing efforts to ban bottom trawling on the high seas, largely because Ottawa doesn't want to accept any restrictions on the right to bottom trawl our own waters.

Then there's Canada's attempt to obstruct worldwide efforts to establish that people have a right to clean water. For more than a decade, negotiations have been under way at the UN to recognize water as a basic human right. But Canada has resisted, protesting that the law could be used to force Canada to give away some of its water. Boyd dismisses Canada's position as indefensible and unconscionable. "Fears about being forced to export water are bogus. Does the human right to food force us to export food?" he asks. "I think the real fear is that recognition of a right to clean water would put the feds on the hot seat for failing to ensure that Canadians enjoy the right to clean water, especially Aboriginal Canadians." On this issue, Canada has been virtually alone, the one nation in the world that has repeatedly voted against resolutions supporting the human right to clean water.[7]

"Do you believe that torturing terror suspects is a more effective national security strategy than, say, securing our ports and borders?"

This question was posed one evening in September 2006 on the popular CNN suppertime news program *Lou Dobbs Tonight*. Now, it's horrifying enough to realize that the subject of torture would be considered suitable for the "Question of the Day" on a major U.S. TV news show, since this suggests there could be legitimate views on both sides of the issue. Could we imagine a CNN "Question of the Day" about the pros and cons of slavery, child rape or cannibalism?

But note that the question posed here isn't even about the *morality* of torture—that is, the morality of deliberately inflicting pain and suffering on another human being. The moral issue has simply been set aside, as if it's irrelevant. Instead, the question is a purely practical one about the *effectiveness* of torture. Does torture work? Will it deliver the results we want? Do we have any stats on this? How does torture stack up against other methods of protecting ourselves, like tighter port and border security? (Or how about nuclear war? Might that be more effective?)

That a purely practical question about perhaps the most inhumane of human activities was breezily aired on a prime-time U.S. news program, without stirring public comment, reveals the moral abyss into which America has fallen.

In the United States, torture has gone mainstream. It is no longer a universally condemned activity like slavery, child rape, cannibalism, bestiality, incest. It is now possible to argue that, in the case of torture, there are shades of grey, situations where torture might be okay—not ideal, but defensible—as long as it's not too extreme, or doesn't leave permanent damage. Perhaps some day, CNN will ask whether child rape is okay in some cases, as long as the child isn't permanently damaged, or if bestiality is permissible if no other sex partner is available.

This casual attitude towards torture has been actively encouraged by the U.S. government and lawmakers in the wake of 9/11. In September 2002, a joint session of the House and Senate intelligence committees heard Cofer Black, the CIA's counterterrorism chief, describe how America's handling of captives had changed after the September 11 attacks. As Black put it: "There was a before 9/11, and there was an after 9/11. After 9/11 the gloves came off." It's hard to imagine anything much clearer than this statement by a high-level official of the U.S. government's intelligence service. What did the senators and congressmen think the senior CIA official meant by "the gloves came off"—that detainees would no longer be addressed as "sir" during interrogations?

And the gloves did come off. *New York Times* reporter Carlotta Gall reported from Afghanistan in early 2003 that the death of a young detainee in U.S. custody had in fact been a homicide. In a press release, the U.S. military had attributed the death of the twenty-two-year-old Afghan taxi driver named Dilawar to a heart attack. But Gall contacted Dilawar's family and discovered that the U.S. military death certificate accompanying his body had indicated in English that his death was a "homicide." The heart attack had come after Dilawar had been beaten so severely that his legs had "basically been pulpified," a coroner later testified. Incredibly, the *Times* held Gall's news report of the murder of a prisoner in U.S. custody for a number of weeks before publishing it, apparently because some editors simply refused to believe that U.S. forces would behave in such a way. U.S. officials later acknowledged that Dilawar was in fact innocent.[8]

The tone for this new gloves-off era was set by the White House itself, which openly scorned the notion that prisoners in its "war on terror" had rights. The purpose of building a special prison camp at Guantánamo Bay was clearly to put detainees beyond the reach of U.S. law. Of course, the Geneva Conventions should have applied there, but the Bush administration simply announced that the detainees were "enemy combatants"—a newly defined category of human being arbitrarily stripped of all legal rights. What possible reason would there be to hold prisoners in a law-free, offshore enclave except to do things to them that the law doesn't permit—to apply the very gloves-off treatment that Cofer Black set out to members of the U.S. Congress as the new normal?

It was in this new climate—with open declarations that the gloves were off and the Geneva rulebook tossed aside—that the now-famous grinning crew of American soldiers took up their posts inside Abu Ghraib. This was clearly a sadistic bunch, with their obvious delight in piling naked, hooded men on top of each other, threatening these men with vicious dogs and attaching electrodes to their penises. But it's hard to avoid noticing the green light flashing at these U.S. soldiers from Congress and the White House, which had communicated in words and deeds that all was fair in the "war on terror."

There was a flurry of outrage over Abu Ghraib in the U.S. Congress and the U.S. media before the White House was able to prevail with its insistence that the punishment of a "few bad apples" would be sufficient to deal with the problem. After that, the Abu Ghraib photos and the issues they raised—while hugely inflaming the Muslim world—mostly disappeared from the U.S. mainstream media. Congress quickly closed ranks with the administration in deciding not to draw further attention to what had been going on in U.S. prisons. Additional photos of apparently even more horrific mistreatment at Abu Ghraib were shown exclusively to members of Congress, who decided against releasing them publicly. "It was disgusting," said Texas senator Kay Bailey Hutchison after the private congressional screening. "There were new ones that we hadn't seen before, and they're bad. I mean there's no doubt about that." These unreleased photos reportedly depict "assault, coerced sexual activity, rape, even dead bodies."[9]

The torture and killing by U.S. soldiers didn't stop, however. By the summer of 2006, some ninety-eight terror-related detainees were reported to have died in prisons operated by the United States in Guantánamo, as well as in Iraq, Afghanistan and other CIA-operated "black sites" around the world, with six hundred U.S. personnel implicated in some sort of abuse.[10] And there are almost certainly other deaths—and more torture—by U.S. soldiers that have simply not been recorded.

With torture apparently encountering little resistance from the American public, the Bush administration was emboldened in the fall of 2006 to assert its right to torture terror suspects, and the U.S. Congress went along. In the Military Commissions Act, passed by both the House and the Senate at the end of September 2006 and signed into law by the president the following month, the administration has been given sweeping powers that overturn human rights protections dating all the way back to the Magna

Carta, signed in Britain in 1215. Under the new act, which a *New York Times* editorial described as "a tyrannical law," the administration can designate any non-citizen an enemy combatant.[11] This person is then stripped of all rights, and can be locked up indefinitely, without recourse to the courts.

This amounts to a repudiation of *habeas corpus*, which has for centuries been the fundamental legal protection a person has had against arbitrary detention by the state. Here's how Winston Churchill described the importance of *habeas corpus*: "The power of the executive to cast a man into prison without formulating any charge known to the law, and particularly to deny him the judgment of his peers, is in the highest degree odious, and the foundation of all totalitarian government whether Nazi or Communist." Or as Beverley McLachlin, chief justice of the Supreme Court of Canada, has put it: "The oldest human right is the right to be free from arbitrary arrest and imprisonment. Chapter 33 of the *Magna Carta* of 1215 banned arbitrary arrest and imprisonment and established the right to call upon a judge to be freed—the right of *habeas corpus*."[12]

The new U.S. Military Commissions Act also opens the door for the administration to do things to detainees that, by any reasonable definition, constitute torture. The act tries to muddy the clearly articulated standard of the Geneva Conventions banning "cruel, inhuman and degrading" treatment of those held in the custody of governments. The need for such a standard in preventing abuse and torture is obvious, but the Bush administration and co-operative U.S. lawmakers worked out wording that opened up some wiggle room. The act opens up a distinction between pain that is "severe" as opposed to merely "serious," and appears to permit techniques like sleep deprivation, exposure to extreme cold and water-boarding (mock drowning) as long as they don't cause lasting harm. What kind of hairsplitting nonsense is this? One would have thought that any pain, deliberately caused by the state in order to coerce, intimidate or punish a person in its custody would be unacceptable to a civilized society.

By permitting some level of pain, the act clearly opens the floodgates. Who, after all, will determine whether the pain is "severe" as opposed to "serious"? Certainly not the person experiencing the pain. That determination, ultimately, will be made by the person inflicting the pain, who may well believe that the pain he is administering is not all that severe or serious—or at least not more than the detainee deserves. The interrogator may well have sadistic tendencies, which would help explain his attraction to a job where he enjoys such power over another human being.

With the passing of the Military Commissions Act, the descent into barbarism begun after 9/11 has now been codified into law. Of course, many countries in the world are far more barbaric in their treatment of prisoners. But for the United States—a nation founded on principles of human and civil rights—the implications are immense. Tragically, Americans are so poorly served by their mainstream media that, even as Congress was passing this alarming law, stripping them of the centuries-old legal foundations of their democracy, there was little serious media commentary about the profound implications. To the extent that the issue was discussed in the media at all, the focus was on what impact it might have on the upcoming mid-term elections, the key question being: would the Republicans be able to tar Democrats who voted against the bill with being "soft on terror"? The day after the bill cleared the Senate, the media had already lost interest; the story dominating the news was the resignation of Florida congressman Mark Foley over emails he had sent to a teenaged congressional page.

While the Foley scandal went on to be a big item in the mid-term campaign—along with the war in Iraq and stem cell research—the Democrats kept silent on the Military Commissions Act. Although they had tried to stop the bill from passing, the

Democrats lacked the political courage to make torture an issue in the campaign, fearful that it would help the pro-torture Republicans position themselves as better able to handle national security. The right of the U.S. government to torture "evil-doers" had apparently become so accepted in the American mainstream that politicians were afraid to challenge it at all during an election campaign. Thus, with barely a murmur raised, some of the most basic fundamental legal and human rights protections disappeared from the United States, which, paradoxically, still billed itself as the world's leading democracy.

———

For Canada, the implications are immense. Under the Military Commissions Act, any non-U.S. citizen—including Canadians—can be designated an enemy combatant and detained indefinitely. So Canadians considered terrorists by Washington have no legal protections in the U.S. And yet Ottawa, rather than protesting this lawlessness and the danger it poses to Canadians, is actively co-operating with the U.S. in its fight against "terror."

Indeed, as noted in chapter 2, Canada has already become complicit in some of the worst aspects of the U.S. "war on terror" through our failure to ensure that suspected insurgents we detain in Afghanistan are not subjected to torture.

Meanwhile, Prime Minister Stephen Harper loudly proclaims his deep concern about human rights abuses—in China, that is. On his trip to the international summit in Hanoi in November 2006, Harper tried to seize the moral high ground, going out of his way to tell reporters that he planned to be vocal in his criticisms of China's abuses, and not "sell out" Canadian concerns "to the almighty dollar," as previous Canadian governments had. Harper followed through. In his brief meeting with Chinese president Hu Jintao, Harper raised the case of Canadian Huseyin Celil, imprisoned in China on terrorism charges.

But Harper's booming voice has been strangely silent when it comes to the human rights violations of our ally the United States. Protesting the U.S. abuses is a far more pertinent and urgent responsibility for Ottawa, because Canada is actually complicit in them, whereas we are not complicit in China's abuses. In addition to Ottawa's indifference to what happens to Canadian detainees in Afghanistan, Ottawa has also failed to take up the case of Canadian citizen Omar Kadr, held in Guantánamo Bay since 2002. Kadr was only fifteen when he was taken into U.S. custody, after allegedly killing a U.S. soldier in a firefight in Afghanistan. Lawyers for Kadr have tried to get Ottawa to intervene on his behalf and to point out that, under international law, a fifteen-year-old is entitled to special protections for children set out in a UN protocol (which the United States ignores). So while the Harper government loudly proclaims its deep concern about human rights abuses in China, and confronts the president of China directly about an imprisoned Canadian, it abandons a Canadian teenager to fend for himself in the Guantánamo gulag run by our friend and ally.

This Canadian failure to challenge U.S. abuses is not confined to the Conservatives. It was the Liberal government that initially failed to take up Kadr's case (beyond urging Washington to spare Kadr the death penalty). More recently, the prominence of Michael Ignatieff in the 2006 Liberal leadership race suggested a certain level of tolerance—among Liberal delegates at least—for U.S. lawlessness. Although Ignatieff attempted to be careful in his statements during the leadership race, he had come out clearly in favour of the U.S. invasion of Iraq at the time, even extolling the virtues of U.S. global hegemony in January 2003 in an article in the *New York Times Magazine*. "The 21st century imperium," he wrote, "is a new invention in the annals of political science, an empire lite, a global hegemony whose grace notes are money, free markets, human rights and democracy enforced by the most awesome military power the world has ever known."[13] Ignatieff, who was director of the Carr Center for Human Rights Policy at Harvard, never seemed bothered by the illegality of the U.S. invasion. Indeed, he soured on the war only later, as did other neoconservatives, because Washington's strategy was ineffective and failed to produce a U.S. victory.

Ignatieff also seemed comfortable with other aspects of U.S. lawlessness, including torture. He protests that he is against torture, but he has come up with convoluted arguments that defend certain kinds of torture. He has striven to make his pro-torture arguments appear sophisticated and nuanced. In reality, they seem awfully similar to the thinking behind the U.S. Military Commissions Act, setting out acceptable levels of torture, under which maximum stress can be created in detainees without leaving them permanently damaged, at least in any detectable way. The similarity of positions between Ignatieff and the U.S. military is perhaps not surprising since, as *Toronto Star* reporter Linda Diebel pointed out in a profile of Ignatieff, the Carr Center has focused on "the continuing dialogue between rights workers and the military."[14] Here's what Ignatieff had to say in another article in the *New York Times Magazine:* "To keep faith with this commitment, we need a presidential order or Congressional legislation that defines exactly what constitutes acceptable degrees of coercive interrogation. Here we are deep into lesser-evil territory. Permissible duress might include forms of sleep deprivation that do not result in lasting harm to mental or physical health, together with disinformation and disorientation (like keeping prisoners in hoods) that would produce stress."[15]

Ignatieff's thoughts on what might constitute acceptable levels of torture are revealing. It's hard to imagine that he would find such coercive methods of interrogation acceptable if they were, say, applied to him. If he were arrested in a foreign country on suspicion of having committed a crime, would he think it all right

for police to keep him sleep-deprived, disinformed and disori-
ented, with a hood over his head, in order to produce stress?
Would he object to any of his relatives being treated in this way?
My guess is that he would, that he'd be outraged by such indigni-
ties and deliberate attempts to terrorize and intimidate him or
others he cared about. And yet he seems unable or unwilling to
apply this standard to people suspected of terrorism—who may,
for that matter, be no more guilty than he would be. As a "professor of human rights" does he not understand that, by its very
definition, a human right is one that belongs to all humans, that
we can't have one set of human rights for those we like and
another set for those we don't?

If the danger of this sort of casual approach to torture—an
approach that permeates the U.S. "war on terror"—isn't obvious,
the case of Maher Arar brings it into sharp relief.

———

While thousands of people have been subjected to the arbitrary
lawlessness and abuse of the U.S. "war on terror," few of these
cases have been investigated. Certainly none of them has been
investigated as thoroughly as the case of Maher Arar.

The Arar case gives us a glimpse inside this dark, disturbing
and little-known world. It also shows the ease with which
Canadian authorities, in their zeal to co-operate in tracking down
"terrorists," ended up delivering an innocent Canadian man into
this hell. It should be seen above all as a wake-up call to the dangers of Canadian complicity in the "war on terror."

It's also interesting to note that what is perhaps the only in-
depth investigation of the fate of a victim of the "war on terror"
was carried out in Canada—and only because the Canadian public demanded it.

As a result of the thorough investigation by Justice Dennis
O'Connor, Arar's innocence has been firmly established, as well as

the facts that led to his ordeal. It was in the heightened security-conscious atmosphere following 9/11 that officials of our Royal Canadian Mounted Police took an interest in Arar, because he had had some contact with another individual they were investigating. Although the RCMP found nothing to implicate Arar with any questionable activity, they requested that U.S. authorities post "border lookouts" for Arar and his wife, Monia Mazigh. Along with this request, the RCMP provided inaccurate information that portrayed Arar in a highly negative light. Most seriously, the RCMP officers told U.S. authorities that Arar and Mazigh were "Islamic Extremist individuals suspected of being linked to the Al Qaeda terrorist movement." As Justice O'Connor notes: "The RCMP had no basis for this description, which had the potential to create serious consequences for Mr. Arar in light of American attitudes and practices at the time."[16]

When Arar entered the United States a year later, changing planes in New York on his way home from a trip to Tunisia, he was detained by U.S. authorities. He was now in very serious trouble, given the al Qaeda allegation made against him by the RCMP—the only information that U.S. authorities apparently had on him. With Arar's plane about to land in New York, U.S. authorities contacted the RCMP and asked them to provide a list of questions to put to Arar. Surely, at this point, the Mounties must have realized the gravity of what they had done, even if they hadn't somehow realized it earlier. Arar, a Canadian who was not even under investigation in Canada, was about to be detained and interviewed by U.S. agents who would almost surely be abusive to him, given the allegation that he was connected to al Qaeda. Clearly, there was a responsibility on the part of the Mounties at this point to correct their earlier error and state unequivocally that they had no basis for saying Arar had ties to al Qaeda or was an Islamic extremist.

But that's not what the Mounties did. Instead, within an hour of receiving the U.S. request, they had assembled a list of questions to be put to Arar and faxed them off to New York. One new piece of information the Mounties included was that, on September 11, 2001, Arar had been in the Washington, D.C., area. Of course, that's not in any way proof that he was involved in the terrorist attacks on Washington and New York that day. But it would certainly heighten suspicions on the part of U.S. officials. In fact, however, the information was completely false. Arar had been in San Diego, not Washington, that day. Yet, apparently on the basis of this and other false information provided by the RCMP, U.S. authorities delivered Arar to a military prison in Syria, where he was beaten with metal cables and kept for months in a dark, rat-infested cell not much bigger than a grave. O'Connor concluded that it was "very likely" that U.S. authorities, in making their decision to hand Arar over to Syria, had "relied on" the false and inflammatory information about Arar supplied by the RCMP.

Once Arar's ordeal in Syria began, other Canadian authorities behaved in ways that also drew sharp criticism from Justice O'Connor. One would have thought that the responsibility of the Canadian officials involved—in the Canadian embassy in Syria, as well as in the Canadian Department of Foreign Affairs and Canadian intelligence agencies—would be to do everything possible to secure the release of a Canadian citizen who was being held by military authorities in a country with an extremely bad human rights record. Yet, reading the report, it is hard not to be struck by what seems to be an unconcerned attitude on the part of some Canadian officials. I couldn't help feeling that, if I'm ever in the custody of a brutal foreign military police, I certainly hope my file isn't handed over to these particular Canadian officials.

Technically, the Canadian ambassador and his staff in Syria pressed Syrian authorities to release Arar. But they also sent other, contradictory signals to the Syrians, indicating a willingness to cooperate with Syrian authorities in order to get information from Arar. And they failed to communicate to Ottawa the seriousness of Arar's situation, thereby minimizing the chances that senior government officials would intervene forcefully on his behalf. At the beginning of his ordeal in Syria, Arar was held incommunicado for about twelve days, without Syrian officials even acknowledging to Canadian authorities that he was in Syrian custody. When Syria finally acknowledged it was holding Arar, it told the Canadian ambassador that Arar had already confessed to having connections with terrorist organizations. Given Syria's abysmal human rights record, particularly in relation to terror suspects, any reasonable person would have suspected that Arar's "confession" was given under torture. Among other things, this would suggest his confession was meaningless.

But the Canadian ambassador, Franco Pillarella, was reluctant to come to this apparently obvious conclusion. This meant that communications from the embassy not only failed to alert Ottawa to the seriousness of Arar's plight but also tended to give some credence to the notion that Arar was connected to terrorism, since, after all, he had confessed! The failure of Pillarella to be suspicious of torture is striking, especially after Canada was allowed a consular visit with Arar two weeks into his detention. At the meeting with Canadian consul Leo Martel, things were very tightly controlled, with Syrian officials present at all times. Furthermore, Arar was not allowed to speak with Martel in English, but was obliged to speak in Arabic, through an interpreter, thereby increasing Syria's control over what he was able to communicate. Martel noted that Arar attempted to make eye signals indicating that he couldn't speak freely. Martel also reported that Arar, through the interpreter, said: "I am proud of my country of origin and I am also proud of Canada, my country of adoption. I have been respected by my Syrian brothers and I am happy to have come back to Syria." Surely, anyone would realize that Arar's statement was preposterous, and obviously said under duress. No matter what feelings Arar may have had for his native

Syria, clearly he would not be happy to be held in a notorious Syrian military prison, rather than being allowed to complete his trip home to his family in Canada.

As Justice O'Connor noted, such a statement was "ridiculous" under the circumstances, and obviously pointed to Arar's inability to communicate what was really going on. O'Connor concludes that these factors, coupled with Syria's poor human rights record, "paint a very strong, virtually overwhelming picture of interrogation and torture."[17] While some Canadian officials in Syria reached this conclusion, the key Canadian official—Pillarella—didn't. As O'Connor notes, "The Ambassador seemed strangely reluctant to conclude that it was even likely that Mr. Arar had been abused or tortured."[18]

This reluctance to admit the likelihood of torture persisted. O'Connor notes that in an email to Ottawa many months later, "Ambassador Pillarella made the troubling comment that the meeting 'should help us rebut the recent charges of torture.'"[19] Help us rebut the charges? Why on earth was this ambassador focused on rebutting the charges rather than working on the assumption that they were very likely true and putting his efforts into trying to protect a Canadian from being subjected to such horrific treatment? After all, that was the ambassador's job—to defend the interests of Canada and Canadians in Syria. That's what we were paying him to do. But Pillarella appeared reluctant to accept that Arar was being mistreated. Indeed, the ambassador seemed strangely trusting of Syrian authorities, to the point of naivety. In his testimony at the inquiry, Pillarella stated that he was not aware that Syria committed serious human rights abuses. (This prompted a rebuke by a prominent former Canadian diplomat, Paul Heinbecker, who said that Syria's bad human rights record was well known and that Pillarella's failure to acknowledge this reality cast a pall over the entire Canadian foreign service.)

Pillarella's reports to Ottawa led Foreign Affairs Minister Bill Graham to conclude that Arar's situation was not that serious. In

August 2003, while Arar was still in custody, Graham told reporters that, contrary to reports from human rights groups, Arar had not been tortured. Of course, Graham must have been enormously out of touch with world events himself to be unaware of Syria's reputation as a brutal dictatorship. Even if his own ambassador had also been unaware of what was common knowledge, Graham could have easily learned about the nature of the Syrian regime from countless other sources at his command. Had Graham, for instance, taken a minute to check the website of the U.S. State Department—or have an underling check it—he would have found a 2003 report on Syria detailing human rights abuses: "Continuing serious abuses included the use of torture in detention; poor prison conditions; arbitrary arrest and detention; prolonged detention without trial, etc." If Graham had read a few paragraphs further, he would have encountered some graphic descriptions of torture methods reported by previous detainees in Syrian custody: "Administering electrical shocks; pulling out fingernails; forcing objects into the rectum; beating, sometimes while the victim is suspended from the ceiling; hyper-extending the spine; bending the detainees into the frame of a wheel and whipping exposed body parts; using a chair that bends backwards to asphyxiate the victim or fracture the victim's spine." The site went on to note that in Syria "torture was most likely to occur while detainees were being held at one of the many detention centers run by the various security services throughout the country, particularly while the authorities were attempting to extract a confession or information."

In addition to misleading reports from ambassador Pillarella, both the RCMP and CSIS, the Canadian Security and Intelligence Service, behaved in ways that seemed to hurt Arar's chances of being released from Syrian custody. Both these agencies declined to support a letter, proposed by the foreign affairs department, that would have presented a united Canadian voice to

Syria, requesting Arar's return. Among their reasons for not co-operating with the "one voice letter," notes O'Connor, was the "concern that Mr. Arar's release might send the wrong message to the United States . . . about Canada's motives and resolve in the fight against terrorism."[20] This raises the possibility that Arar's detention in Syria may have been prolonged because officials in the RCMP and CSIS were anxious to convince U.S. authorities that Canada was committed to the "war on terror."

After Arar's release in October 2003 and his return to Canada, after almost a year in Syrian captivity, Canadian authorities continued to act in ways that seemed to prolong his torment. Some officials, who have not been identified, leaked information to the media in an apparent attempt to discredit Arar's claim of torture and to suggest he was indeed linked to terrorism. The sheer malevolence of this is striking. By this point, stories of Arar's innocence and his ordeal were causing outrage across the country. By planting conflicting stories in the media, these officials seemed to be hoping to convince the public that Arar was a dangerous character after all, and therefore deserving of his imprisonment. The ultimate goal was presumably to take the heat off themselves or off other Canadian officials for what they had done to Arar—acted in ways that had led to his torture and imprisonment in Syria, and then failed to act on his behalf once he was there. And now, in a final callous act, someone was trying to shift the blame onto Arar, rather than allow it to fall where it properly should—on Canadian officials.

For months in early 2004, the new Liberal government of Paul Martin had circled the wagons, trying to fend off never-ending assaults from Opposition parties and the media over the "sponsorship scandal." The essence of the scandal, laid out by the auditor general in a scathing report, was that the Liberal government of

Jean Chrétien had taken public money and funnelled it into Liberal coffers and advertising firms, defrauding Canadian taxpayers of tens of millions of dollars in the process. The scandal dominated public debate for almost a year and led to the public disgrace and firing of high-level officials, as well as to jail sentences for two ad executives and one senior civil servant. It also ultimately led to the fall of the Martin government in the January 2006 election.

Should we assume that all that outrage would have disappeared if, say, Alfonso Gagliano, the politician who'd been responsible for the sponsorship program, had announced that he really was very sorry about the whole thing?

Of course not. And yet, oddly enough, the Harper government seemed to think it was sufficient that RCMP Commissioner Giuliano Zaccardelli apologized to Maher Arar at a parliamentary committee in September 2006 for what members of his force had done. Under questioning, Zaccardelli also told the parliamentary committee he'd learned at the outset of Arar's detention in Syria that RCMP officers had provided false information about Arar. He also admitted that none of the officers involved in the case had been fired, and that indeed some of them had been promoted! Despite Zaccardelli's startling testimony, revealing his failure to treat the case seriously, the Harper government declared immediately afterwards that it had full confidence in him to run our national police force.

It was two and a half months later that Zaccardelli resigned— not because of his failure to act properly in the Arar case, but because he ended up changing his version of events. Testifying again before the parliamentary committee in early December, the commissioner withdrew his earlier statement that he'd known about the RCMP misinformation on Arar at the outset of Arar's Syrian imprisonment, and insisted instead that he'd only found out about it after the release of the O'Connor report. This was bizarre, to say the least, since it suggested that he had confessed to knowing about his force's misdeeds, and only later realized his confession was wrong and that he hadn't really known about the misdeeds until an inquiry had uncovered them. It was the contradiction in his version of events, not his failure to take steps to defend Arar's rights, that finally prompted the Harper government to withdraw its support for him. As *Toronto Star* columnist Thomas Walkom put it: "In effect, he is being penalized for being a political goof."[21] In announcing Zaccardelli's resignation, Harper seemed regretful rather than outraged over Zaccardelli's gross mishandling of the case, and thanked the commissioner for his years of service.

The Harper government's failure to show the same level of outrage over the Arar scandal that it showed over the sponsorship scandal is telling. Both were scandals that the previous Liberal government was responsible for, so both should have been grist for the mill of the Conservatives. But while Harper hounded the Liberals relentlessly on the sponsorship issue, he was much more subdued about the Arar case, and showed a reluctance to take any punitive action even after the strong and damning O'Connor report. The issue at stake in the sponsorship scandal was a breach of trust by government officials in defrauding the public of tens of millions of dollars. This is a very serious matter. But so is the breach of trust by government officials in providing false information that led to the torture and imprisonment of an innocent Canadian citizen. As citizens, we have to be able to count on government officials to defend our interests on both these fronts—our interests in having our public finances handled properly and our interests in having our most basic human rights protected.

The reason for Harper's muted response to the Arar scandal, one suspects, was that it exposes the danger—and moral depravity—of Canada's increasingly deep co-operation with the U.S. "war on terror." As noted earlier in this chapter, in the wake of 9/11, Canada has developed an elaborate new infrastructure of security co-operation with Washington. The Arar case reveals just where all this co-operation can lead. Indeed, the Arar case may be the tip of an iceberg. In his report, Justice O'Connor also pointed to three other Muslim men—Abdullah Almalki, Ahmad El Maati, Muayyed Nureddin—who were investigated by Canadian authorities and who were also imprisoned and tortured in Syria. Wrote O'Connor: "The cases of each of the three other men . . . raise troubling questions about what role Canadian officials may have played in the events that befell them."[22]

But Canada's co-operation with the U.S. "war on terror" lies at the very heart of Stephen Harper's agenda, and Harper would fiercely resist any move to fundamentally alter this co-operation. As we saw, RCMP and CSIS officials resisted efforts to present a united Canadian front in getting Arar released from Syrian detention, partly because they feared Arar's release might send a message to the United States that Canada wasn't committed to fighting terrorism. Certainly, any Canadian retreat on collaboration with Washington over terror would anger Washington. From the beginning, Washington opposed Canada's holding an inquiry into the Arar affair, and once the inquiry was established, Washington refused to co-operate with it. Washington's resentment over the inquiry was evident in a document called *Country Reports on Terrorism 2005*, which concluded that the "principal threat to the close U.S.–Canadian co-operative relationship remains the fallout from the Arar case . . . that prompted the Canadian government to review and restrict information-sharing arrangements with the United States."[23] For Washington, Canada's willingness to co-operate fully in dealing with "terror" is key to America's ongoing close relationship with us.

In addition, in exposing the details of what happened to Arar, Canada has drawn attention to American behaviour that Washington wants to keep shrouded in secrecy. After all, as mentioned, the Arar inquiry was the first real attempt to shine a penetrating light on the fate of someone who fell into the hands of those conducting the "war on terror." And it revealed not only how brutally U.S. authorities treat terror suspects, but also how they detain people based on only the flimsiest of evidence. If the Arar case is typical, it suggests that many of those imprisoned and tortured in the "war on terror" may be completely innocent.

Arar was ultimately the victim of the secretive U.S. practice known as extraordinary rendition, under which terror suspects are shipped for interrogation to countries known to perform torture, presumably to avoid any possible legal consequences or bad publicity that could arise from U.S. officials' actually performing the torture themselves. While the Bush administration has acknowledged the practice, it refuses to release any information about the victims or what happens to them. The Arar case brings some desperately needed light into this curtained-off world of U.S. depravity—light that Washington desperately wants turned off.

So the Arar case presented Harper with a huge dilemma. The Canadian public clearly showed its revulsion for what happened to Arar and the role Canadian officials played. But the case also pointed to Canada's complicity in the U.S. "war on terror." The Harper government is deeply committed to that war, and Washington is also adamant that Canada be fully onside. Caught between Canadian public opinion and Harper's desire for Canada to remain a loyal ally in the "war on terror," Harper dealt with the Arar scandal in a half-hearted, tepid way, showing none of the extravagant outrage that we know he is capable of.

The Harper government did act on Justice O'Connor's recommendation that a formal protest be lodged with the U.S. government, but seems to have tried to soften the impact of this protest as much as possible. Unlike other foreign policy statements, where Harper has often been quick and forceful in his criticism—such as his insistence that he wouldn't "sell out" Canadian concerns over a Canadian imprisoned in China "to the almighty dollar"—in the Arar case, the protest was slow in coming and soft around the edges. Harper waited several weeks after the release of the O'Connor report, and then phoned Bush to notify him that a protest was coming, and perhaps to assure the president privately that the move was necessary to soothe agitated Canadian public opinion but didn't reflect the feelings of the Harper government. The actual formal protest was to follow in a communication between Canadian Foreign Affairs Minister Peter MacKay and U.S. Secretary of State Condoleezza Rice, who had last been seen publicly exhibiting an unusual level of affection for each other in an official walkabout in Nova Scotia, ostensibly to celebrate the kindness of the Canadian public to U.S. passengers stranded here after 9/11. (The site of the walkabout—MacKay's riding—seemed to have been selected to help out his political prospects, since it was far from where any actual U.S. passengers had been stranded.)

Given the depth of the moral abyss that the U.S. "war on terror" represents, and the devastating ordeal of a Canadian who was victimized in that war, it would have been more appropriate for Canada's protest to be dealt with at the very highest levels. The protest should have come from the Prime Minister's Office and been directed to the Oval Office, rather than becoming perhaps just another opportunity for contact between our foreign affairs minister and the U.S. secretary of state.

———

One alarming possible explanation that has surfaced for the government's slowness in taking action against Zaccardelli is that the Harper government was in some way beholden to the RCMP for the role the force played in the winter 2005–2006 election campaign that brought Harper to power.

The evidence centres on the RCMP's somewhat odd decision to publicly launch a criminal investigation involving the Liberal government—right in the midst of an election campaign. That was the turning point in an otherwise fairly uneventful campaign. *Montreal Gazette* columnist Don MacPherson, a seasoned observer of the political scene, noted that the explosive words "criminal investigation" utterly undermined Martin's attempt to distance his government from the corruption-tainted Liberal government of Jean Chrétien, effectively handing the election to Harper's Conservatives. MacPherson went on to point out how "curious" the RCMP's behaviour was in the whole affair.[24]

The RCMP investigation centred on the question of whether a tip from a government source had led to a spike in stock trading hours before Finance Minister Ralph Goodale had announced the government's plan to change the taxation of income trusts in November 2005. There had been some media speculation about a possible leak from inside the finance department, and NDP MPP Judy Wasylycia-Leis had asked the RCMP to investigate. The Mounties had investigated and, after an initial review, reported in a statement a month later that they found "no evidence of wrongdoing or illegal activity on the part of anyone associated to this investigation, including the Minister of Finance Ralph Goodale."

Now, one would have thought that that finding would have been the end of the matter. But instead the RCMP, having found no evidence of wrongdoing, decided to proceed with a criminal investigation anyway! This was certainly odd, but even odder was Zaccardelli's decision to make the investigation public—a criminal investigation is typically not made public until a suspect is arrested or a warrant issued—by mentioning it in a letter to Wasylycia-Leis, who then predictably informed the media. After that, the Liberal campaign largely collapsed.

Could it be that the RCMP deliberately undermined Paul Martin's Liberal government? The RCMP's curious handling of the income trust case certainly raises some questions about what the Mounties were thinking at the time. It might also be relevant that there is evidence that the RCMP was very unhappy with the Martin government over its decision to call the Arar inquiry, since the inquiry was likely to uncover the RCMP's gross mishandling of the case.

It appears that the RCMP had applied pressure on Martin not to call the inquiry. In the months before the inquiry was announced, Peter Marwitz, a veteran intelligence officer who had worked for the RCMP and CSIS, had sent a series of confidential letters to Martin urging him to resist the growing public calls for an inquiry. In the letters, Marwitz, who went on to run a security consulting firm, urged Martin not to "bend to the wind" on matters involving national security. He also pointed to the defeat of Pierre Trudeau's Liberal government in 1979 after it had "abandoned the Mounties" by calling the McDonald inquiry into RCMP wrongdoing two years earlier. In what sounds perhaps like a veiled threat, Marwitz wrote in one of his letters to Martin: "To pursue a public inquiry into the Arar affair is to court political dangers to your government leading into the next election."[25]

As Marwitz predicted, the Martin government did lose the next election, with the strange actions of RCMP commissioner Giuliano Zaccardelli creating the turning point in the campaign.

———

With the publication of Samuel Huntington's influential 1994 book, *The Clash of Civilizations*, a new enemy came into view. Huntington, a Harvard political scientist, rejected the idea that the end of the Cold War represented an opening for peace. Instead, he argued that it had provided an opening for the revival of the clash between ancient civilizations—that is, between the civilizations that had grown out of the world's major religions. The Cold War, with its political and economic ideological fault line, was giving way to a religious fault line that had divided the world in earlier centuries. Building on ideas pioneered a few decades earlier by historian Bernard Lewis, Huntington predicted a revival of conflict between the Muslim world and the West. And he was clear about which side was to blame. "Islam has bloody borders," he argued. To Huntington, the Judaeo-Christian or Western world was a more advanced form of civilization, and was inevitably headed for a confrontation with the primitive and bloody world of Islam.

The views of Huntington and Lewis have held sway in the West. But some scholars of Middle Eastern history have started to question the notion of an inevitable clash of civilizations. Columbia University historian Richard Bulliet takes issue with the prevailing view of the Muslim world as stuck in rigid, vengeful medievalism. In his book *The Case for Islamo-Christian Civilization*, Bulliet challenges the negative view of Islam portrayed by Lewis and Huntington, and points to a tolerant side of Islam, noting the role that Islamic religious scholars and institutions played through the centuries as a bulwark against domestic political tyranny in the Arab world. Ironically, this tolerant, moderating role of Islam began to fade in the late nineteenth and early twentieth centuries, when Western legal structures and armies were imposed on the region and Islam was devalued. What emerged out of this Western influence and marginalization of Islam wasn't modernization but rather tyranny. In other words, without the moderating influence of Islam, the armies and governments put in place by the West became tyrannical.

The West played a central role in creating these tyrannies, beginning at the end of World War I, when the British and the French arbitrarily divided up the Arab world into nation-states run by political dictatorships chosen for their amenability to Western interests. When democratic reform movements eventually did emerge to challenge this despotism, the West took steps to stamp them out—most noticeably in Iran in the early 1950s. Thus, as we saw in chapter 2, Muslim resistance to the West is more likely resistance to Western intervention and imperialism than resistance to its "modernity." Bulliet insists that, far from being a monolithic, backward-looking civilization, there is considerable diversity in modern Islam, and a potential within Islamic societies to develop on a moderate, peaceful path, favouring co-existence with the West.

Indeed, it is striking to note that the Islamic world tried in the late 1990s to head off the looming "clash of civilizations," only to be rebuffed by the West. Ironically, this effort came out of Iran, long a hotbed of Muslim fundamentalism and resistance to the United States. In August 1997, moderate reformer Seyyed Mohammad Khatami won a landslide victory in the Iranian presidential election after campaigning for the rule of law and for expanding democracy within Iran—a direct challenge to the fundamentalist religious leaders who dominate the Iranian political system. Crucially, Khatami rejected the notion of a "clash of civilizations" and proposed instead a "dialogue of civilizations"—an idea that, it turned out, resonated with Iranians and with many others in the Muslim world and beyond. In 1998, a year after his election, Khatami took his proposal for a "dialogue of civilizations" to the UN, where it found strong support among members of the General Assembly and with Secretary-General Kofi Annan. With apparent determination to avoid the clash that Huntington and Lewis had predicted, the General Assembly designated a "year of dialogue among civilizations." As it turned out, the year designated was 2001.

But if the concept of such a dialogue was gaining momentum in the less developed world, it was not nearly so popular in the West, where Huntington's analysis had been seized upon and celebrated as the coming thing. In particular, Washington was unresponsive to the notion of a dialogue with the Muslim world, and showed little interest in helping Khatami, either in his quest to launch that dialogue or in his battle against hard-line religious leaders at home. Indeed, Washington did nothing to boost Khatami's stature on the international stage. Yet, if the West were trying to avoid conflict with the Islamic world, Khatami seemed like a lifeline—a popularly elected Muslim leader trying to challenge the fundamentalists, while holding out an olive branch to the West.

With the terrorist attacks on New York and Washington that September, the stage was set for a "clash of civilizations" to begin in earnest. Still, Khatami tried to head off the clash. He quickly condemned the 9/11 attacks and announced that Iran would join with the West in fighting terrorism. A moment of silence was declared at an Iranian soccer match in honour of the 9/11 victims, and a candlelight vigil held in Tehran. But the Bush administration showed little interest in these gestures of sympathy and support from the Iranian president and the Iranian people (and from other parts of the Muslim world as well), or in avoiding a confrontation with the Muslim world.

On the contrary, apparently delighted to have a new enemy in the crosshairs, Bush seized the moment. Among other things, he quickly introduced a new National Security Strategy that gave Washington far-reaching powers to pre-emptively attack nations it considered threatening or potentially threatening—a strategy that was directly built on the ideas of pre-emption and unilateralism developed by Paul Wolfowitz in his 1992 "Defense Planning Guidance." And the president soon made clear that the Muslim world figured prominently among Washington's list of threatening nations. Despite the fact that there was no evidence of an Iranian role in the 9/11 attacks, Bush brushed aside Khatami's continuing pleas for a dialogue with the West. In his State of the Union address the following January, the president simply declared Iran (as well as Muslim Iraq) part of the "axis of evil."

Washington was clear. There would be no dialogue with the Muslim world. There would be war.

For members of the Bush administration, the emergence of the new Muslim arch-enemy was a godsend that allowed them to reshape the nation in ways long dreamed of by the right wing of the Republican Party. Certainly for the military establishment and war hawks who had been left adrift and rudderless by the sudden disappearance of the Soviet enemy, it was reassuring to have a clear-cut foe again. All that annoying talk about a "peace dividend," about diverting resources away from the military and from new weaponry, could be shut down (and was). Military budgets could be ramped up (and were). And the public could be rallied behind a new version of "total war"—the "war on terror" that the Bush administration stressed was key to the survival of America and would go on for a very, very long time.

The Canadian military too warmed enthusiastically to the task ahead. The fear of irrelevance that had permeated the Canadian Forces since the end of the Cold War was gone. Suddenly there was a new set of bad guys even if it was only a band of unarmed outlaws on the run, hiding in caves in the far reaches of Afghanistan and Pakistan. As Gen. Rick Hillier told the Canadian troops at his inauguration in Ottawa, the Soviet "bear" had been replaced by a "bag of snakes." While a bear might seem like a more solid foe to rally against, a "bag of snakes" would also do in a pinch. An enemy, at last!

Of course, to rally the public for a new version of "total war," the enemy had to be more than a bunch of outlaws hiding in caves. The enemy had to be the equivalent of a massive army ready to take on the West. But there was no such army, so it was necessary to make the band of outlaws seem as threatening as an army. Hence, it was repeatedly pointed out that these outlaws could become very threatening if they managed to get their hands on nuclear or chemical weapons. Furthermore, although there might not be that many of these outlaws now, their ranks could grow. Recall that U.S. Lt.-Gen. Thomas Metz, who spoke to the

Canadian military gathering mentioned in chapter 2, described the enemy broadly as "radical Islamic terrorism." As he noted, there are a billion Muslims in the world, and if only one per cent of them are radical, "that's ten million radicals." Suddenly there wasn't just a bag of snakes, but ten million snakes. Now *there's* an enemy.

The notion of a "clash of civilizations" proved useful in enhancing the dimensions of this new enemy. The West wasn't just fighting Muslim terrorists; it was ultimately fighting the whole Muslim civilization—a civilization that was hostile to the West's advanced, enlightened ways and that fed the hatred of the terrorists. The perception of the Muslim world as backward and medieval was reinforced by images of furious Muslims on Western TV screens. Rarely was any context given for their anger. Accordingly, when Muslims around the world rioted in response to Danish cartoons mocking Muslim religious figures, many Westerners appeared to believe that the rage began with the publication of the cartoons, rather than being a response to a historical pattern of Western condescension and interference in the Muslim world.

With these images creating a lurid backdrop, the "war on terror" could be made to seem like a compelling battle to save civilization. The fact that the Islamic world happened to sit on the world's biggest oil deposits could be deemed irrelevant when bigger issues like fighting for Western values and our way of life were said to be at stake. Indeed, anyone who drew a connection between America's desire for oil and America's war against the oil-rich Muslim world was quickly marginalized, dismissed as a conspiracy theorist. And yet, occasionally even those orchestrating the "war on terror" would allude to the importance of oil to America. As we saw, Lt.-Gen. Metz, in his speech about radical Islamic terror, emphasized oil as essential to America's prosperity. Even Bush himself finally started to publicly make the connection between oil and the occupation of Iraq in the fall of 2006. As public pressure to bring the troops home grew during the mid-term election campaign, Bush began pointing to oil as a reason for the U.S. to stay in Iraq, arguing that otherwise all that oil would fall into the hands of the terrorists. "You can imagine a world in which all these extremists and radicals got control of energy resources," said Bush.[26] The flipside—that Washington also wanted to get control of all that energy—remained unmentioned in the North American media, even as the U.S. and the International Monetary Fund pressured Iraq to pass a "hydrocarbon law" opening up its vast oil reserves to private foreign investment.[27]

Plans for getting control of Iraq's oil also showed up in the December 2006 report of the Iraq Study Group, the bipartisan group set up to advise the administration on how to deal with the Iraq fiasco. The report noted right at the beginning that Iraq has "the world's second-largest known oil reserves." Recommendation 63 of the report called for Washington to "assist Iraqi leaders to reorganize the national oil industry as a commercial enterprise" and "to encourage investment in Iraq's oil sector by the international community and by international energy companies."

Thus, the notion of a compelling and inevitable "clash of civilizations" may have become a convenient cloak for aggressive Western actions against the Muslim world—actions that perhaps have more to do with geopolitical concerns like controlling the oil-rich Middle East, weakening foes of Israel and allowing the U.S. military to extend its control over a strategic corner of the world.

As Canada has increasingly lined up with America in its "war on terror"—a war in which we are being urged to ready ourselves for battle against ten million Muslims—we should examine whether we are really fighting "terror" or simply fighting on behalf of a new imperialism.

―――――

In vilifying the Muslim enemy, we have attempted to sanitize our own behaviour. Indeed, much of the commentary about the "war on terror" and the "clash of civilizations" is rife with a sense of our moral superiority, with the notion that, whatever grievances separate the West and the Muslim world, we in the West are ultimately decent while they are ultimately barbaric. The proof of this is said to be obvious: they are capable of being cold-blooded in a way we can barely comprehend. They cut off people's heads, and deliberately set bombs in subways and marketplaces packed with innocent civilians.

These actions are indeed barbaric. That's easy enough to see. What's odd is our inability to see our own Western actions with a similarly critical eye.

In a thoughtful essay in *Le Monde Diplomatique*, writer Tom Engelhardt points out that the West has simply declared our way of making war not barbaric, even though there is little reason to do so. "We have mostly achieved non-barbaric status . . . by removing the most essential aspect of the American . . . way of war from the category of the barbaric. I'm talking about air power."[28]

Clearly, waging war by dropping bombs from the sky has the potential to create immense suffering, as well as death and destruction. This was obvious from the very early days of air power. It's hard to imagine anything much more horrific than what some 100,000 Tokyo residents experienced in March 1945 when they awoke to find firebombs raining down on their city from U.S. jet fighters. Survivors later recalled men, women and children on fire, writhing in agony, jumping into rivers to douse their burning flesh, only to find themselves boiled alive. In the following months, even though there was ample evidence that Japan was on the verge of surrender, the U.S. unleashed similar air assaults on more than sixty Japanese cities, all leading up to the dropping of nuclear bombs on Hiroshima and Nagasaki.

Since then, dropping bombs from airplanes has been the West's major means of waging war, from Korea to Vietnam, from Kosovo to Iraq. One of the reasons for its popularity may be that an air campaign can be conducted with minimal risk of Western lives. Pilots drop their enormous loads of destruction and then usually return home unscathed. Engelhardt notes: "The result has been the development of the most barbaric style of warfare imaginable, one that has seldom succeeded in breaking any society's will, though it has destroyed innumerable bodies, lives, stretches of countryside, villages, towns and cities."

As we Westerners have developed the capacity to drop devastating bombs from great heights with little risk to ourselves, we marvel at the barbarity of people who murder with old-fashioned face-to-face brutality.

———

"We are stumped by the failure of our democratic concepts to gain a foothold in the Arab world," wrote Michael Bell, a former Canadian ambassador to Israel, in an op-ed in the *Globe and Mail* in February 2006.[29]

This sort of dismissive statement, dripping with the notion of our superior Western ways, is standard fare in our media—so standard that we often fail to detect the enormous hypocrisy that lies behind it. It's not quite clear, for instance, which "democratic concepts" Bell thinks have failed to gain a foothold in the Middle East. Surely he's not referring to the democratic concept that people are free to elect the government they choose. This is the most basic democratic concept of all. And it clearly *has* gained a foothold among Palestinian Arabs, who exercised this democratic right in January 2006 by rejecting a corrupt government that had failed to make any progress towards the establishment of a Palestinian state, and electing the Hamas party. The Hamas victory was in fact the subject of Bell's commentary, but he focused only on what he found objectionable in the new government—its refusal to recognize Israel—and ignored the fact that it had been democratically elected by the Palestinian people.

Obviously the Palestinians had failed to understand the subtle nuances of Western "democratic concepts." Just because the West urges them to elect a government doesn't mean they're free to elect a government the West doesn't like. As the *New York Times* reported, the "United States and Israel are discussing ways to destabilize the Palestinian government so that newly elected Hamas officials will fail and elections will be called again."[30]

If only the Palestinians would get it right the first time, it wouldn't be necessary for the West to intervene in their democratic process. But since they got it wrong, the West, led by Canada and the United States, proceeded to destabilize their democracy.

The Harper government made it clear that Ottawa was cutting off financial support because Hamas refused to renounce violence, recognize Israel and accept previous Israeli-Palestinian peace agreements. At first glance, this position may have seemed reasonable, since it appeared to support peace in the region. But why are these demands placed only on Palestinians? Shouldn't Israel also have to renounce violence? As the World Council of Churches has argued, "If violence is incompatible with democracy and with peace, it is incompatible for both the Israeli and Palestinian authorities."[31] As for recognizing Israel, Hamas had implicitly indicated on a number of occasions a willingness to do this—if Israel ended its occupation. But the Harper government made no demand that Israel end its illegal occupation.

The lopsided nature of Ottawa's demands was striking, particularly since Israel already exists as a country, with secure borders and the unwavering support of the most powerful nation on earth. Meanwhile, Palestinians, after forty years of living under military occupation, are essentially powerless.

This context is so often missing from mainstream commentaries like Michael Bell's. While he seemed to be urging moderation on both sides, his notion of moderation apparently consisted of demanding that Palestinians renounce their resistance to Israeli occupation, while making no demand that Israel end its occupation. He didn't even mention that Israel continues to build settlements on Palestinian land and continues to construct a massive wall incorporating large chunks of Palestinian territory permanently inside Israel.

Rather than belittling others for allegedly failing to grasp our "democratic concepts," we in the West could begin by showing we grasp these concepts ourselves.

———

Meanwhile, the Harper government continued to reshape Canada's traditional role in the Middle East, siding vigorously and unequivocally with Israel in Israeli–Arab disputes. In its voting at the United Nations, Canada reversed long-standing positions, voting against or abstaining on a number of resolutions supporting Palestinian rights. This shift, which began under the Martin government, has put Canada in the company of the United States and only a handful of tiny U.S.-dependent states like Micronesia and Palau.

With the cut-off of Western aid and the stepped-up Israeli attacks in the Gaza Strip, the situation became increasingly bloody and dire for the Palestinians in the summer and fall of 2006, as they faced severe food, water and medicine shortages as well as coming under almost constant attack. By late November, 370 Palestinians, many of them women and children, had been killed by the Israeli army since the previous June, compared to two Israeli civilians who had died from rockets fired by Palestinian militants into Israel.

As the Palestinians were abandoned by Western governments and ignored by the Western media, the UN remained one of the few bodies still taking an interest in the fate of these long-suffering people. In late November, UN High Commissioner for Refugees Louise Arbour made a trip to the Gaza Strip, bringing some much-needed media attention to the devastated area. In the town of Beit Hanoun, she toured the ruins of a building where, two weeks earlier, Israeli shells had killed eighteen members of the Athamna family. Arbour was clearly moved as she watched survivor Tahani Athamna weep uncontrollably over her lost relatives. "The violation of human rights I think in this territory is massive," said Arbour, as reporters and a crowd of Palestinians gathered around her.

The next day, touring southern Israel even as it came under rocket attack from Palestinians, Arbour did not back down. She acknowledged that Israel had a right to defend its citizens but insisted that it "has to do so only by legal means . . . It has to do so in line with international law, including international humanitarian law."

Arbour is a former Canadian Supreme Court justice, and her actions and words were more in keeping with Canada's traditional role in the region than that of the Harper government. As a UN official, she has no power to alter what is happening in the Gaza Strip. But her presence there was a principled act aimed at drawing world attention to the gross human rights violations being perpetrated on a defenceless civilian population. It may also keep alive the notion that, even if the Harper government has abandoned the Palestinians, not all Canadians have.

———

Far from the secret trysts of the U.S. and Canadian elites and from the battlefronts in the "clash of civilization" lies another world. It is the world set out by Justice O'Connor in his report on the Arar scandal.

While our government officials, commentators and business leaders have tried to draw us deeper into the compromised moral world of the U.S. empire and its "war on terror," O'Connor steers us in a different direction. With an intellectual rigour and a steady moral compass, O'Connor leads us back from the abyss, reminding us of the basic moral and legal principles that underlie Canadian society, and indeed civilized society.

Justice O'Connor was clearly appalled by what he uncovered when he looked into what happened to Maher Arar, at how Canadian officials, caught up in their zeal to nail a terrorist, had acted in a way that ultimately led to Arar's torture and imprisonment.

As the notion of acceptable levels of torture or acceptable circumstances for torture has crept into the public dialogue in North America, it is worth noting O'Connor's words: "The infliction of torture, for any purpose, is so fundamental a violation of human dignity that it can never be legally justified." He cites the UN secretary-general: "Let us be clear: torture can never be an instrument to fight terror, for torture is an instrument *of* terror."[32]

O'Connor points to the unequivocal ban on torture in a number of international treaties Canada has signed and supported, including the Universal Declaration of Human Rights, the International Covenant on Civil and Political Rights, the Geneva Conventions of 1949 and their two Additional Protocols, the United Nations Torture Declaration and the Convention Against Torture. To those who see room for leeway on torture in certain circumstances, such as tracking down terrorists in the wake of 9/11, the Convention Against Torture speaks clearly: "No exceptional circumstances whatsoever, whether a state of war or a threat of war, internal political instability or any other public emergency, may be invoked as a justification for torture." O'Connor points out that the prohibition against torture in international law is so fundamental that it has acquired the status of what is known as a *jus cogens* norm—a body of "higher law" that, because of its importance to the international community, overrides all other laws, treaties or state practices.

O'Connor notes that, in addition to international law, Canada's own Charter of Rights and Freedoms also absolutely rejects torture. The Supreme Court of Canada has characterized torture as "so inherently repugnant that it could never be an appropriate punishment, however egregious the offence."

In sharp contrast to the moral clarity of Justice O'Connor is the moral fog of rationalizations for the U.S. "war on terror," as reflected in the U.S. Military Commissions Act and in the thinking of our own Michael Ignatieff, who achieved considerable stature in the United States by providing the American empire with intellectually inventive but morally incoherent justifications for imperial lawlessness. While Justice O'Connor shows how international law unequivocally rejects torture in all circumstances, Ignatieff, adhering to the doctrine of American exceptionalism, looks for a way to give Washington a little extra manoeuvring room in dealing with its enemies. So, for instance, Ignatieff has argued that if torture is being administered by a "non-sadistic" and "patriotic American," then the torturer should be made to stand trial for his crime—but be allowed the legal defence of "mitigation."[33] We should be willing to cut the torturer a little slack, in other words, as long as he means well and is advancing the cause of America.

Powerful forces in this country are encouraging us to accept the notion of American exceptionalism and a role for Canada as adjunct to the U.S. empire. Indeed, they want us to believe that, in the wake of 9/11, we've already embraced a new approach to the world, abandoning our traditional vision of ourselves. Rudyard Griffiths, executive director of a think tank called the Dominion Institute, has argued, for instance, that "the country's most cherished myths seem to be melting away." Asks Griffiths: "If we are not what we were, what now defines us as a nation? Put another way, what new national touchstones do we want to forge together to replace, say, universal health care or peacekeeping?"

Griffiths points to the election of Stephen Harper's Conservatives as indicative of "seismic shifts" under way in the country and of "a hunger for a new formulation of what it means to be a Canadian."[34] (More careful analysts have attributed the Harper victory largely to the public's disgust over Liberal corruption.)

My guess is that Canadians have no interest in abandoning universal health care or peacekeeping as national touchstones. I'd also guess that we're hungry not for a new neoconservative formulation of what it means to be a Canadian but rather for political leaders who will adhere to the values Canadians have long held.

Personally, I'd be satisfied with the vision of being Canadian that emerges from the moral clarity of Justice O'Connor's report, or from the determined quest for justice by Maher Arar and his wife, or from Louise Arbour's gutsy walk through the Palestinian rubble—a vision committed to fair treatment and equality, to decency and to the rule of law. I'd take that simple notion of what it means to be Canadian any day over what many members of our elite appear to have in mind for us—a helpmate's role, with a lucrative perch inside the U.S. empire, obligingly assisting the bully as he goes about trying to subdue the world.

NOTES

INTRODUCTION

1 Philippe Sands, *Lawless World* (London: Penguin Books, 2005), p. xii.

2 Greg Jaffe, "Rumsfeld Details Big Military Shift in New Document," *Wall Street Journal*, March 11, 2005.

3 Mary McGrory, "Pit-stop Presidency," *Washington Post*, October 27, 2002.

4 Philip Resnick, *The European Roots of Canadian Identity* (Peterborough, Ontario: Broadview Press, 2005), p.97.

5. Bill Graveland, "Civilian Deaths Hurt Cause in Afghanistan," *Edmonton Sun*, January 4, 2007.

6 John Mueller, "A False Sense of Insecurity," *Regulation*, Vol. 27, No. 33 (Fall 2004), pp. 42–46. Available at http://ssrn.com/abstract=604063

7 Clayton Ruby, speech to the Law Society of Upper Canada, Toronto, July 20, 2006.

8 Nikolai Lanine, "We're Still Dying in Afghanistan," *Globe and Mail*, November 30, 2006.

CHAPTER ONE: Anti-Canadians at Home and Abroad

1. Doug Saunders and Jane Taber, "Harper reroutes his jet to bring Canadians home," *Globe and Mail*, July 20, 2006.

2. Clifford Krauss, "Letter from the Americas; Canada's Prophets of Pessimism," *New York Times*, September 29, 2004.

3. Interview with the author, Ottawa, November 14, 2006.

4. Jane Taber, "'Steve' blessed; Rae goes north," *Globe and Mail*, October 7, 2006.

5. From a speech Michael Byers delivered October 5, 2006 to Members of Parliament and Senators as part of a "Breakfast on the Hill" lecture series organized by the Canadian Federation for the Humanities and Social Sciences.

6. Telephone interview with the author, January 23, 2007.

7. Telephone interview with the author, November 22, 2006.

8. Telephone interview with the author, November 7, 2006. See also David R. Boyd, "Canada: an ecological scofflaw?" *Toronto Star*, October 17, 2006.

9. George Monbiot, lecture, University of Toronto, November 13, 2006. Monbiot is the author of *Heat* (Toronto: Doubleday Canada, 2006).

10. Steven Staples and Bill Robinson, *It's Never Enough: Canada's alarming rise in military spending* (Ottawa: Polaris Institute, October 2005).

11. Richard A. Preston, *The Defence of the Undefended Border: Planning for War in North America 1867–1939* (Montreal: McGill-Queen's University Press, 1977), pp. 216–217.

12. Floyd Rudmin, "War on Canada: Secret War Plans and the Malady of American Militarism," *CounterPunch*, vol. 13, no. 1, January 1–15, 2006. Posted at www.counterpunch.org/rudmin02172006.html. For fuller version, see Floyd Rudmin, *Bordering on Aggression: Evidence of U.S. Military Preparations Against Canada* (Hull, Quebec: Voyageur Publishing, 1993).

13. National Archives, Microfilm Publications, Microfilm Publication M1421. Records of the Joint Board, 1903–1947, Roll 10, J.B. Serial 435 through Serial 641. National Archives and Records Administration. Washington, D.C. 1986.

14. Rudmin, "War on Canada" and email correspondence with the author.

15. Margaret Wente, "The road to UN hell is paved with good intentions," *Globe and Mail*, September 23, 2004.

16. Robert Fulford, "The values battle," *National Post*, September 24, 2005.

17. Robert Fulford, "Anti-Americanism, bred in the bone," *National Post*, November 17, 2005.

18. Alan Freeman, "Bush admits to secret prisons," *Globe and Mail*, September 7, 2006.

19. Institute for Energy and Environmental Research, Lawyers' Committee on Nuclear Policy, *Rule of Power or Rule of Law?: An Assessment of U.S. Policies and Actions Regarding Security-Related Treaties* (New York: The Apex Press, 2003), p. 91.

20. Quoted in Samantha Power, "Boltonism," *The New Yorker*, March 21, 2005.

21. Allan Gotlieb, "Romanticism and Realism in Canada's Foreign Policy," lecture, C.D. Howe Institute, November 3, 2004.

22. The calculations on foreign ownership have been done for this book by Jerome Klassen, a Ph.d. student in political science at York University. The percentages have been rounded off to the nearest whole number.

23. Ajay Kapur, Niall Macleod, and Narendra Singh (Citigroup Research), "Plutonomy: Buying Luxury, Explaining Global Imbalances," Citigroup Global Markets, New York, October 16, 2005.

24. Michael Adams, *Fire and Ice: The United States, Canada and the Myth of Converging Values* (Toronto: Penguin, 2003), pp. 51–52.

CHAPTER TWO: No More Girlie-Man Peacekeeping

1. J.L. Granatstein, *Who Killed the Canadian Military?* (Toronto: HarperCollins Publishers, 2004), p. 34.

2. James Travers, "In full retreat on Darfur: Military told Martin they'd be ready. A year later, peacekeeper pledge fades," *Toronto Star,* May 11, 2006.

3. Michael Ignatieff, "Ignatieff on the Record: Peacekeeping died in Rwanda,'" *Toronto Star,* August, 30, 2006.

4. Interview with the author, UN headquarters, New York, April 21, 2006.

5. Robert A. Pape, *Dying to Win: The Strategic Logic of Suicide Terrorism* (New York: Random House, 2005), p. 4.

6. Project for a New American Century (PNAC), *Rebuilding America's Defenses,* (September 2000), p. 14.

7. John F. Burns, "Villagers Say U.S. Should Have Looked, Not Leapt," *New York Times,* February 17, 2002.

8. Michael Mandel, *How America Gets Away with Murder* (Ann Arbor, Michigan: Pluto Press, 2004).

9. Two UN Security Council resolutions were passed about terrorism following 9/11 and before the U.S. invasion of Afghanistan on October 7, 2001, but neither of these authorized military force against Afghanistan, nor even mentioned Afghanistan. See Mandel, p. 33.

10. Mandel, *How America Gets Away with Murder,* p. 41.

11. Rory McCarthy, "New bin Laden Offer," *The Guardian,* October 17, 2001.

12. Mandel, *How America Gets Away with Murder,* p. 31.

13. *Ibid.,* p. 49.

14. *Ibid.,* p. 31.

15. *Ibid.*, p. 48.

16. Abdullah Shahin, "Axe Attack Highlights Resentment," *Afghan Recovery Report*, Institute for War and Peace Reporting, April 14, 2006.

17. J. L. Granatstein, "Wake up! This is our war too," *Globe and Mail*, February 28, 2006.

18. "General warns of 20-year mission in Afghanistan," CBC news online, August 8, 2005.

19. Sean Maloney and Tom Fennell, "Soldiers, Not Peacekeepers," *The Walrus*, March 2006.

20. Granatstein, *Who Killed the Canadian Military?*, p. 30.

21. A. Walter Dorn, "Canadian Peacekeeping: Proud Tradition, Strong Future?," *Canadian Foreign Policy*, Vol. 12, No. 2 (Fall 2005) pp. 7–32.

22. Telephone interview with the author, January 2006.

23 John Polanyi, "From War to Law via Science," *Toronto Star*, February 19, 2006.

CHAPTER THREE: All Opposed to Nuclear Disarmament, Please Stand Up

1. Survey conducted by Angus Reid Strategies, reported in Ken MacQueen, "They like us! They really like us!" *Maclean's*, November 20, 2006.

2. Christopher S. Raj, *Stalking Terror: Landmines in Peace and War* (Delhi: Wordsmiths, 2000), p. 91.

3. *Ibid.*, p. 15.

4. *Ibid.*, pp. 15–16.

5. Lydia Monin and Andrew Gallimore, *The Devil's Garden: A History of Landmines* (London: Random House, 2002), p. 1.

6. Lloyd Axworthy, *Navigating a New World: Canada's Global Future* (Toronto: Random House, 2004), p.132. Raj, *Stalking Terror*, p. 91.

7. Axworthy, *Navigating a New World*, pp. 133–134, and interview with the author, Calgary, April 27, 2006.

8. Axworthy, *Navigating a New World*, p. 136.

9. Edward Greenspon and Anthony Wilson-Smith, *Double Vision: The Inside Story of the Liberals in Power* (Toronto: Doubleday Canada, 1996), p. 250.

10. Jody Williams, Nobel Lecture, Oslo, December 10, 1997.

11. Cited in Monin and Gallimore, *The Devil's Garden*, pp 13–14.

12. Cited in Monin and Gallimore, *The Devil's Garden*, p. 22.

13. Axworthy, *Navigating a New World*, p.146.

14. Interview with the author, Ottawa, November 14, 2005.

15. Axworthy, *Navigating a New World*, p.155.

16. Interview with the author, Washington, D. C., May 19, 2006.

17. Interview with the author, Ottawa, November 15, 2006.

18. Telephone interview with the author, November 2006.

19. Email correspondence with the author.

20. Mark MacKinnon, "'We love Canada,'" *Globe and Mail*, March 16, 2006.

21. Anne Trowell Hillmer, "'Here I Am in the Middle,' Lester Pearson and the Origins of Canada's Diplomatic Involvement in the Middle East," in David Taras and David H. Goldberg (eds.) *The Domestic Battleground: Canada and the Arab-Israeli Conflict* (Kingston: McGill-Queen's University Press, 1989), p. 129.

22. *Ibid.*, p 131.

23. *Ibid.*, p. 134.

24. *Ibid.*, p. 131.

25. *Ibid.*, p. 137.

26. Menachem Begin, *The Revolt* (New York: Nash Publishing, 1977), p. 148.

27. *Ibid.*, p. xxv.

28. John Kirton and Peyton Lyon, "Perceptions of the Middle East in External Affairs," in Taras and Goldberg, *Domestic Battleground*, p. 198.

29. Lloyd Axworthy, "Losing our way in the world," *Globe and Mail*, July 22, 2006.

30. George Takach, "Clark and the Jerusalem Embassy Affair," in Taras and Goldberg, *Domestic Battle*, pp. 159–160. See also Irving Abella and John Sigler, "Canada and the Arab-Israeli Conflict: A Discussion with Irving Abella and John Sigler," in Taras and Goldberg, *Domestic Battle*, p. 231.

CHAPTER FOUR: The Most Dangerous Man in the English-Speaking World

1. Lester Pearson, *Mike: the Memoirs of the Right Honourable Lester B. Pearson, 1957–68, Vol. 3*, edited by John A. Munro and Alex I. Inglis (Toronto: University of Toronto Press, 1975), p. 149.

2. Lester Pearson, *Mike: the Memoirs of the Right Honourable Lester B. Pearson, 1948–1957, Vol. 2*, (Toronto: University of Toronto Press, 1973), p.123

3. Quoted in John English, *The Worldly Years: The Life of Lester Pearson, Vol. II: 1949–1972* (Toronto: Alfred A. Knopf Canada, 1992), p. 88.

4. Pearson, *Memoirs, Vol. 2*, p. 53.

5. English, *The Worldly Years*, p. 110.

6. Quoted in Howard Peter Langille, *In Pursuit of Common Security*, (doctoral thesis, University of Bradford, 1999.) p. 27.

7. Pearson, *Memoirs, Vol. 2*, p. 46

8. *Ibid.*, p. 44

9. Quoted in Bruce Thordarson, *Lester Pearson: Diplomat and Politician* (Toronto: University of Toronto Press, 1974), p. 69.

10. Quoted in Geoffrey A.H. Pearson, *Seize the Day: Lester B. Pearson and Crisis Diplomacy* (Ottawa: Carleton University Press, 1993), p. 75.

11. Quoted in Pearson, *Seize the Day*, p. 73.

12. Quoted in *Ibid.*, p. 75.

13. Quoted in Thomas Walkom, "The problem with losing perspective," *Toronto Star*, June 12, 2006.

14. Quoted in Thordarson, *Lester Pearson*, pp. 78–79.

15. *Ibid.*, p. 79.

16 Quoted in John English, *The Worldly Years, Vol. 2.*, pp. 107–108.

17. Robert Bothwell, *Pearson: His Life and World* (Toronto: McGraw-Hill Ryerson Ltd., 1978), p. 77.

18. Bothwell, *Pearson*, p. 80.

19. Pearson, *Memoirs, Vol. 3*, p. 122.

20. *Ibid.*, p. 152.

21. Victor Levant, *Quiet Complicity: Canadian Involvement in the Vietnam War* (Toronto: Between the Lines, 1986).

22 Cited in *Ibid.*, pp. 153–154.

23. *Ibid.*, p. 167.

24. Joseph T. Jockel and Joel J. Sokolsky, *Canada and Collective Security: Odd Man Out* (New York: Praeger Publishers, 1986). pp. 60–61.

25. J. L. Granatstein, "Canada and Peacekpeeing: Image and Reality" in Granatstein (ed.) *Canadian Foreign Policy: Historical Readings (1986)* , pp. 238–239, 186.

26. Cited in Langille, *In Pursuit of Common Security*, p. 279.

27. The quotes in this paragraph are drawn from various parts of Chapter One in Granatstein, *Who Killed the Canadian Military?* (Toronto: HarperCollins Publishers, 2004).

28. Howard Peter Langille, *Changing the Guard: Canada's Defence in a World of Transition* (Toronto: University of Toronto Press, 1990), p. 109.

29. Cited in *Ibid.*, p. 91

30. *Ibid.*, p. 108.

31. Telephone interview with the author, December 2006.

32. Background material provided by DIPTF to the BCNI Task Force on Foreign and Defence Policy, cited in Langille, *Changing the Guard*, p. 89.

33. Letter to BCNI from Erik Nielsen February 5, 1986, cited in Langille, *Changing the Guard*, p. 113.

34. Cited in Steven Staples, *Missile Defence: Round One* (Toronto: James Lorimer & Company, 2006), p. 41.

35. Quoted in Langille, *Changing the Guard*, p. 115.

36. *Ibid.*, p.115.

37. *Ibid.*, p.117.

38. Quoted in Granatstein, *Who Killed the Canadian Military?*, p. 136.

CHAPTER FIVE: The Threat of Peace

1. CATO Handbook for Congress, 105th Congress, Washington D.C.,1997–98.

2. Cited in Gerard Piel, "Globalopolies," *The Nation*, May 18, 1992.

3. Patrick Tyler, "U.S. Strategy Plan Calls for Insuring No Rivals Develop a One-Superpower World," *New York Times*, March 8, 1992.

4. Langille, *In Pursuit of Common Security*, p.57.

5. Interview with author, Montreal, May 30, 2006.

6. Canada 21 Council, *Canada and Common Security in the Twenty-first Century* (Toronto: Centre for International Studies, University of Toronto, 1994.)

7. David Harries, "Challenges in Military Futures," *Canadian Defence Quarterly*, December 1993, p. 21, cited in Langille, *In Pursuit of Common Security*, p. 145.

8. Allen G. Sens, "Canadian Defence Policy After the Cold War: Old Dimensions and New Realities," *Canadian Foreign Policy*, vol. 1, no. 3, Fall 1993, cited in Langille, *In Pursuit of Common Security*, p. 313.

9. John de Chastelain, "Wing-Walking Revisited: Canadian Defence Policy after the Cold War," *Canadian Defence Quarterly*, Vol. 2, No. 3, June 1992.

10. Brigadier-General Lalonde, "Peacekeeping," Force Mobile Command, 3450–1 (COS OPS), cited in Langille, *In Pursuit of Common Security*, p. 139.

11. Handwritten memo from Fowler, June 22, 1992, cited in Langille, *In Pursuit of Common Security*, p. 208.

12. Senator Colin Kenny, Minutes of Proceedings and Evidence of the Special Joint Committee, Issue no. 8, May 4, 1994, p. 50, cited in Langille, *In Pursuit of Common Security*, p. 150.

13. Col. Douglas Bland, Minutes of Proceedings and Evidence of the Special Joint Committee, p. 50, cited in Langille, *In Pursuit of Common Security*, p. 150.

14. Langille, *In Pursuit of Common Security*, p. 168.

15. Yves Engler and Anthony Fenton, *Canada in Haiti*, (Vancouver: Red Publishing; Black Point, Nova Scotia: Fenwood Publishing, 2005), pp. 41–46.

16. Denis Paradis interviewed by freelance journalist Anthony Fenton, September 11, 2004. Transcript available online at the Dominion Daily weblog dominionpaper.ca/weblog/2004/09interview.

17. Telephone interview with the author, December 2006.

18. *Human Security Report 2005*, Liu Institute for Global Issues, University of British Columbia, pp. 8, 153, 155.

19. Telephone interviews and email correspondence with the author.

20. Robert C. Johansen, "UN peacekeeping: the changing utility of military force," *Third World Quarterly*, vol. 12, no. 2, April 1990, p. 58.

21. Anatol Rapoport, *Peace: An Idea whose Time has Come*, (Ann Arbor: University of Michigan, 1992), p. 178.

22. John Mueller, *Retreat from Doomsday: The Obsolescence of Major War*, New York: Basic Books, 1988), pp 9–10.

23. *Ibid.*, p. 13.

24. Both Engerman and Drescher cited *Ibid.*, p. 12.

25. Mueller, *Retreat from Doomsday*, p. 12.

26. Anatol Rapoport and Leonard Johnson, "Peacekeeping as a conversion opportunity," *Peace Magazine*, September/October 1993.

CHAPTER SIX: Back from the Abyss

1. The Banff meeting, which received almost no coverage in the mainstream media, was brought to public attention by Canadian author and former book publisher Mel Hurtig. It was also reported by Maude Barlow, "Getting closer to Uncle Sam," *Toronto Star*, September 20, 2006.

2. Linda McQuaig, *It's the Crude, Dude: War, Big Oil and the Fight for the Planet*, (Toronto: Doubleday Canada, 2004) p, 46.

3. For a discussion of the role and process of the IPCC, see Linda McQuaig, *It's the Crude, Dude* pp. 150–157.

4. Rex Murphy, "Overheated climate arithmetic," *Globe and Mail*, November 4, 2006.

5. George Monbiot, *Heat: How to Stop the Planet from Burning.* (Toronto: Doubleday Canada, 2006), pp. ix-x, xix.

6. David R. Boyd, "Canada: An ecological scofflaw?," *Toronto Star*, October 17, 2006. See also David R. Boyd, "Canada is exporting death," *Globe and Mail*, October 10, 2006.

7. Boyd, "Canada: An ecological scofflaw?," *Toronto Star*, October 17, 2006.

8. Eric Umansky, "Failure of Imagination," *Columbia Journalism Review*, September/October 2006.

9. Quoted in Ari Berman, "More Images of Abu Ghraib," *The Nation*, August 22, 2005.

10. Eliza Girswold, "American Gulag: Prisoners' tales from the War on Terror," *Harper's Magazine*, September 2006.

11. "Rushing Off a Cliff," Editorial, *New York Times*, September 28, 2006.

12. Beverley McLachlin, Speech to the Vietnam-Canadian Business Association, November 28, 2003. Available at www.scc-csc.gc.a/aboutcourt/judges/speeches/vietnam_e.asp.

13. Michael Ignatieff, "The Burden," *New York Times Magazine*, January 5, 2003.

14. Linda Diebel, "A cosmopolitan with a thirst for adventure," *Toronto Star*, November 19, 2006.

15. Michael Ignatieff, "Lesser Evils," *New York Times Magazine*, May 2, 2004.

16. Government of Canada, Commision of Inquiry into the Actions of Canadian Officials in Relation to Maher Arar, *Report of the Events Relating to Maher Arar, Analysis and Recommendations*, p. 13.

17. *Ibid.*, pp. 186–189.

18. *Ibid.*, p. 191.

19. *Ibid.*, p. 236.

20. *Ibid.*, p. 222.

21. Thomas Walkom, "Gone, but for wrong reasons," *Toronto Star*, December 7, 2006.

22. *Report of the Events Relating to Maher Arar,* pp. 268–276.

23. Paul Koring, "Citing 'liberal' immigration laws, U.S. blasts Canada on terrorism," *Globe and Mail*, April 29, 2006.

24. Don MacPherson, "RCMP probe into 'allegations' grows curiouser," *Montreal Gazette*, January 11, 2006.

25. Andrew McIntosh, "Arar probe will harm RCMP, CSIS, ex-agent warns," *National Post*, February 2, 2004.

26. Peter Baker, "Bush cites oil as reason to stay in Iraq," *Washington Post*, November 5, 2006.

27. Pepe Escobar, "Stability first: Newspeak for rape of Iraq," *Asia Times Online*, October 26, 2006. www.atimes.com

28. Tom Englelhardt, "The contemporary barbarism of air power," *Le Monde Diplomatique*, August 2006.

29. Michael Bell, "Harnessing the forces of moderation," *Globe and Mail*, February 16, 2006.

30. Steven Erlanger, "U.S. and Israelis said to talk of Hamas ouster," *New York Times*, February 14, 2006.

31. Letter from the general secretary of the World Council of Churches to members of the UN "Middle East quartet," Geneva, February 8, 2006. Available at www.oikoumene.org

32. *Report of the Events Relating to Maher Arar*, p. 51.

33. Michael Ignatieff, interview, ABC Radio National (Australia), Sunday April 24, 2005.

34. Rudyard Griffiths, "Canadian mood is changing dramatically," *Toronto Star*, April 2, 2006.

ACKNOWLEDGMENTS

I'm grateful to a number of people who generously gave their time, expertise and insights to help me with this book, notably Peter Langille, Graeme MacQueen, Thomas Walkom, Michael Mandel, John Sigler, Walter Dorn and Peggy Mason.

I also want to thank the very competent crew at Doubleday, who were highly professional and a pleasure to deal with, despite an extremely tight editing and production schedule. This talented and creative cast includes: Brad Martin, Maya Mavjee, Martha Kanya-Forstner, whose thoughtful editing suggestions were particularly helpful, Martha Leonard, Scott Richardson, Colleen Clarke, Lara Hinchberger, Tim Rostron, Susan Burns, as well as Nick Massey-Garrison, and freelance copy editor Shaun Oakey. The help of Bruce Westwood and Natasha Daneman of Westwood Creative Artists is also much appreciated.

I'm indebted to my longtime editor, David Kilgour, who applied his usual talents, his keen eye and his good humour, and to my great friend Barbara Nichol, for insightful editing suggestions—on the book and also on my weekly columns in the *Toronto Star*—and for coming up with the title of the book.

I'd also like to thank Ish Theilheimer and Michael Cowley-Owen of *Straightgoods.com* for their generosity in creating a website for me.

My personal life was full of sadness this year, due to the unexpected illness and death of my wonderful brother Donnie, to whom this book is dedicated. Donnie was a magnetic character, with an infectious energy and enthusiasm about life and people, particularly those he most loved—his wife Diane and daughters Kate, Laura, Margot and Jacqueline. Even when Donnie was very sick, his focus remained on what was going on in other people's lives. When I visited him in the hospital, his first question was always about how this book was progressing.

I'd like to thank a number of people who have been very supportive, including my parents, Audrey and Jack McQuaig, brothers Peter and John, and sister Wendy; as well as Fred Fedorsen (and Tasha), David Cole, Linda Diebel, Gord Evans, Wallis Millar-Blanchaer, Lorraine Telford, Christine Hartmann and Stephanie Chan, and my old friends from Mellowville.

I'd also like to thank Andrzej Tarnas, for magical moments on Baldwin Street, in the Elmhirst sun and in Calabogie park.

And finally, my thanks go to my very precious daughter Amy, whom I love with all my heart.

INDEX